THE FIRST INDOCHINA WAR

The First Indochina War

FRENCH AND AMERICAN POLICY 1945-54

R. E. M. IRVING

CROOM HELM LONDON

Croom Helm Ltd
2-10 St. Johns Road, London SW11

ISBN: 0-85664-286-X

For Alison, Susan, Jane and Caroline.

Printed by Biddles of Guildford

CONTENTS

INDOCHINA

French Indochina (the Indochinese Union of 1886) consisted of the protectorates of Laos, Cambodia, Tonkin and Annam, and the colony of Cochinchina. In 1949 the three *kys* of Vietnam (Tonkin, Annam and Cochinchina) were united, and the new State of Vietnam, together with Laos and Cambodia, became Associated States of the French Union. As a result of the Geneva Agreement of 1954 Vietnam, Laos and Cambodia became independent, but Vietnam was divided at the seventeenth parallel into a Communist North and a non-Communist South. This state of affairs pertains in 1975, although many parts of South Vietnam are now under Communist control.

ABBREVIATIONS

DST	Direction de la surveillance du territoire
CNIP	Centre national des indépendants et paysans (Conservatives)
MRP	Mouvement Républicain Populaire (Christian Democrats)
OSS	Office of Strategic Services
PCF	Parti communiste français (Communists)
RPF	Rassemblement du peuple français (Gaullists)
SDECE	Section de documentation extérieure et de contre-espionnage
SFIO	Section française de l'internationale ouvrière (Socialists)
UDSR	Union démocratique et socialiste de la résistance
Viet Minh	Viet Nam Doc Lap Dong Minh
VNQDD	Viet Nam Quoc Dan Dang

PREFACE

A number of important books have been written about the decolonisation of French Indochina between 1945-54,[1] but until the present study none has focused specifically on the role and influence of French political parties in making and implementing Indochina policy.

It should, of course, be emphasised at the outset that the unstable coalition governments of the Fourth French Republic (1946-58) were rarely in full control of their colonial policy. Both in Indochina and in North Africa examples abound of French soldiers and administrators taking the law into their own hands and presenting their governments with *faits accomplis*. Moreover, during the last two years of the first Indochina War, which lasted in all from 1946-54, French policy was considerably influenced by the attitude of the United States' Government. Nevertheless, this study shows that at certain crucial moments French governments and French political parties played a vital part in defining and influencing Indochina policy. Indeed, as regards the first Indochina War, there is a considerable element of truth in Ho Chi Minh's claim of 1947 that 'the key to the problem of Indochina is to be found in the domestic political situation in France'.[2]

This book, then, is primarily a study of French policy in Indochina between 1945-54, with particular reference to the role and influence of the political parties, but increasingly it develops into a study of American policy as well, because by the end of the war the United States were almost as deeply involved in Indochina as France, although, unlike France, the United States were never *directly* involved in the first Indochina War. By 1953-54, however, the Americans were paying for two-thirds of the cost of the war, and their commitment to Indochina, and in particular to Vietnam, had grown to such an extent that it was almost inevitable that the United States took over France's role in the fight against communism after the abortive Geneva Agreement of 1954.

This book sets out to provide answers to three important questions. To what extent and in what ways did French political parties influence Indochina policy? What were the motives behind the policies pursued by France, the United States and Vietnam in the period 1945-54? And in what ways were these three countries affected, both at the time and subsequently, by their involvement in the process of decolonising Indochina?

No definitive answers can be given to these questions. Indeed, none ever will be, for even when all the documents have been released, they will be interpreted in different ways. The French cabinet papers [at present not normally published until fifty years after the events in question] will undoubtedly shed more light on the whole period of decolonisation. But in the meantime, thanks to the large number of documents and other primary sources already available for study,[3] it is possible for one to make a serious attempt to answer the above questions.

The bulk of the research for this book was done at the Fondation Nationale des Sciences Politiques, the Bibliothothèque Nationale, the Assemblée Nationale, and the Sénat, Paris; at the Royal Institute of International Affairs, Chatham House, London; and at Nuffield College, Oxford. I would like to thank the librarians of these institutions for the help they have given me over the years in locating the appropriate documents, parliamentary debates, parliamentary reports, newspapers, journals and periodicals. I would also like to acknowledge my gratitude to the large number of politicians and scholars who have discussed the decolonisation of Indochina with me; I am particularly grateful to those French politicians who allowed me to consult their private papers. My principal debt of gratitude, however, is to those who have been kind enough to read and criticize the various drafts of my book: Philip Williams, Official Fellow in European Politics, Nuffield College, Oxford; Dennis Duncanson, Reader in South East Asian Studies, University of Kent, Canterbury; and Patrick Honey, Reader in Vietnamese Studies, School of Oriental and African Studies, University of London.

I should add that the views expressed are my own and that none of the persons or institutions mentioned above can be held responsible for any factual mistakes or errors of judgement.

University of Edinburgh, January 1975. R. E. M. Irving

NOTES

1. See Bibliography, part 1, pp.157-60.
2. P. Devillers, *Histoire du Vietnam de 1940 à 1952* (Seuil, 1952), p.371, n.18. [The first time a book is cited, its author, title and publisher will be stated in full. Thereafter only the author's name will be given unless there is a possibility of confusion, in which case the book's full or short title will also be given. For a full list of books, see Bibliography, pp.157-60].
3. For a full list of sources consulted, see Bibliography, pp.157-63.

1.   THE FOURTH FRENCH REPUBLIC AND THE PROBLEM OF DECOLONISATION

> The Fourth Republic was born with the war in Indochina. It died
> with the war in Algeria. Amongst all the errors of the Republic, the
> most fatal was its failure to establish new relationships with the
> overseas territories.[1]

The Fourth French Republic (1946-58) was arguably the most
successful of all French republics, except that it failed. Major economic
and social reforms were carried out. The 'stalemate society' and
'Maginot' attitudes of the inter-war years were abandoned as France
began to adapt herself to the economic conditions of the post-Keynesian
industrial West. The hand of friendship was extended to Germany as
French governments played a leading part in the early steps towards the
integration of Western Europe. And although parliamentary democracy
continued to function in a rather desultory manner, the vast majority of
French Catholics at last became fully reconciled to republicanism and
democracy after a hundred and fifty years of hesitant support or overt
opposition. But the Republic failed to solve the problem of decolonisation, which ultimately proved to be its Spanish Ulcer. The Army revolt
in Algiers in May 1958, which led to the downfall of the Fourth
Republic, was in effect the last despairing reaction of those who refused
to face up to the 'wind of change' in colonial relationships. The professional soldiers, who believed that they had been betrayed by the
politicians over Indochina and Suez, finally broke the traditional *grande
muette* of the French Army by revolting against the so-called 'government of abandon' of Pierre Pflimlin. But ironically the government
which came to power as a result of the Army *coup*, namely that of
General de Gaulle, continued the progressive colonial policy of its
immediate predecessors, although with one major difference: it had the
authority to implement its policies. After four years of bloodshed
(including two more attempted Army *coups*), Algeria finally achieved
its independence. That great pragmatist, General de Gaulle who in
1946 and 1947 had threatened any politician responsible for losing any
part of the French Empire with impeachment, himself granted independence to the last great French colonial territory.

The first stage in the tragic history of French decolonisation began
in Indochina in 1946. Colonial policy was, of course, the concern of
all the parties which participated in the French coalition governments
of 1945-54, but the political party which played the key role in

1

defining and executing Indochina policy throughout this period was the
Christian Democratic *Mouvement Républicain Populaire* (MRP). The
MRP was the child of the Resistance, in which Catholic laymen had
played a role second only to that of the Communists. As a Catholic
Resistance party, blessed with the tacit approval of General de Gaulle,
the MRP had a mushroom growth in the post-Liberation period. It was
the largest party in the National Assembly from June to November
1946 with 169 deputies (out of 586), and the second largest (after the
Communists) from 1946-51 with 167. Although less successful at the
General Elections of 1951 and 1956, the MRP never had less than 85
deputies in the National Assemblies of the Fourth Republic. The MRP
participated in 23 of the 27 governments from 1944-58, and supported
all but that of Pierre Mendès-France (June 1954– February 1955), and
the party provided the Fourth Republic with three Prime Ministers,
George Bidault, Robert Schuman and Pierre Pflimlin.

In a way it was ironic that the MRP became so heavily involved in
the problems of decolonisation, for unlike the Radicals and Conservatives (i.e. members of the Independent and Peasant parties), and to a
lesser extent the Socialists, the Christian Democrats had no vested
interests in the old Empire. They knew almost nothing about the
colonies, and yet Indochina became an MRP fief after the elimination
of Socialist influence during the Generals' Affair of 1950-51. For
almost six of the seven-and-a-half years of the war, MRP Ministers were
responsible for Indochina;[2] the party also held the Ministry of Foreign
Affairs without a break until the last month of hostilities,[3] and at
various times ran the Ministries of Defence and War;[4] in addition seven
of the twelve Colonial Ministers (Overseas France) were Christian
Democrats.[5]

French colonial policy in the immediate post-war period was based
on a mixture of idealism and quasi-federalism. At the Brazzaville
Conference of Colonial Governors in January 1944 a break was made
with the pre-war doctrine of assimilation, but the French stopped well
short of conceding anything comparable to dominion status to their
former colonies. Instead they talked of 'progressive federalism', i.e. the
maximum economic, social and political progress compatible with a
federal structure of which France was clearly the head. In practice this
looked all too like old-fashioned paternalism. As the Catholic Church
believes in national Catholic churches within a unified structure under
the control of the Papacy, so the Catholic Christian Democrats (and
others) favoured a family of nations and territories within the unified
structure of the French Union. But, as with the Catholic Church, there
was to be no question of secession: Paris was to be to the French Union
(as the Empire was now called) what Rome is to the Catholic Church,
both spiritual home and supreme authority.

2

With the hindsight of history it is easy to accuse the French politicians responsible for decolonisation of naiveté and blindness. It is now clear that the Second World War had acted as a powerful stimulant to nationalism amongst colonial peoples. This was particularly true of the Far East, where the Japanese had both propagated the slogan 'Asia for the Asians' and shown that the white races were far from invincible. Another powerful stimulant to decolonisation was the fact that the Americans and the Russians were in full agreement on one thing — if only on one thing — namely that the old European colonial empires should be liquidated as quickly as possible. At the same time the word 'independence' suddenly aquired a new significance as *the* qualification for entry into the United Nations.

In fairness to France it must be conceded that the process of decolonisation was almost inevitably more painful for her than it was for Britain. In the first place France was anxious to reassert herself after the humiliations of the Second World War. In spite of General de Gaulle and the Resistance, France in effect lost the war, although she came out of it on the winning side. In contrast to Britain, therefore, it was difficult for France to be generous in 1945. She had to prove herself after the defeat of 1940, and the only way she could apparently do this was by consolidating the French Union with its hundred million inhabitants.[6] Moreover, France had scarcely begun to recover from the ravages of the war in Europe when the first colonial struggle was upon her with the opening of hostilities in Indochina in late 1946. But even without the psychological problem created by the defeat of 1940 (which incidentally affected the soldiers at least as much as the politicians)[7] and the practical problem of a 'premature' colonial war, France would have encountered greater difficulties than Britain in granting independence to her colonial territories owing to the very different colonial traditions of the two countries.

Since the Durham Report of 1840 Britain had always contended that her long-term objective was some form of self-government for her colonies. France, on the other hand, emphasised the Jacobin concept of 'the one and indivisible Republic' (including all the overseas territories). Imbued with French culture, her overseas subjects would eventually aspire to full French citizenship, but this would not entail independence or even dominion status. Thus, although France adhered to the Atlantic Charter, whose third principle emphasised the right of all peoples to choose freely the form of government under which they wanted to live, and although she signed the United Nations Charter, which laid down that independence was the inevitable and only morally justifiable goal of colonisation, she also, in the person of General de Gaulle, signed the Brazzaville Declaration (January 1944), which proclaimed a quite different objective:

3

Whereas the aims of the work of civilisation accomplished by France in her colonies rule out all idea of autonomy and all possibility of development outside the French Empire; [therefore] the eventual constitution, even in the far-off future, of self-government in the colonies is out of the question.[8]

It is true that the Brazzaville Conference also proposed generous economic and social policies throughout the Empire, but in the post-war world in which 'independence' became *the* magic word for colonial peoples, the Brazzaville Declaration, devoid as it was of political content, soon appeared obsolete. The same was true of the French Provisional Government's proposals for the future government of Indochina (Declaration of 24 March 1945). In its preamble the Declaration referred to the economic and social rights of all the peoples of Indochina, but its political proposals for an Indochinese Federation (Cochinchina, Annam, Tonkin, Cambodia and Laos) within the French Union were very conservative. The French Governor-General was to preside over a government consisting of French and native ministers, and this government was to be assisted by (but not responsible to) an assembly representing the five constituent parts of the Federation. However, certain matters, notably defence and the police, were to be reserved to the Governor-General. The 24 March Declaration was more or less what Edouard Daladier had demanded after the disturbances in Indochina in 1930.[9] Coming a fortnight after the 9 March 1945 *coup*, in which the Japanese had overthrown the Vichy régime in Indochina, and immediately after Emperor Bao Dai's declaration of Vietnamese independence, the proposals were frankly anachronistic. And they became even more anachronistic after Ho Chi Minh took over the government of Vietnam in September 1945.

France was further hindered in working out a new relationship with her former colonies by a much more pernicious tradition than the concept of the indivisible Republic, namely the colonial administrators' habit of disobeying or ignoring instructions from Paris. The tradition had been established by Marshal Lyautey in Morocco in the 1920s. In the Fourth Republic it was continued by Admiral d'Argenlieu and General Valluy in Indochina, by Marshal Juin in Morocco, and finally by Generals Massu and Salan in Algeria. In a famous article in *La Nef* in 1953 Robert Schuman, who as Foreign Minister had been responsible for the protectorates (Morocco and Tunisia) from 1948-52, complained of the 'independence' (i.e. disobedience) of various governor-generals during his time as Foreign Minister.[10] Indeed, throughout any discussion of French colonial policy in the Fourth Republic it is essential to bear in mind the words of Philip Williams and Martin Harrison:

Ministers in Paris were generally well-intentioned, often liberal, rarely blind or reactionary. But time and again they were too weak to impose their will upon a local administration, often supported by settlers in the colony and by powerful politicians and business interests in the capital.[11]

This leads us to one of the fundamental problems of the Fourth Republic. In spite of its success in the economic and social fields, the Republic suffered, like its predecessor, from governmental instability. This did not necessarily mean ministerial instability. Indeed, France had only two Foreign Ministers in the decade 1944-54 (although she had fifteen Prime Ministers), but it did produce ministerial weakness which made it difficult for a minister to implement any policy which was opposed by one of the powerful pressure groups represented in the National Assembly (such as the alcohol lobby or the colonial settlers' lobby).

French governments were weak because they represented all too accurately the political divisions of the nation. Approximately two-fifths of the French electorate regularly voted for parties which were opposed to the Fourth Republican system (one-fifth each for the Communists and the Gaullists). At first the three major Resistance parties (Communists, Socialists and Christian Democrats) worked together in tripartite governments, but the degree of unity achieved in the Resistance was greatly reduced when de Gaulle resigned as Prime Minister in January 1946 on the ground that he was opposed to the Assembly-dominated system of government being drawn up by the left-inclined constitutional committee. Tripartism continued to function in a desultory manner until May 1947 when the Communists were evicted from the government as France finally opted for the West in the Cold War. From then on, until the end of the Republic, the Communists concentrated solely on destructive criticism. The year 1947 also saw the foundation of General de Gaulle's *Rassemblement du Peuple Français* (RPF), which soon achieved spectacular success by taking 40 per cent of the votes at the municipal elections in October. In the National Assembly various Conservatives and Radicals joined the RPF intergroup. The result was that the centre governments of the *troisième force* (basically Christian Democrats, Socialists and Radicals) came under constant pressure from both the Left and the Right: from the Left because the Socialists and Communists vied with each other for the same electorate, from the Right because the Christian Democrats and Gaullists shared much the same electorate. With the eviction of the Communists from the government the political centre of gravity inevitably moved rightwards, and this tendency continued as Conservatism and Gaullism, largely synonymous at that time, increased in strength in the late 1940s. The 1951 General Election produced a further shift to the Right, largely because of an electoral law specifically

5

designed to strengthen the *troisième force,* and although the Gaullist party (which won 120 seats in 1951) disintegrated in 1952-53, this did not affect the political balance in the National Assembly, as most Gaullists simply joined other conservative parliamentary groups. The upshot of these political developments was that the coalition governments of the Fourth Republic were (a) unstable, and therefore relatively weak; and (b) particularly susceptible to right-wing pressure, at least after 1947.

As far as colonial policy was concerned, the Communists normally demanded what amounted to a straightforward sell-out, at least after they were evicted from the government in May 1947. The fact that Ho Chi Minh was a Communist inevitably aggravated the problem of working out a new relationship with the former colonies of Indochina, but despite this embarrassing fact — no other nationalist leader in the French Union was a Communist — it is possible that an agreement of some sort could have been worked out with Ho Chi Minh if his claims had *not* been so vociferously championed by the French Communist Party (PCF). The Communists had only to advocate a particular line of action to put most others off it. It was indeed ironic that the most enthusiastic decolonisers unwittingly made the process of decolonising more difficult. At the other end of the political spectrum were the Gaullists, who were outspokenly anti-Communist in the late 1940s and early 1950s. They insisted that no concessions should be made to nationalists in the colonies, whatever their political views: 'The Union must be French, which means that the authority, I repeat authority, of France must be exercised decisively . . . in the fields of public order, national defence, foreign policy and economics'.[12] In the political centre were the governments of the *troisième force,* dominated by Christian Democrats and Socialists (at least until 1951). Both parties were well-meaning in their desire to work out new relationships with the former colonies, but they were relatively ignorant about the problems they were tackling, particularly during the first few years after the war, and above all they were indecisive about implementing their policies owing to constant uncertainty about the strength and reliability of their parliamentary and electoral support.

The clauses on the French Union in the Constitution of the Fourth Republic (October 1946) reflected this party indecision,[13] which was almost as much a characteristic of the tripartite coalition governments of 1944-47 as it was of their *troisième force* successors. It is true that the main emphasis of the Constitution was on the predominant role of the French Government within the Union. Thus article 62 stated that: 'The members of the French Union shall pool their resources in order to guarantee the defence of the whole Union. The Government of the Republic shall undertake the coordination of these resources . . .' But article 61 implied that the relationship between France and the more advanced territories within the Union, the Associated States,[14] would be open to negotiation, whilst the role of the Union's three institutions – the Assembly, the High Council and the President[15] – was not defined with any precision.

Clearly there was room for manoeuvre. The crucial question was how far the French Government would 'federalise' the Union. What exactly did the politicians mean by the phrase 'progressive federalism'? Would the Union develop into a close-knit federation from which secession would be impossible, or into a loose association of states joined to the mother-country only by economic and cultural ties? The first and crucial test came within two months of the promulgation of the Constitution, in far-off Indochina.

Indochina: the Historical Background

Before going on to discuss the post-war problem of Indochina, a brief comment must be made about the historical background in order to set the problem in its proper context.[16]

In 1945 the population of French Indochina was about 25 million, of whom three-quarters were Vietnamese, the rest being Laos and Khmers, together with a small number of Rhades and other ethnically diverse groups (about eighty in all). Laos had a population of about 1 million and was similar in area to the United Kingdom, 90,000 square miles. Cambodia's respective figures were about 3 million and 70,000. But the main part of French Indochina was Vietnam, not only because of her population, about 20 million, and size, 130,000 square miles, but because of the dominant influence of the Vietnamese people with their two thousand years of recorded history, their intelligence, their culture and their energy. The Vietnamese part of French Indochina consisted of three territories (*kys*): Tonkin (in the North), Annam (in the centre) and Cochinchina (in the South). There were differences between the vigorous northerners and the more easygoing southerners, but the Vietnamese were very conscious of their ethnic unity. Two Vietnamese Prime Ministers of the 1950s, Tran Van Huu and Nguyen Nan Tam, both Cochinchinese, and one of Ho Chi Minh's former Ministers, Nguyen Manh Ha, a Tonkinese, emphasised strongly that Vietnam was, and is, one nation.[17] The French, applying the well-worn imperial strategy of 'divide and rule', had encouraged the innate separatist tendencies of Tonkin and Cochinchina, but it should be remembered that these tendencies *preceded* French colonial rule. As Dennis Duncanson has pointed out, 'the present division of Vietnam at the seventeenth parallel is normal, not exceptional, as unhappily is the state of war between the two halves'.[18]

7

Vietnam has a long history, much of it a struggle to gain or retain national identity in the face of external threats. By the time that Rome emerged as the dominant Mediterranean power, a rudimentary Vietnamese State was already in existence. Viet tribes had migrated from the Yangtse river basin in the fourth century B.C., settling in the northern part of present-day Vietnam under their Emperor. Although the Empire of Annam was a Chinese satellite for almost a thousand years (111 B.C. - 939 A.D.), the Vietnamese were never properly assimilated. Foreign occupation seems only to have stimulated national consciousness, and suspicion of foreigners has ever since been a Vietnamese characteristic. After various risings against the Chinese, Ngo Quyen freed the country for five centuries (939 - 1413 A.D.), and although the Chinese Mings reconquered the Vietnamese in 1413, Le Loi led a rebellion against them in 1418, and after ten years of guerrilla fighting succeeded in driving the Chinese out. It is interesting to note that Ho Chi Minh was later to refer frequently to the exploits of Ngo Quyen and Le Loi.

The Vietnamese gradually expanded southwards, destroying the kingdom of Champa in central-southern Vietnam in the seventeenth century, and by the middle of the eighteenth century they controlled all of present-day North and South Vietnam and were making inroads into Khmer territory (now Cambodia) to the west of the River Mekong. Dynastic quarrels in the second half of the eighteenth century, notably the civil war which followed the revolt of the Tay Son brothers, put an end to this expansion, for the Empire of Annam depended to a large extent on the personal ability of its rulers. The political upheavals of the eighteenth century were halted by Nguyen Anh, a southerner who, with French support, defeated the Tay Son brothers. He adopted the imperial title of Gia Long in 1802 and founded the last of the Vietnamese dynasties, the Nguyen. However, with the exception of Gia Long, the Nguyen Emperors of the nineteenth century were no more competent than their predecessors of the eighteenth; indeed, 'in retrospect the Nguyen dynasty appears the most disastrous of all the Vietnamese dynasties, being cruel, oppressive and ineffective in domestic policy, and wilfully blind to events taking place beyond the frontiers of Vietnam'.[19] Moreover, the mandarins, who were responsible for the administration, and who were at one time respected for their interest in learning, had become renowned for their cruelty and slothfulness. In these circumstances it was not surprising that the Empire of Annam fell easily to the French, for, as Patrick Honey has written:

In the world of the nineteenth century, with colonial expansion proceeding apace even in neighbouring China, Vietnam remained turned in on herself, defenceless, decaying, and ripe for seizure by any colonial power which cared to undertake the task.[20]

It was not surprising that the colonial power was France, because the French had had links with Annam since the early seventeenth century when Alexandre de Rhodes established a successful Jesuit mission at Tourane (Danang). From then until the present day Catholicism has been a significant factor in Vietnamese politics. Indeed, persecution of the Catholics by the Nguyen was one of the main reasons why France occupied Indochina in the 1880s. Jules Ferry, the French Prime Minister chiefly responsible for the annexation of Indochina, was personally no lover of the Church, but he was anxious to strengthen France politically and economically by establishing an Empire. By the time Ferry fell from power (1885) Indochina was French, despite the euphemistic 'protectorate' status of four of its five territories. Cochinchina was a colony; Annam, Tonkin, Laos and Cambodia were protectorates. In practice, they were all integral parts of the Indochinese Union, wholly under French control.

The French brought many benefits to Vietnam. New roads were built; mineral resources were developed; rubber was introduced, as were better methods of cultivating rice; many hospitals were built, and the famous Pasteur Institute at Hanoi did much to check the ravages of disease. But the French did nothing to develop Indochina politically. The Emperor of Annam and the Kings of Cambodia and Laos were puppets; no native, however well-qualified, could rise above a very junior level in the administration, which was staffed almost exclusively by Frenchmen. This situation was much resented, especially by the Vietnamese with their long tradition of self-government, and there were nationalist revolts in 1908, 1916 and 1930.

When the Second World War began French Indochina was quiet and peaceful, but the 1930s had shown that just below the surface there was considerable dissatisfaction. There was no popular basis for the political structure and no evidence that the French intended creating one. Young nationalists and intellectuals were becoming increasingly restive, resenting their exclusion from all posts of political power. Indeed, the edifice of the Indochinese Union, like the Habsburg Empire on the eve of the First World War, was much more infected with woodworm than was immediately apparent. And, as with the Habsburg Empire, war was to be the blow which brought the building down.

The Second World War had three important effects on Indochina. It showed that the Europeans were not invincible; it stimulated nationalism; and it created a political vacuum.

After her defeat in Europe in 1940 France was forced to make concessions in Asia. In September 1940 the Japanese were granted the right to station troops and aircraft in Indochina, and by the Darlan-Kato Agreement of July 1941 Indochina was fully integrated into the Japanese military system, although the French continued to administer the country. But on 9 March 1945 the Japanese, worried by signs of nascent Gaullism in the French community, deposed the French administration and appointed Bao Dai (hitherto Emperor of Annam) head of the 'independent' State of Vietnam (Tonkin, Annam and Cochinchina being reunited). The March *coup* was of major importance in the history of French Indochina, for it was a body-blow to the French, whose soldiers and administrators were arrested within a few hours. The peoples of Indochina were shown the weakness of the Europeans; nationalism was stimulated by the Japanese slogan 'Asia for the Asians'; and administrative chaos increased over the next five months until Hiroshima created a complete vacuum into which the Viet Minh stepped.

The Viet Minh (short for Viet Nam Doc Lap Dong Minh, or National Front for the Independence of Vietnam) was one of two major anti-Japanese resistance groups. The other was the VNQDD (Viet Nam Quoc Dan Dang, or Vietnamese Nationalist Party). The Viet Minh was Communist-controlled, whereas the VNQDD professed to follow the triple aims of Sun Yat Sen and the Kuomintang, i.e. nationalism, socialism and democracy.

The Viet Minh was founded in 1941 by Nguyen Ai Quoc (as Ho Chi Minh was then known) in order to implement the new world directives of the Comintern, i.e. the establishment of Communist liberation movements in all occupied countries in preparation for Communist take-overs after the war. As a known Communist Nguyen Ai Quoc was arrested (ostensibly because he had no valid travel document) when he entered China in 1942 to organise the Viet Minh, but he was released in 1943. It was then that he adopted the pseudonym Ho Chi Minh ('He who enlightens') and succeeded in persuading the American OSS officers, who were aiding the anti-Japanese resistance movements, that he was no more than an energetic nationalist leader imbued with strong anti-colonialist sentiments.

Chiang Kai Shek at first gave his support to the VNQDD leader Nguyen Hai Than, but the latter proved so incompetent that the Kuomintang Generalissimo was persuaded to give overall control of the Vietnamese resistance to Ho Chi Minh, without apparently realising that he was none other than Nguyen Ai Quoc, the Vietnamese Communist leader. This was a remarkable stroke of luck for Ho Chi Minh, who found himself fully supported by the Chinese and Americans. He set to work with great skill and determination, helped by the men who were to be his closest colleagues for the next twenty-five years, Vo Nguyen Giap and Pham Van Dong, both Communists and former political prisoners of the French. Indeed

Communists held most of the key posts in the Viet Minh, although until 1951 the Viet Minh leaders, as already mentioned, played down their Communism, emphasising only their nationalism. By violent propaganda and the murder of their opponents the Viet Minh gained a considerable foothold in Tonkin, although in Annam and Cochinchina they were much less successful. The French had planned a campaign against them, due to begin on 12 March 1945, but they were forestalled by the Japanese *coup* of 9 March.

When the war ended five months later, France had no troops available to send to Indochina to organise the Japanese surrender. As this had been foreseen, the Allies had already decided at the Potsdam conference (to which France had not been invited) that Indochina should be temporarily occupied to the north of the sixteenth parallel by the Chinese and to the south by the British. Jean Sainteny was later to argue that if the French had been ready to send troops to Indochina immediately after the Japanese surrender, many of the problems of post-war Indochina might not have arisen.[21] But, even if the French had got to Hanoi before Ho Chi Minh, a revolutionary change of some sort was as inevitable as it was in India or Indonesia. Vietnamese historical tradition and national consciousness had shown before the war that France's colonial policy would have to be revised; the effect of the war was to demonstrate the weakness of France and to stimulate the Vietnamese desire for independence. A rapid French return to Indochina might have shelved the problem of the country's future status; it would not have solved it, unless the French had been prepared to adopt a completely new colonial policy.

NOTES

1. J. Fauvet, *La Quatrième République* (Fayard, 1959), p.12.
2. Coste-Floret, Minister of Overseas France, November 1947 to October 1949. Letourneau, Minister of Overseas France, October 1949 to June 1950; Minister with Special Responsibility for Indochina, July 1950 - May 1953.
3. Bidault, September 1944 to July 1948 (except for Blum's one-month Government in December 1946); Schuman, July 1948 to December 1952; Bidault, January 1953 to June 1954.
4. Coste-Floret, Minister of the Army, January to November 1947; Teitgen, Minister of the Armed Forces and National Defence, November 1947 to July 1948; Bidault, Minister of National Defence, August 1951 to February 1952; Chevigné, Minister of State for War, July 1951 to June 1954.
5. Apart from Coste-Floret and Letourneau (note 1 above), MRP Ministers of Overseas France were Pflimlin, March 1952 to June 1953; Buron, June 1954 to January 1955; Juglas, January to February 1955; Teitgen, February 1955 to January 1956; Colin, May to June 1958. Other Ministers of Overseas France were Moutet (Soc.) 1946-7; Mitterrand (UDSR), July 1950 to August 1951; Jacquinot (Ind.) August 1951 to June 1954 except for Pflimlin's interlude under Pinay in 1952; Defferre (Soc.) January 1956 to June 1957; Jaquet (Soc.), June 1957 to May 1958.

6. Interview with Jean Lacouture, February 1967. (Lacouture is a *Le Monde* journalist who has specialised on decolonisation, both in Indochina and North Africa). This point was also made by several other French scholars and politicians.

7. See, for example, J. S. Ambler, *The French Army in Politics, 1945-62* (Ohio State University Press, 1966), and J. Planchais, *Une Histoire Politique de l'Armée, 1940-67* (Seuil, 1967).

8. *La Conférence de Brazzaville,* Janvier-Février 1944 (Ministère des Colonies, Paris, 1945), p.32.

9. *Journal Officiel* (Débats parlementaires, Chambre des Députés), 27 June 1930.

10. *La Nef,* March, 1953, pp. 7-9.

11. P. M. Williams and M. Harrison, *De Gaulle's Republic* (Longmans, 1961), p.22.

12. General de Gaulle at Bordeaux in May 1947. It should be noted in passing that the Gaullist attitude to decolonisation changed to one of liberal pragmatism in the mid 1950s, but the change came too late to contribute anything to the solution of the Indochina problem.

13. See in particular F. Borella, *L'Evolution Politique et Juridique de l'Union Francaise* (Nancy doctoral thesis, 1957), and D. Bruce Marshall, *The French Colonial Myth and Constitution-making in the Fourth Republic* (Yale University Press, 1973).

14. Apart from Vietnam, Laos and Cambodia, which became Associated States in 1950, the nominally independent protectorates, Morocco and Tunisia, were Associated States, but they boycotted the institutions of the French Union from the start on the grounds that they did nothing to reduce their dependence on France.
    All the other territories of the Union were Departments or Overseas Territories. They were under direct French control, being the responsibility of the Ministry of the Interior.

15. In practice the Assembly was virtually powerless; the High Council did not meet until 1951; and the President of the Union was simply the President of France.

16. For detailed accounts of the historical background, see P. J. Honey, *Genesis of a Tragedy: the Historical Background to the Vietnam War* (Benn, 1968), or Le Thanh Khoi, *Le Vietnam: Histoire et Civilisation* (Seuil, 1965). See also the Bibliography, Part 1, p.157-60.

17. Interviews with Tran Van Huu, Nguyen Van Tam and Nguyen Manh Ha, December and January 1967.

18. *The World Today,* October 1967, p.410. See also Dennis Duncanson's excellent *Government and Revolution in Vietnam* (Oxford University Press/Royal Institute of International Affairs, 1967).

19. Honey, p.39.

20. ibid.

21. J. Sainteny, *Histoire d'une Paix Manquée: Indochine, 1945-47* (Amiot-Dumont, 1953), pp.80-102.

THE SCRIPT SYSTEM IS A LONG RUN PLAN. WE CAN LOCK PRICES AND SUBSIDISE THEM DOWN AND THEN SUBSIDISE FULL EMPLOYMENT. WE CAN THEN INTRODUCE A RIGHTS SYSTEM. IF THE PEOPLE HAVE A ONE CHILD FAMILY FOR 5 GENERATIONS THE POPULATION WILL FALL TO 3½ MILLION AND THIS WILL TAKE 175 YEARS AND WE CAN AFFORD TO BUILD EVERYBODY A HOUSE LIKE BUCKINGHAM PALACE EACH. THE SCRIPT SYSTEM IS A MILITARY SOCIAL CONTROL PLAN WHICH CONTROLS KNOWLEDGE, EDUCATION AND ECONOMICS AND IT IS STRUCTURED.

2   THE POST-WAR PROBLEM OF INDOCHINA

Ho Chi Minh declared the independence of Vietnam on 2 September, 1945. In a sense the Provisional Government he set up was the logical result of Vietnamese history; the Vietnamese were determined, sooner or later, to run their own country again. The fact that it was sooner rather than later was due to the catalytic effect of the war — European defeats in Asia, Japanese encouragement of nationalism, American anti-colonialism. The Potsdam decision to divide Vietnam aggravated the situation but was not one of the main reasons why the French failed to reassert themselves in Indochina. From France's point of view the Indochina situation did not look promising, but there were a few hopeful signs. It is true that France had to concentrate first on building up her own war-ravaged economy, and that Indochina ranked low on her list of priorities. The first full parliamentary debate on Indochina did not take place till March 1947. It is also true that de Gaulle's 24 March 1945 Declaration (proposing an Indochinese Federation within the French Union)[1] was unlikely to satisfy the nationalists, whilst the appointment of the ultra-conservative Admiral d'Argenlieu as High Commissioner was even less likely to conciliate them. At the same time Ho Chi Minh needed aid and protection, and he preferred the French to the Chinese;[2] a few far-sighted Frenchmen, such as Sainteny and Leclerc, were sent out to Indochina immediately after the war; and the Left, although divided, was in power in France with a Socialist, Marius Moutet, as Colonial Minister. It seemed possible that a way might be found for a new era of co-operation between France and Indochina.

Admiral d'Argenlieu

Admiral Thierry d'Argenlieu was appointed by General de Gaulle as High Commissioner of Indochina, a post he held from 17 August 1945 to 27 March 1947. Like his patron, de Gaulle, d'Argenlieu was a man of very definite opinions; once he had made up his mind about something there was very little point in suggesting to him that there might be another side to the question. Léon Pignon, his chief political adviser, illustrated this by emphasising that d'Argenlieu was determined to apply to the letter de Gaulle's 24 March Declaration without listening to any Vietnamese opinions about it. To d'Argenlieu, 'the Declaration was a Bible'.[3] Like de Gaulle, too, d'Argenlieu was a

13

man with fixed ideas about the meaning of 'French greatness'. He was also a devout Catholic. Indeed he had spent seventeen years as a monk before the war. In 1940 he was one of the first men to join de Gaulle, and ended the war as an Admiral in command of the Free French navy.

Almost all historians of Indochina are agreed that d'Argenlieu's appointment was at best unfortunate, at worst a major blunder by de Gaulle.[4] Jean Lacouture wrote that the only virtues possessed by d'Argenlieu were 'icy determination and fearlessness'.[5] The conservative Claude Paillat saw him as a man with 'a passionate belief in national greatness and fanatical confidence in his own judgement, . . . but he had few of the qualities required for tackling such complex problems.'[6] This is about as favourable a comment as can be found on d'Argenlieu. Men of the Left, like Claude Bourdet, were much less charitable, describing d'Argenlieu as the key figure in the 'sabotage' of the 1946 negotiations.[7] Politicians of the centre parties were later to make full use of d'Argenlieu's potential as a scapegoat for the failure of French policy in Indochina, although their attitude at the time was rather different. Max André of the MRP, for example, later criticised d'Argenlieu for summoning the second Dalat Conference (August 1946) without asking the French Government for permission to take this step.[8] But one looks in vain for MRP criticisms of d'Argenlieu in 1946. The fact of the matter is that d'Argenlieu's 'Gaullist' views were not so very different from those held by MRP leaders like Bidault, Teitgen and Coste-Floret in the immediate post-war period. They backed the wrong horse, and when it lost they blamed it, not themselves.

D'Argenlieu arrived in Saigon on 31 October 1945. His first act was unfortunate, for he carried out a purge of all administrators tainted with 'Vichyism', replacing them with inexperienced Gaullists. If he had not done this he would no doubt have been blamed for allowing France to be identified with collaboration, but the public humiliation of Frenchmen by Frenchmen was probably a great mistake in a country where it was important to avoid 'loss of face'.[9] The rump of experienced administrators retained by the Admiral were men whose views agreed with his own, namely that the nationalist disturbances could be dealt with by strong government and the exploitation of Vietnamese personal, political and regional differences. The French Security Services and the *colons* informed d'Argenlieu that this was all that was required to reassert French authority, an assumption questioned by *Le Monde* in August 1946,[10] but by that time d'Argenlieu had already decided on a certain course of action and would not listen to anyone else's criticisms.[11] Marius Moutet was later very critical of d'Argenlieu's advisers who presented only one side of the case[12] — in particular he mentioned the harmful influence of

14

Raymond Dronne, then a colonial administrator, later a prominent Gaullist deputy. D'Argenlieu also appears to have made no effort to understand the nature of the Tonkin problem. Having installed himself in Saigon he refused to visit Hanoi and did not meet Ho Chi Minh until 24 March 1946, appropriately enough on a battleship in Along Bay.

D'Argenlieu's aim, then, was to reassert French authority and to implement de Gaulle's 24 March 1945 Declaration. On the face of it this seemed a reasonable objective to the south of the sixteenth parallel, where the 'Provisional Executive Committee of South Vietnam', set up by Tran Van Giau on 25 August, had been driven out of Saigon by the forces of Generals Gracey and Leclerc at the end of September. Leclerc's armoured columns ranged throughout Cochinchina for the next two months, meeting only spasmodic resistance. The Viet Minh were not prepared for effective fighting in the South, but Leclerc was not deceived. He seems to have quickly realised that the nationalist movement had affected the masses and not just their leaders. Although he announced at a press conference on 5 February 1946 that 'Cochinchina and southern Vietnam have been completely pacified',[13] he had seen enough of the nationalist movement to have become convinced that France would be foolish to try to reassert her authority in Vietnam by military means: 'France is no longer in a position to control by arms an entity of 24 million people, amongst whom xenophobia and perhaps even nationalism have taken root'.[14]

It is interesting that two men of such similar backgrounds should have come to such different conclusions about the Vietnamese problem, because d'Argenlieu and Leclerc were both members of the French aristocracy; both were devout Catholics; both immediately rallied to de Gaulle in 1940; both were appointed to Indochina commands knowing nothing of Indochina. But there the similarity ended, for d'Argenlieu, given the senior and political job as High Commissioner, seems only to have thought of a military solution, whereas Leclerc, given the purely military post of Commander-in-Chief, soon realised that only a political solution was possible.[15] D'Argenlieu's response to Leclerc's suggestion that France should negotiate with Ho Chi Minh's Provisional Government was to send a report to de Gaulle complaining of Leclerc's 'defeatist attitude'.[16] D'Argenlieu's intransigent approach to the very delicate problem of post-war Indochina certainly did not augur well for the talks with Ho Chi Minh, which were bound to occur simply because France did not have sufficient troops to attempt a forcible take-over in the North, where Ho Chi Minh's Government was showing an increasing ability to govern, and where in any case there were 180,000 Chinese occupation troops. If Vietnam had ended at the sixteenth parallel d'Argenlieu's policy of implementing the 24 March Declaration might have

15

succeeded — at least for a few years. As it was, he reluctantly had to agree to negotiations with Ho Chi Minh, but he insisted on regarding the latter as a rebel, an attitude which hardly helped to alleviate the distrust between Vietnamese and French.

Northern Vietnam

The real Indochinese problem lay in the North of Vietnam. A *de facto* government had been established (unlike Tran Van Giau's abortive Executive Committee in the South); the Viet Minh were much more strongly organised than they had ever been in Cochinchina; the Chinese forces of occupation were unsympathetic to French aims (unlike the British under Gracey).

It was fortunate for France that her representative, who arrived in Hanoi on 22 August 1945, was a far-sighted and intelligent man, Jean Sainteny. Not that he could do much in the early stages because he remained a virtual prisoner first of the Japanese, then of the Chinese, and finally of the Viet Minh. In these unpromising circumstances, made worse by American obstruction, notably by Major Patti of the OSS,[17] Sainteny's tasks during the winter of 1945-6 were to prevent the 25,000 Frenchmen in Hanoi compounds from being massacred by the Viet Minh or Chinese, get rid of the Chinese peacefully, and work out an understanding with Ho Chi Minh.

It soon became obvious to Sainteny that Ho Chi Minh's Government was there to stay, that France would have to negotiate with it, and that a completely new policy would have to be evolved with regard to Indochina. The determination of Ho Chi Minh's Government to govern had been shown from the start. One week after the atomic bomb was dropped on Hiroshima (6 August 1945) the Viet Minh proclaimed its intention of 'disarming the Japanese before the arrival of the Allies in Indochina; taking over the power that was in the hands of the Japanese and their puppets . . . and receiving, as the authority in control of the country, the Allied forces coming to demobilize the Japanese.'[18] This was precisely what the Viet Minh did, proclaiming a provisional government four days later, and the independence of Vietnam on 2 September.

Despite famine and administrative chaos Ho Chi Minh's Provisional Government set about gaining control of the country and implementing a 'revolution'. The French administrative system was retained provisionally, but the Notables' Councils, which had been abolished by Bao Dai in the summer of 1945, were now replaced by Peoples' Committees (in theory elected, in practice appointed by the Viet Minh), and the mandarinal administrative system was also abolished. There was talk of a general election, although there is no

16

evidence that one actually took place in spite of Viet Minh claims.[19] Social reforms were promised, such as an eight hour working day and more schools. But the Government had to face tremendous difficulties, notably severe inflation and a famine. To add to these difficulties the Chinese looted the country as if they were an invading force rather than an army of occupation. The Chinese also replaced many of the Viet Minh People's Committees by nationalists, i.e. members of the VNQDD. In these circumstances Ho Chi Minh persuaded the Central Committee to abolish the Indochinese Communist Party in November and to form a government of national union with the VNQDD.

In all the confusion of the winter of 1945-6 two things stood out — the leadership of Ho Chi Minh and the fact that a revolution was occurring. Sainteny, like Leclerc, was wise enough to see that Vietnam could no more go back to 1939 than the French Convention of 1793 could have gone back to 1789. In the absence of d'Argenlieu, who had returned to France in February 1946 to defend his policies, Leclerc was acting High Commissioner as well as Commander-in-Chief. Leclerc cabled to Paris on 14 February 1946 that negotiations must be opened with Ho Chi Minh (which d'Argenlieu had opposed on the grounds that these would merely legitimise a rebel government), and that 'independence' must be pronounced forthwith (which d'Argenlieu had opposed on the grounds that it would destroy the whole basis of the French Union). On 18 February Marius Moutet cabled to Leclerc that negotiations could be opened with Ho Chi Minh's Government on the basis that Vietnam should have the right to 'self-government' within the framework of the Indochinese Federation and the French Union, Vietnam guaranteeing in return economic and cultural privileges to the French; Ho Chi Minh's Government must also agree to the return of the French Army, when it came to relieve the Chinese in accordance with the Chungking Agreement; Cochinchina was to have the right to decide about its own future. On these bases Ho Chi Minh agreed to negotiate with the French.

The 1946 negotiations

France and Vietnam continued to balance on a tight-rope during the summer and autumn of 1946, the tension of the situation being increased by men at both ends who wanted to cut the rope. Unwilling to try this balancing-act were 'all those who, grouped around the MRP, retained nostalgic feelings about the old Empire'.[20] They agreed with Admiral d'Argenlieu's words to General Valluy (8 March 1946): 'I am amazed, General, that is the only word I can use, amazed that France's leaders prefer negotiations to action when we have such a

17

magnificent expeditionary force in Indochina'.[21] The French colonial administrators were also opposed to the policy of negotiations; they knew that they stood to lose their jobs without having to read Ho Chi Minh's statement to *Le Monde:* 'We look forward to having French teachers, journalists and engineers. But no more administrators'.[22]

At the other end of the rope were men like Pham Van Dong and Vo Nguyen Giap, who considered that the only way to get rid of the French was by force. Even the more moderate members of the Viet Minh were reconciled to the fact that the negotiations might well fail. Their views were expressed in articles like one in the Hanoi newspaper, *Quyet Chien,* on 5 March 1946, entitled 'Calm but Ready': 'France has proposed negotiations. We are happy to negotiate in accordance with France's wishes. We are preparing to negotiate, but at the same time we are preparing to resist, and the negotiations will succeed only if we get independence and freedom'.

The March 1946 Agreement

The 6 March Agreement, signed at Hanoi by Sainteny and Ho Chi Minh, was only a preliminary agreement, but it was a promising start. France recognised the Democratic Republic of Vietnam as 'a free State, having its own Government and Parliament, and forming part of the Indochinese Federation within the French Union'.[23] France also promised a referendum to decide whether the three 'Kys' — Tonkin, Annam and Cochinchina — should be united. In return, the Vietnamese agreed that the French army should relieve the Chinese north of the sixteenth parallel.

This Agreement left many questions unanswered, but superficially it stabilised the situation. D'Argenlieu wrote to Alexandre Varenne, President of the National Association of French Indochina, giving his qualified approval: 'By a narrow margin we have avoided the definitive secession of Tonkin and Annam . . . they will now remain within the framework of the Indochinese Federation and the French Union'.[24] D'Argenlieu, persuaded by Leclerc, also agreed to meet Ho Chi Minh on board the French warship *Emile-Bertin* in Along Bay (24-5 March).[25] Sainteny later wrote that good progress was made at this meeting, and it was agreed that a preliminary conference should be held at Dalat in April, to be followed by the main conference in Paris shortly afterwards. Sainteny supported Ho Chi Minh's request (in the face of opposition from d'Argenlieu) that the main conference should be held in France, well away from both Vietnamese hotheads and *colon* reactionaries.[26]

Leclerc also demonstrated his wish that the 6 March Agreement should be a success. He insisted that the French armoured vehicles returning to Hanoi (9 March) should fly both French and Viet Minh flags. He seemed delighted when Giap, with a spontaneous gesture, shook his hand before the Tomb of the Unknown Soldier in Hanoi — a gesture cheered by the Vietnamese, although ominously not by the French.[27] The March Agreement seemed to bear out the optimism and generosity expressed by the Socialist Félix Gouin when he became Prime Minister of France in January 1946: 'We have achieved much for the peoples of distant Indochina . . . However let us be clear about this; we have but one end there: to ensure a sufficient degree of order and civilisation that all citizens, in accordance with the principles of the U.N. Charter, can make a free choice about the political future of their country'.[28]

Perhaps Indochina would be independent before India or Indonesia; France might be the first great power to fulfil the aims of the U.N. Charter and enter into a new relationship with her former colonies. It all seemed to depend on the degree of magnanimity with which the Government interpreted the March 1946 Agreement. On 27 March Leclerc sent a report advocating a generous approach and exhorting moderation (as in his 14 February telegram).[29] He warned that in the climate of world opinion in 1946, and with the troops available, 'the reconquest of Tonkin, even in part, is impossible'; the March Agreement must be loyally implemented; progress towards a negotiated solution, even if it meant pronouncing the word 'independence', was essential.[30] The report was strongly worded, perhaps betraying Leclerc's anxiety, but as it was to fall on the ears of a Socialist Minister of Overseas France (as the Colonies were now called) there seemed some grounds for optimism.

But all was not well. It did not require a *Le Monde* leader-writer to point out that there was no agreement on fundamentals.[31] Ho Chi Minh made this clear when he told Sainteny that the 6 March Agreement was a 'victory' for France: 'My position is difficult, because you know very well that basically you have won. You know that I wanted more than has been granted . . . Nevertheless, I realise that one cannot achieve everything in one day'.[32] Sainteny was equally apprehensive. Returning to France, he tried to persuade people of the importance of the developments in Indochina, of the need for a radically revised colonial policy, of the need for progress towards 'dominion status', at least for Vietnam. He held press conferences, spoke on the radio, went to meetings of the 'Comité de l'Indochine', but could not convince French politicians of 'the immense importance of the Indochina problem'.[33] The influential economic interests had their eyes obstinately fixed on the past, whilst the politicians had their eyes glued to the domestic present. André Colin, who was then Secretary-General of the MRP, recalled that as far as his party was concerned there was little real interest in colonial affairs during 1946 in spite of signs of impending trouble in Indochina. Only men like Max André, with his Far Eastern connections, and Georges Bidault, with his responsibilities as Foreign Minister and later as Prime Minister, paid much attention to the situation in Indochina before the Viet Minh *coup* of 19 December 1946.[34]

Meanwhile, in Hanoi dismay was being expressed because the March Agreement had not included the word 'independence', whilst rumours were even circulating that 'Uncle Ho' had become 'Viet Gian' (the betrayer of the fatherland). Ho Chi Minh had to use all his crafty eloquence to regain the cheers of the crowd: 'You know that I, Ho Chi Minh, have always led you on the path to freedom and that I have struggled all my life for the independence of our country. You know that I would rather die than betray our country. I swear to you that I have not sold it'.[35] Despite the applause with which this statement was received, the uneasiness of the Vietnamese population was shown by continued, though spasmodic, Viet Minh outrages.

Leclerc, too, had expressed fears as well as hopes in his report of 27 March: 'If I insist on these facts (i.e. the need for a political solution), it is only because I have suddenly realised the extent to which the Government has been misinformed about the gravity of the situation'. A man who warns his Government that it is being 'misinformed' is clearly worried. And Leclerc had good reason to be worried by the actions of d'Argenlieu and Cédile, the Governor of Cochinchina. D'Argenlieu gave provisional approval of the March Agreement and then sent a criticism of it to the Government in Paris. He also began to persuade Marius Moutet of the advantages of setting up an 'independent' Cochinchinese Republic, a proposal encouraged by Moutet in several telegrams during March, 1946.[36]

D'Argenlieu and Cédile were playing the old game of French colonial administrators: decide on a policy without reference to Paris; persuade Paris that the policy is both feasible and beneficial to all concerned, including the natives; if persuasion fails, carry out the policy all the same. That d'Argenlieu had embarked on this course was indicated by his telegrams to Moutet and by the dispatch to Paris of a four-man commission to plead for Cochinchinese autonomy; it was confirmed by Cédile's assurance (12 March) to the provisional Advisory Council in Cochinchina that the March Agreement was no more than a local agreement between the Hanoi authorities and the French Commissioner in Tonkin – a statement apparently confirmed by Moutet's declaration in the National Assembly on 14 March.

The attitude of Marius Moutet remained equivocal throughout 1946. This Socialist Minister, who had expressed such liberal views in the 1930s, notably as Colonial Minister in the Popular Front Government, seems to have followed a path previously well-trodden by left-wing idealists, i.e. a drift to the Right. It is not surprising that this new J. H. Thomas was retained at the Ministry of Overseas France (Colonies) when Georges Bidault became Prime Minister on 25 June 1946, nor perhaps that he allowed the situation to drift out of control, for it always required a Colonial Minister of exceptional character and skill to control colonial administrators.[37] Moutet would have to have been a Minister of outstanding foresight and determination to have heeded the warnings of Leclerc in the summer of 1946.

Moutet's own explanation of his conduct in 1946 was that basically he agreed with Leclerc's views; he believed in a policy of negotiations and concessions, but to some extent his hands were tied. Two factors were important here: the first was the constant state of unrest in Indochina throughout 1946, which meant that Moutet tended to formulate his policy in consultation with Bidault (Foreign Minister till 28 November) and Michelet (Minister of the Armed Forces till the same date) instead of on his own initiative; and secondly, although d'Argenlieu had been appointed High Commissioner by de Gaulle, Moutet thought it would be an error to replace him so soon after his arrival in Indochina. Moutet never seems to have trusted d'Argenlieu, but he lacked the ruthlessness to get rid of him. In any case, Moutet emphasised strongly the *legal* difference between Cochinchina and the other two *Kys* (Annam and Tonkin), pointing out that the former was a 'colony,' and hence constitutionally he was not in a position to grant Ho Chi Minh's demand for immediate Vietnamese unity: only the French National Assembly could decide whether a change in Cochinchina's status should be accepted. If this change were agreed to by the National Assembly, he had no objection to a referendum in Cochinchina and the subsequent unification of Vietnam. Moutet, however, was opposed to 'independence' being pronounced for Vietnam in 1946-7. He favoured a large measure of autonomy for Vietnam, but felt that the Indochinese states were not ready for full independence, although ultimately, he claimed, the French Union should have consisted of 'autonomous' states.[38]

Moutet denied that he was influenced by the MRP in 1946, but in fact he almost certainly was. On his own admission he worked out much of his policy in consultation with Bidault and Michelet. It was Michelet, who, as Minister for the Army, sent Max André to Indochina in January 1946: 'I sent him to see Ho Chi Minh. It was a mistake . . . his influence was extremely bad. I had thought that he was a man of conciliatory views . . . He was a lamentable choice.'[39] Michelet went on to say that he paid considerable attention to André's reports from Indochina, when in fact he would have done better to have listened to the advice of Jean d'Arcy, his own *chef de cabinet,* who was sceptical about the inflexible policies advocated by André. Jean Sainteny was equally critical of the role played by André in 1946: 'His influence was important and bad . . . He was Bidault's adviser rather than his spokesman . . . He also advised Michelet

21

badly — Michelet who was basically rather liberal'.[40] André maintained
that he, Bidault and Moutet were always in agreement when they discussed
Indochina. If this was the case — and there seems no reason to doubt it — it
is clear that Moutet must have done the 'agreeing' with Bidault and André,
and by so doing he betrayed the liberal ideas he had expressed in the 1930s.
In general, Moutet seems to have been rather a weak character — shown,
for example, by his failure to dismiss d'Argenlieu when the Admiral
summoned the second Dalat Conference without consulting him. Thus, all
the evidence suggests that the well-intentioned Moutet was much more
influenced by the MRP — in particular by Bidault, Michelet and André —
than he realised (or admitted). The MRP's influence on Indochina policy in
1946 was important, because a few MRP leaders knew what they wanted,
whilst Moutet and the Socialists were hesitant, and the other major
government party, the Communists, were frankly not interested.

Dalat and Fontainebleau

After the negotiations leading to the March Agreement (1946) two further
conferences were held, the Dalat preliminary Conference (18 April - 11
May) and the Fontainebleau Conference (July - August). The Dalat
Conference went badly. The Vietnamese delegation was theoretically led
jointly by Nguyen Tuong Tam of the VNQDD and Vo Nguyen Giap of the
Viet Minh; in fact the former was ill throughout the conference, possibly
diplomatically, so that the latter alone put the Vietnamese case. Giap
began by demanding the suspension of operations against the Viet Minh
in Cochinchina; the French replied that any such operations were police
actions against people who were committing breaches of the peace. But
this was a superficial matter compared with the completely different
concepts of the French Union held by the two sides. Max André, the MRP
leader of the French delegation, spoke of a compact Union with one
foreign policy; the Vietnamese of a loose association of equal states.
France wanted an Indochinese Federation of five 'Free' States with a
Federal Assembly of sixty, whose main task would be to work out the
federal budget. The Five States were to control their internal affairs, with
the important proviso that Justice, Hygiene, Social Security, Economic
Planning, Transport, Customs, Communications and Immigration were to
be the responsibility of the High Commissioner and his administration. To
the Vietnamese these conditions were unacceptable; they realised that they
were going to be accorded only second degree independence.

The Dalat Conference was really a failure, and Vo Nguyen Giap drew
his conclusions; the French were not to be trusted, the Vietnamese
Government must be on its guard. Giap was so outspoken and belligerent
that Ho Chi Minh decided to omit him from the Vietnamese delegation due
to leave for France on 31 May. But in a sense Giap was only being
realistic; Max André later described Giap as 'extremely bitter and hard, but

very intelligent'.[41] In his attitude after Dalat Giap certainly showed both bitterness and a perceptive grasp of the realities of the situation. It was clear that if the French would not modify their views as put forward at Dalat there was little chance of a peaceful settlement. That they were unlikely to do so was indicated by Andre''s communiqué describing the concessions made at Dalat as 'major' and 'final'[42]. If André really believed that France had made 'major concessions' at Dalat, it is not difficult to see why the Fontainebleau Conference failed. In fact, André later admitted privately that he thought Fontainebleau was bound to fail after Dalat had shown the radically different objectives of the two sides. However, he also maintained that he did all he could to prevent a breakdown at Fontainebleau.[43]

What chance there might have been of preventing failure at the Fontainebleau Conference was virtually ruined by the man who had rather prematurely declared that the Dalat Conference had been 'highly successful'.[44] For on 1 June 1946 d'Argenlieu proclaimed the 'autonomous' Cochinchinese Republic. Dr Thinh was appointed Prime Minister; the ministers he chose were to be responsible only to him, whilst the Consultative Council (elected on a very restricted basis) had only two tasks — to select the Prime Minister by a two-thirds majority and vote the budget. The whole set-up was merely a facade behind which the real *deus ex machina* was the French High Commissioner.

D'Argenlieu's action put the French Government in an embarrassing position. On the eve of negotiations it would have been difficult for the Government to dismiss its representative in Indochina (even had it wanted to do so); at the same time the new 'republic', still legally a colony, could not even be recognised by the Government without the approval of the National Assembly. Worst of all, the proclamation of an 'autonomous' Cochinchina infuriated the Vietnamese provisional government, which regarded this action as a stab in the back, for Cochinchina was 'a symbol both of the unity of Vietnam and of the sincerity of France'.[45] Conferences such as Fontainebleau require mutual confidence if they are to succeed; the 'autonomous' Cochinchinese republic destroyed this essential basis before the negotiations began. But at the time d'Argenlieu's action attracted little attention, although the Communist paper, *L'Humanité,* justifiably asked: 'What is going on in Saigon? It seems that a tiny number of Cochinchinese autonomists, who represent no one but themselves, are wielding disproportionate influence'.[46]

On his arrival in France Ho Chi Minh continued to profess optimism. He was willing to refer to the 'autonomous' Cochinchinese republic as 'a misunderstanding', which could be cleared up at the Fontainebleau Conference.[47] He was even willing to comment favourably on the results of Dalat (as no other Vietnamese nationalist would do): 'We agree with the idea of a federation so long as each constituent part is permitted to consider its own interests first, whilst at the same time remaining closely linked to the other members. Having reached agreement in principle, we must now work out the means by which the federation can be built'.[48] Unfortunately no real agreement in principle had been reached despite Ho Chi Minh's assertion, and without it the two sides could hardly go on to work out the means for realising the new federation. Ho Chi Minh may have reached some 'agreement in principle' with Sainteny and Leclerc; but they were not the French Government, and by July 1946 were even less representative of its views than they had been in March. For the rejection of the first Constitutional draft in May, followed by the General Election of June, had led to a stronger MRP and weaker Socialists; the Communists gained a little and the Radicals and Conservatives showed signs of revival. The result was that the axis of the Assembly moved to the Right, and the new Provisional Government was headed by the first MRP Prime Minister, Georges Bidault.

The Vietnamese delegation could hardly have been cheered by the results of the June election in view of General Xuan's statement to *Paris - Saigon* (29 May).'The Cochinchinese delegation', he said, 'has received a warm welcome from the Radicals and Conservatives and a very enthusiastic welcome from the MRP'. Even the Communists had welcomed the proposals for Cochinchinese autonomy: 'Remarkably enough, M. Thorez, the deputy Prime Minister, assured me that the Communist Party had no intention of liquidating French positions in Indochina, and he hopes to see the tricolour continuing to fly in all parts of the French Empire. The only opposition we have encountered has been amongst Socialists. . .'.[49] In other words, only the Socialists were likely to listen sympathetically to Ho Chi Minh's delegation (not to be confused with the Cochinchinese 'autonomists'), but the Socialists had been weakened by their electoral setback in June. Moreover, the only Socialist Minister directly concerned with Indochina was the indecisive Marius Moutet. The Communists' attitude may seem surprising, especially in view of their later condemnation of *la sale guerre,* but Communists from Lenin to the present day have had little difficulty in accepting imperialism if they are in power. The French Communists only became enthusiastic supporters of Ho Chi Minh after being evicted from the Government in May 1947. Meanwhile, in Bidault's Cabinet of June-December 1946 there were 9 Christian Democrats, 5 Socialists, 7 Communists and 2 Radicals. Such a cabinet would clearly make only minimal concessions to the Vietnamese nationalists.

From Ho Chi Minh's point of view it was unfortunate that the new French premier, Georges Bidault, was highly intelligent, strongly anti-Communist, and absolutely determined to build a 'one and indivisible' French Union. Of all French politicians, Bidault was the least likely to be deceived by Ho's apparent moderation. Moreover, Bidault was a man of enormous influence in French politics in the immediate post-war period, largely owing to the fact that he had been President of the National Resistance Council in 1943-4. It was a strange paradox that the former leader of the French Resistance was to prove the most implacable opponent of the leaders of national resistance movements throughout the French Union. Later, as Bidault moved further to the Right, his influence within the MRP gradually declined, but he did not finally break with the Christian Democrats until 1958 when his extreme *Algérie Française* views were at complete variance with those of most of his party colleagues.[50]

Marius Moutet and Georges Le Brun-Kéris claimed that Bidault was not *au fond* illiberal in the immediate post-war period. It was only when it became fully apparent that Ho Chi Minh was first and foremost a Communist that Bidault refused to consider making any concessions.[51] But the only evidence to support the Moutet-Le Brun-Kéris thesis about Bidault's 'liberalism' is that in January 1947 Bidault tried to persuade Leclerc to take over from d'Argenlieu as High Commissioner. Leclerc, however, refused, almost certainly because de Gaulle (having resigned in January 1946 as Head of the Provisional Government) advised Leclerc not to accept on the grounds that he (Leclerc) would not be a free agent, but would be subject to constant government interference. Leclerc seems to have been in a curious position in 1946-7, normally advocating liberal policies in Indochina, but at other times opposing them on the advice of his old wartime commander, de Gaulle. A possible explanation for Bidault's attempt to persuade Leclerc to return to Indochina is that he was using Leclerc as a pawn in his quarrel with de Gaulle. Bidault and de Gaulle disliked each other from the time they first met in 1944, even although they co-operated in government until January 1946, and Robert Buron made the plausible suggestion that Bidault wanted to replace d'Argenlieu with Leclerc in January 1947 only because d'Argenlieu was a de Gaulle appointee and not because he preferred Leclerc's 'liberalism' to d'Argenlieu's intransigence.[52] There is no evidence to suggest that Bidault favoured 'independence' or 'dominion status' for Vietnam at this or any other stage. Le Brun-Kéris's description of Bidault in 1946 — 'in reality more liberal than was apparent' — thus seems to be accurate only in the sense that Bidault's colonial policy was marginally more flexible than that of de Gaulle or d'Argenlieu. It was hardly likely to be flexible enough to satisfy Ho Chi Minh's delegation at Fontainbleau. A more accurate assessment of Bidault's position in 1946 was probably that of Maurice Schumann, who maintained that from the start there were two basic attitudes towards decolonisation within the MRP: those against it, led by Georges Bidault and Alfred Coste-Floret, and those for it, led by Robert Schuman and Robert Buron.[53]

In the political circumstances of the summer of 1946, therefore, the Fontainebleau Congress was virtually doomed before it started. It is true that Ho Chi Minh continued to express optimism, for example at his press conference of 13 July, when he said that he was 'convinced of the ultimate success of the Franco-Vietnamese negotiations'.[54] It is also true that Bidault's speech of welcome augured quite well, even if in a rather platitudinous way; for example, he addressed Ho Chi Minh as 'Head of the Provisional Government of Vietnam',[55] thus implicitly recognising the legitimacy of the régime set up in September 1945. On the other hand, he made no reference to 'independence' or even to 'internal autonomy'.

If Bidault and Moutet really wanted Fontainebleau to succeed, they chose their negotiators badly. Nearly all were men of secondary importance, 'technicians rather than diplomats or senior politicians capable of representing France in negotiations with another State'.[56] Not one politician of cabinet rank was chosen; yet, as Paul Mus later emphasised, the problem was essentially political not technical.[57] Bidault's decision to choose Max André as leader of the French delegation was particularly unfortunate. Claude Bourdet later described André as 'the representative of financial interests and Catholic interests in Indochina'.[58] André was an agnostic[59], one of the very few in the largely Catholic MRP, so it is hardly reasonable to accuse him personally of being swayed by Catholic interests,[60] but he was certainly a man of the *colon* class. He had been a director of the Franco-Chinese Bank from 1923-35, returning to France as financial adviser to the government in 1936. A close friend of Bidault's since the Munich crisis, he was appointed head of the Paris Resistance Co-ordinating Committee by Bidault in 1943. Like Bidault, André was a founder-member of the MRP in 1944. His only qualifications to lead the French negotiating team at Fontainebleau were that he knew something about pre-war Indochina and that he was a trusted colleague of Bidault's. Nguyen Manh Ha, one of Ho Chi Minh's Ministers in 1945-6, tells the story of the first meeting he arranged between André and Ho Chi Minh. After André had left the room Ho Chi Minh asked Nguyen Manh Ha: 'What is André's background?' – 'He is a former director of the (Franco-Chinese) Bank' – 'That does not surprise me in the least', replied Ho, 'We will have difficulty in getting very far with people like him'.[61]

At Fontainebleau André claims he was given 'a very wide brief' by Bidault, but on the eve of the conference Bidault warned André that although he could make a large number of detailed concessions, he was

to 'give away nothing in the field of diplomacy'.[62] In other words Ho
Chi Minh was to be refused what he regarded as *the* essential attribute
of independence. At this stage Ho Chi Minh would have been quite
prepared to have remained within the French Union, provided his
country could also have joined the United Nations. It seems reasonable
to accept André's statement that he did not deliberately sabotage the
Fontainebleau negotiations,[63] as was later claimed by the Socialist Paul
Rivet,[64] but at the same time the position adopted by André and
Bidault was far too rigid and 'traditional' to satisfy the Vietnamese.
Moreover, André's background as a *colon* certainly did not help; he was
incapable of creating an atmosphere of mutual confidence.

To make matters worse, the 'swing to the Right', which had occurred
at the General Election of June 1946, and in particular the decline of the
Socialists, encouraged intransigence on the part of the Government. The
Christian Democrats obtained 28 per cent of the votes cast, their highest
ever figure, and rightly or wrongly this no doubt seemed to Bidault like
a mandate for his policies *in toto*. But Fontainebleau really only
demonstrated what Dalat had already proved – that the differences
between the two sides were so great as to be irreconcilable without a
major shift of position by one or the other. And in the summer of 1946
neither side would, or could, concede enough to satisfy the other.
Vietnam had experienced a 'revolution' since the departure of the
Japanese; Ho Chi Minh's Government could not accept less than unity
and independence, albeit within the framework of the French Union.
France, on the other hand, was just recovering her self-respect after the
years of wartime humiliation; she could hardly be expected to agree to
secession, or even partial secession, from her new Union of a hundred
million Frenchmen before it had even been tried out. When Ho Chi Minh
told *Franc-Tireur* (15 August) that all that was needed was one word, 'I
repeat . . . one word: independence', he was asking for the one thing that
no French Government would have conceded at that time.

The 'entente' Breaks Down

Max André later maintained that the Conference of Fontainebleau failed
because the Vietnamese Communists arrived at the conference table with
set opinions from which they refused to deviate. Argument and discussion
in the accepted sense were thus impossible. The Communists were
therefore almost entirely responsible for the failure of the conference.[65]
To some extent this appears to be an *ex post facto* judgement, for although
it is true that the Vietnamese leader, Pham Van Dong, was a diehard
Communist and therefore particularly suspect in the eyes of the French
negotiators, it is clear that the Fontainebleau Conference failed primarily
because Pham Van Dong put forward what were regarded as excessively
nationalist demands, namely complete unity and independence, at a time

27

when virtually no French politician, not even from the Communist Party, was prepared to concede them.

The tone was set on the first day when, after platitudinous introductory remarks by André and Pham Van Dong, the latter launched into an attack on France for 'mutilating Vietnam' and breaking the March Agreement by condoning the setting-up of the Cochinchinese Republic.[66] André replied that the status of Cochinchina was a legal matter requiring a decision by the French National Assembly. The talking continued on parallel lines (with various suspensions) until 27 August, the French regarding the problem of the status of Vietnam essentially as one of internal constitutional law, and the Vietnamese seeing it in terms of international law: for the former it was a question of 'autonomy within the French bloc', whereas for the latter it was a question of 'independence complemented with association with France'.[67] The insuperable stumbling block was Cochinchina — to the French a colony, to Ho Chi Minh 'Vietnamese territory . . . flesh of our flesh and blood of our blood . . . Before Corsica was French, Cochinchina was Vietnamese'.[68] It was all very well for André to maintain that the French did all they could to keep the negotiations open, for example by special restricted evening sessions.[69] So long as the two sides continued to talk different languages there was no hope of agreement.

Leclerc's resignation of his command in July 1946, like the second Dalat Conference in August (summoned without Moutet's permission), was a clear sign that those in favour of confrontation were getting their way. On 3 August d'Argenlieu said to Devillers in Saigon: 'I can assure you that if General de Gaulle were still Prime Minister of France, Ho Chi Minh would not get away with such impertinence. He would be obliged to keep his place'.[70] D'Argenlieu also told Devillers that he expected General de Gaulle to return to power in the near future, and in the meantime he had no intention of letting Indochina advance beyond the limits outlined in de Gaulle's 24 March 1945 Declaration.[71] D'Argenlieu had already expressed his preference for a solution by force; he was soon to get his way.

The modus vivendi of 14 September solved nothing. This last-minute arrangement, signed by Ho Chi Minh and Marius Moutet after the departure of the Vietnamese delegation from France, was only 'an agreement to postpone agreement'.[72] Politicians of the Right later regarded the modus vivendi as a mistake, because it gave the Viet Minh more time to prepare their attack of December 1946.[73] Men of the Left later criticised it, because no real concessions were made.[74] Yet Ho Chi Minh continued, at least in public, to profess optimism. When he arrived back in Indochina he told journalists that if the modus vivendi were applied by both sides, another full-scale conference could be arranged in due course to clear up the outstanding differences.[75] But if

28

Ho Chi Minh really wanted peace it is surprising that he rejected Marius Moutet's proposal that he should return to Vietnam by air; he could thus have used his influence for moderation within three days. Instead, he insisted on returning by boat, a six week journey. Meanwhile, the much more extreme Giap remained in charge of the provisional government in Hanoi. Perhaps Ho Chi Minh was more realistic when shortly after Fontainebleau he told the American journalist, David Schoenbrun: 'It will be a war between an elephant and a tiger. If the tiger ever stands still, the elephant will crush him with his mighty tusks. But the tiger will not stand still. . . He will leap upon the back of the elephant, tearing huge chunks from his side, and then he will leap back into the dark jungle. And slowly the elephant will bleed to death. That will be the war of Indochina'.[76]

Whether it was the French or the Vietnamese who brought about the final rupture does not really matter. With both sides sticking to their principles and confident that a trial of strength would lead to victory for themselves, it is of little concern who attacked first. There is no doubt that at the time the French played down their own bombardment of Haiphong (23 November), later appropriately described by Moutet as 'a foolish and criminal mistake',[77] and that they exaggerated the treachery of the Viet Minh at Hanoi (*coup* of 19 December); equally the Viet Minh argued 'vice-versa'. On the whole the evidence indicates that the French allowed an atmosphere of tension to build up, so that they could use force.[78] D'Argenlieu was in Paris at the time of the Haiphong bombardment, in which 6,000 Vietnamese were killed, but he had encouraged General Valluy to take the tough line which led to the latter's famous telegram to General Morlière (22 November): 'The time has come to give a hard lesson to those who are treacherously attacking us. You are to gain complete control of Haiphong, using all the means at your disposal'.[79] The bombardment of Haiphong (23 November), followed by French demands for free movement along the Haiphong-Hanoi road, seemed like a direct challenge to Ho Chi Minh and Giap. Meanwhile, in Paris d'Argenlieu did all he could to persuade the politicians that any signs of weakness would mark the first step in the disintegration of the French Union. He also cabled his support to Valluy: 'You have my complete support. We will not withdraw or concede'.[80] There is little doubt that Bidault also favoured the use of force. D'Argenlieu later told Devillers that Bidault had, in fact, advocated its use on several occasions in the autumn of 1946.[81] And in March 1949 the Communist Charles Tillon, who had been Bidault's Minister of Armaments in 1946, said in the National Assembly: 'In November 1946 I was present at a meeting of the Committee of National Defence. A certain amount of evidence was produced to show that war was by no means inevitable, but Bidault, who was then Prime Minister, insisted: 'Il faut tirer le canon.'[82] Bidault did not refute this allegation. Meanwhile, in 1946, d'Argenlieu had persuaded most of the politicians to close their ranks against a policy of concessions, and influential newspapers such as *Le Figaro* and *L'Aube* supported him. Even Moutet seemed to welcome the idea of a clash between the two sides so that law and order could be restored by force.

On the other hand, the Vietnamese Provisional Government seemed to be equally set on a trial of strength. The Socialist Léon Blum had become Prime Minister of France (16 December), and Blum had stated that: 'There is only one way to maintain our cultural and political influence in Vietnam, and that is to come to a genuine agreement with Vietnam, based on independence and friendship'.[83] Yet, despite such conciliatory statements by the French, Ho Chi Minh apparently continued to prepare for the *coup* of 19 December.[84] It is true that he sent a message to Blum (15 December) with proposals for reducing the tension, but although the message was deliberately held up by the French authorities in Saigon and did not reach Paris until 26 December, Ho Chi Minh could at least have waited for a reply before unleashing his *coup* if he really wanted peace at this stage. Instead he told the Viet Minh to be ready to attack on 19 December, and refused to see his old friend Sainteny after 3 December. The latter fully realised the gravity of the situation, writing to Albert Sarraut on 8 December: 'The situation is deteriorating rapidly. . . There is no question but that all the ground gained with such difficulty before and after 6 March has now been lost'.[85] Finally at 2.00 p.m. on 19 December, i.e. eight hours before the scheduled coup, Giap informed Ho Chi Minh that Marius Moutet was coming out to Vietnam. Did he wish to postpone the attack? The answer was no.[86]

A Missed Opportunity?

Some of those who have written about decolonisation have contended that an opportunity for a peaceful settlement of the Indochina problem was missed in 1946. There is an element of truth in their contention, but the price for a peace settlement would have been so high as to have been unacceptable to any French government at that time. In a sense, therefore, the whole argument is pointless. But in view of the tragic history of Indochina in the years which followed, it is worth commenting briefly on the arguments of the two sides.

Jean Sainteny, a Frenchman who knew Ho Chi Minh well, believes that a deal could have been done with Ho in 1946. His judgement is based on his personal knowledge of the Vietnamese leader,

this ascetic figure, whose features revealed his intelligence, energy and shrewdness . . . Ho Chi Minh was a man of incomparable prestige and popularity. There can be no doubt that it was a disaster that France underestimated this man. All the evidence suggests that in 1946 he

30

wanted to come to an agreement with France, and that his intention was to keep Vietnam within the French Union.[87]

The distinguished historian of Indochina, Jean Lacouture, also maintains that France could have made an 'entente' with Ho Chi Minh, who would probably have developed into the Tito of Asia owing to his strong sense of nationalism combined with his traditional Vietnamese suspicion of China. Lacouture, too, was impressed with Ho Chi Minh's apparent moderation when he interviewed him in January 1946.[88] Philippe Devillers, whilst more cautious in his judgement, supports the view of Leclerc that the only possible solution was a political one, and that if Ho Chi Minh had been granted independence in 1946 within the context of the French Union, a Franco-Vietnamese relationship of friendship and association might have resulted, particularly because Ho Chi Minh realised the feeble economic position of Vietnam and would have preferred French to Chinese or American aid.[89] Paul Mus likewise asserted that a successful peace could have been made in 1946, not because he had any illusions about Ho Chi Minh, 'this intransigent and incorruptible revolutionary, this Saint-Just, embittered by twenty years of struggle against the French',[90] but because it would have been politically and economically expedient for the Viet Minh Government to have come to an agreement with France rather than with anyone else, provided of course that independence and unity could have been wrung from the French.

One thing that does seem certain is that if both sides had stuck to the letter of the March 1946 Agreement and war had been avoided, Vietnam would today be a wholly Communist state. As Bernard Fall put it: 'Ho Chi Minh *might* have become a national Communist leader, but it is also clear that he would have run all Vietnam as a Communist state'.[91] The evidence seems to show that Ho Chi Minh was a totally committed Communist from the time of his 'conversion' in the early 1920s, and that during 1946 (and later) he kept quiet about his Communism only because it was politically expedient to do so. Sainteny was almost certainly naive in his assumption that Ho's Government might have developed into an essentially nationalist rather than Communist Government. Ho Chi Minh was always a skilful politician, realising that the essence of successful politics is compromise. He was willing to compromise in November 1945 to the extent of dissolving the Vietnamese Communist Party, but from that date until the official appearance of a new Communist Party, the Lao Dong, in 1951, the Viet Minh Communists nevertheless maintained tight control over the resistance movement. The same has been true since the 1954 Geneva Conference: 'The source of all authority in North Vietnam is and always has been the Head of State and Chairman of the Lao Dong Party, Ho Chi Minh'.[92] Hoang Van Chi maintains even more decisively than Patrick Honey that Ho Chi Minh was first and foremost a Communist, and that as soon as he had got rid of the French he would have set about introducing a fully totalitarian state, and would soon have broken off all contacts with France. Hoang Van Chi bases his arguments on his personal experience of Ho Chi Minh's methods, both in the Viet Minh as a nationalist fighter and in the years after 1954 when Ho Chi Minh carried out his 'thought reform' and 'land reform' campaigns of 1953 and 1954-6.[93] But Hoang Van Chi's arguments are somewhat weakened by two factors. Firstly, his opinions are obviously coloured by his personal animosity towards Ho Chi Minh, which seems to have developed largely after 1954. Secondly, he clearly underestimates the extent to which Ho Chi Minh was a realist, and in 1946 Ho Chi Minh knew that Vietnam could not survive economically without aid from outside. Ho Chi Minh would almost certainly have accepted French economic aid as readily as Tito accepted Marshall aid. Ho said in July 1946 that he wanted co-operation with France:

> The political relationship between France and Vietnam must be defined in a treaty. This treaty must be based on one fundamental principle: the right of people to decide their own destiny. In economic and cultural matters we are in favour of association with France within the framework of the French Union. There can be close co-operation on all matters of common interest.[94]

One is no doubt right to be as sceptical about the publicly expressed views of Ho Chi Minh as about those of any other politician, but this statement does ring true in its emphasis on the Atlantic Charter's self-determination principle and on Indochina's practical need for economic association with a wealthy nation, i.e. France. Further evidence that Ho Chi Minh was interested in an entente with France is that he told the French Communist, Jacques Duclos, that 'one of the things I regret most in life was my failure to come to an agreement with France in 1946'.[95] This statement was made in a private conversation with Duclos at a Communist Party Congress in Moscow in 1958, i.e. several years after Ho Chi Minh had any particular axe to grind with France, and in circumstances which make it likely that he meant what he was saying.

Jean Lacouture, who met Ho Chi Minh on many occasions, maintains that Ho Chi Minh was a nationalist, a Communist and a Francophil, with equal emphasis on the first two and somewhat less on the third. His chief aim was always to achieve independence for a united Vietnam, and this aim did not clash with his belief in Marxist economic and social principles.[96] Patrick Honey, on the other hand, maintains that it is a fiction to assume that the Vietnamese resistance movement was basically a nationalist movement; it was 'a movement dominated and tightly controlled by the Communists'.[97] However, it is equally arguable that it was a nationalist movement made highly efficient and disciplined because it was Communist controlled, similar in fact to Tito's partisan movement in wartime Yugoslavia. Ho Chi Minh, like Tito, was both the symbol and reflection of this nationalist-cum-Communist liberation movement. In addition Ho Chi Minh did have some genuine sympathy for French culture and French egalitarian principles. It was, therefore, natural that he should want the newly independent Vietnam to retain some economic and cultural ties with France. The only alternatives appeared to be the United States or China, but the former soon made it clear that she would give economic aid only if Ho eschewed his Marxism, whilst the latter, besides still being under the Kuomintang, had been Vietnam's traditional enemy for 2,000 years.

Thus, there seems little doubt that a peace could have been achieved in 1946. But the price would have been very heavy from France's point of view: Vietnam would have become independent and Communist, and French influence there would have declined rapidly. Ho Chi Minh would probably have made full use of French aid and expertise for a few years, but there can be little doubt that he would have got rid of the French as soon as possible and transformed Vietnam into a wholly Communist State. Ho admitted as much in 1960. He was always a very talented opportunist, and succeeded in deceiving men like Sainteny and the American Abbot with his apparent moderation in 1945-6.[98] Ho could tell a barefaced lie with tears in his eyes, and this was no small asset in politics. It cut no ice at all with the Chinese, but was most effective in dealing with the French and Americans, or at least with some of them. The French, however, were not blameless for the breakdown of negotiations. D'Argenlieu and the *colons* misunderstood, or refused to understand, the nature of the nationalist movement in Vietnam. They allowed tension to build up, assuming that the rebel Ho Chi Minh could be crushed as easily as his predecessors of 1908, 1916 and 1930. It is possible to explain, if not to justify, the attitude of d'Argenlieu and the *colons*. They, like the vast majority of Frenchmen, were determined to bury the humiliating memory of 1940 by the establishment of a powerful, closely integrated French Union of a hundred million people. Only thus could France hope to be an equal of the Great Powers, and she could hardly start off her ambitious new enterprise by casting away the jewel of her former empire.

In these circumstances it is difficult to apportion blame for the breakdown of negotiations in 1946. On the Vietnamese side the 'hard-liners', Vo Nguyen Giap and Pham Van Dong, were possibly more responsible than Ho Chi Minh for the final rupture. But arguably they were just more realistic, or perhaps only less devious, than Ho Chi Minh. On the French side the Christian Democratic MRP, still considerably influenced by General de Gaulle, led the intransigents. Yet the MRP was 'not really a colonialist party . . . the Christian Democrats were relatively ignorant about the situation in Indochina'.[99] Like the other French parties, the MRP was engrossed in electioneering, with the three elections and two referenda of 1946; like the others, it had to concentrate on the things which concerned the French people most, i.e. economic, social and constitutional problems — in that order. Nevertheless, in spite of their ignorance about overseas France, the Christian Democrats played a more important role than their tripartite partners, the Socialists and Communists, in moulding Indochina policy, both by their influence over Marius Moutet, the Socialist Minister of Overseas France, and through Georges Bidault, who was Prime Minister from 19 June to 28 November 1946, within which period occurred the crucial Fontainebleau Conference.

Pierre de Chevigné, an MRP leader who worked closely with Bidault at that time, suggested that one reason for Bidault's inflexibility in 1946 was that he had been cut off from the outside world during the war. He was thus unaware of the extent to which anti-colonialism and nationalism, encouraged by both Americans and Russians, had grown since 1939.[100] This may be true, but it is also clear that Bidault had always been strongly nationalistic, and that his very definite ideas about the French Union developed out of his pre-war nationalism. Despite his talk of 'progressive federalism' Bidault always intended that the Union should be ruled from Paris.[101] Twelve years later he was to use all his political weight to keep Algeria French. In both 1946 and 1958 he was determined not to be associated with the disintegration of the French Union. He would countenance nothing comparable to dominion status within the Union. Perhaps neither Bidault nor Ho Chi Minh were villains. They simply held totally contradictory views. One was an arch anti-Communist who was determined to preserve France's power overseas. The other was a hard-line Communist who was determined to destroy that power. The almost inevitable consequence was the Haiphong bombardment, the Hanoi *coup,* and eight — arguably twenty-eight (or more) years of war.

NOTES

1. See above, p.4.
2. For the skilful way in which Ho Chi Minh played off the French against the Chinese, and vice versa, see King Chen, *Vietnam and China, 1938-54* (Princeton University Press, 1969), pp.99-154.
3. Interview with Pignon, 1 December 1966.
4. e.g. Lancaster, pp.139-41; Hammer, pp.122-6; Devillers, pp.169-70.
5. *Le Monde,* 19 November 1966.
6. Paillat, p.47.
7. *Les Temps Modernes,* August 1953, pp. 408-11.

8. Interview with André, 3 October 1966.
9. Interview with Sainteny, 3 April 1967.
10. *Le Monde,* 2 August 1946.
11. Interview with Sainteny, 3 April 1967.
12. Interview with Moutet, 18 October 1966.
13. *Figaro*, 24 February 1946.
14. Leclerc Report, 30 April 1946.
15. Although he always advocated a policy of negotiations, Leclerc's attitude hardened in late 1946–early 1947, probably under de Gaulle's influence; see below pp.25, 28.
16. Paillat, p.67.
17. Sainteny, p.66.
18. Viet Minh objectives cited in B. Fall, *Street without Joy, Indochina, 1946-63,* p.26.
19. The Viet Minh claimed that an election took place on 6 January 1946. But it is extremely unlikely that such an event did in fact occur. See D. Duncanson, 'Indochina: the conflict analysed', *Conflict Studies,* October 1973, p.5.
20. Devillers, p.242.
21. ibid., p.242.
22. 28 February 1946.
23. *Année Politique,* 1946, p.50.
24. ibid., 1950, p.50.
25. Lancaster, p.153.
26. Sainteny, pp.192-5.
27. ibid., p.192.
28. *Journal Officiel* (Assemblée Nationale), 29 January 1946.
29. Leclerc Report, 30 April 1946.
30. ibid., pp.453-6.
31. 14 April 1946.
32. Sainteny, p.167.
33. ibid., p.199.
34. Interview with Colin, 18 October 1966; a view supported by Robert Buron on 23 December 1966.
35. Quoted, J. Lacouture, *Cinq Hommes et la France,* p.66.
36. Devillers, pp.244-6.
37. See for example R. Schuman, *La Nef,* March 1953, cited above, p.4.
38. Interviews with Moutet, 18 and 20 October 1966.
39. Interview with Michelet, 25 April 1967.
40. Interview with Sainteny, 3 April 1967.
41. Interview with André, 30 October 1966.
42. *L'Aube,* 11 May 1946.
43. Interview with André, 3 October 1966.
44. D'Argenlieu, quoted in *Année Politique,* 1946, p.130.
45. Devillers, p.264.
46. 3 June 1946.
47. Sainteny, p.200.
48. *Le Monde,* 21 May 1946.
49. *Paris-Saigon,* 29 May 1946.
50. See R.E.M. Irving, *Christian Democracy in France* (Allen & Unwin, 1973), pp.226-8.
51. Interviews with Moutet, 18 October 1966, and Le Brun-Kéris, 14 October 1966.

52. Interview with Buron, 23 December 1966.
53. Interview with Schumann, 21 October 1966.
54. *Le Monde*, 14/15 July 1946.
55. A. Grosser, *La IVe République et sa Politique Extérieure*, p.256.
56. *L'Observateur*, 24 December 1953.
57. ibid.
58. *Les Temps Modernes*, August-September 1953, p.407.
59. Interview with André, 3 October 1966.
60. Such as the powerful *Missions Etrangères*, who had no wish to leave their entrenched position in Tonkin. See below pp.137-40.
61. Interview with Nguyen Manh Ha, 14 January 1967. See also Jean Lacouture, *Ho Chi Minh*, p.118.
62. Interview with André, 3 October 1966.
63. Interview with André, 3 October 1966.
64. *Journal Officiel* (Assemblée Nationale), 10 March 1949.
65. Interview with André, 3 October 1966.
66. *Le Monde*, 7/8 July 1946.
67. J. Lacouture, *Cinq Hommes et la France*, p.75.
68. *Le Monde*, 14 July 1946.
69. Interview with André, 3 October 1966.
70. Devillers, p.301, n.7.
71. Interview with Devillers, 21 December 1966.
72. Hammer, p.174.
73. Interview with André, 3 October 1966.
74. E.g. Claude Bourdet, *Les Temps Modernes*, August 1953, p.408.
75. *Le Monde*, 19 October 1946.
76. D. Schoenbrun, *As France Goes*, p.234.
77. Interview with Moutet, 18 October 1966.
78. J. Lacouture in *Le Monde*, 20/21 October 1966.
79. *Le Conflit Franco-Vietnamien d'après les Documents Officiels*.
80. Quoted Devillers, p.340.
81. Interview with Devillers, 21 December 1966.
82. *Journal Officiel* (Assemblée Nationale), 10 March 1949.
83. *Le Populaire*, 10 December 1946.
84. Hoang Van Chi, p.63.
85. Sainteny, p.220.
86. Hoang Van Chi, p.62.
87. Sainteny, pp.164 and 167.
88. Lacouture, *Cinq Hommes et La France*, p.59.
89. Interview with Devillers, 21 December 1966.
90. P. Mus, *Vietnam: Sociologie d'une Guerre* (Seuil, 1952), p.88.
91. BBC talk on the origins of the war in Vietnam, 3 May 1966.
92. Honey, p.2.
93. Hoang Van Chi, pp.29-74.
94. *Le Monde*, 14 July 1946.
95. Cited, J. R. Tournoux, *Secrets d'Etat*, p.5.
96. Interview Lacouture, 7 February 1967. See also J. Lacouture, *Ho Chi Minh*.
97. Honey, p.15.
98. For Abbot's views, as well as for those of the OSS officers who were taken in by Ho Chi Minh, see below, pp.98-9.
99. Interview with Sainteny, 3 April 1967.
100. Interview with Chevigné, 24 October 1966.
101. The phrase was reputedly coined by Bidault.

3.   WAR: THE FIRST YEAR

Initial Hesitations (December 1946-January 1947)

The Christian Democrats and Gaullists had got their way: negotiations with Ho Chi Minh had been rejected. But it was not yet certain that those who had been united under the leadership of Bidault in 1946 had finally won the day. Throughout 1947 there were rumours of negotiations with Ho Chi Minh, rumours which were not finally scotched until the appointment of Paul Coste-Floret (MRP) as Minister of Overseas France in place of Marius Moutet at the end of November. The MRP had been led by their right wing to a position utterly opposed to colonial concessions. But the MRP was only part of the Government, and between 19 December 1946 and 27 November 1947 there was a constant struggle between those in favour of negotiations with Ho Chi Minh and those opposed to this course. Léon Blum, head of the caretaker government of 13 December 1946 - 16 January 1947, seemed to favour negotiations. His Socialist successor, Paul Ramadier, made a series of contradictory statements, but in practice he swung away from the Blum line. Marius Moutet generally adopted an inflexible attitude towards Ho Chi Minh. In contrast the Socialist militants came increasingly to favour a negotiated solution, especially after the Communists started to condemn the war, following their eviction from the Government in May 1947. But most Socialist parliamentarians were still against making concessions to the Viet Minh. In this period of indecision the MRP leaders, and to their Right, the Gaullists, remained united and uncompromising. They were opposed to negotiations with Ho Chi Minh, a Communist and the perpetrator of the massacre of 19 December. In the end they got their way, but it was only after the Communists had been evicted from the Government and the political pendulum had consequently swung to the Right that the MRP's victory was assured. By the end of 1947 Ho Chi Minh had been definitely transformed from 'Head of State' to 'rebel', and the so-called 'Bao Dai solution' was well on the way to being adopted.

The indecision of the Governments of late 1946 and early 1947 can be illustrated by one or two statements of Blum, Ramadier and Moutet, against which can be contrasted the very definite views of Bidault, André and Schumann. Blum's conciliatory views, as expressed in November 1946, have already been discussed.[1] Even after the *coup* of 19 December he did not allow himself to be carried away by the emotionalism of the Centre and Right. He told the National Assembly (on 23 December) that

> . . . the basic principles of our policy cannot be changed by
> recent harsh events. We will not turn a deaf ear to any proposals for
> ending the present emergency. We remain loyal to the principles
> expressed in the final paragraphs of the preamble of the
> Constitution . . . In our republican doctrine colonialism achieves its
> final objective and true justification only when it ends, i.e. when
> colonial peoples are sufficiently emancipated to govern
> themselves . . . Once the present crisis is over, our objective remains
> as before. It is not a matter of satisfying private interests; even less
> of going back on our principles; it is a matter of faithfully
> completing the work which has been started, that is to build a free
> Vietnam within an Indochinese Union, which will be freely
> associated to the French Union.[2]

In contrast to these generous, if somewhat vague, views of Blum was
the attitude of the MRP leaders. Bidault sent a telegram to d'Argenlieu
on 10 December 1946 encouraging 'une politique de force'. Moutet,
however, emphasised that this telegram was essentially an encouragement to stand firm, and that Bidault did not specifically propose that
d'Argenlieu should take the initiative by using force against the Viet
Minh.[3] Nevertheless, it is clear that Bidault did nothing to *discourage*
d'Argenlieu at this time.[4] His policies, moreover, were fully supported
by the MRP parliamentary group, which met on 13 December to
discuss Indochina, and then sent a letter to Blum emphasising 'the
rights of France in Indochina' and demanding 'the continuation of the
policy of Georges Bidault'.[5]

In December 1946 Maurice Schumann wrote a series of uncompromising articles about Indochina, *L'Aube*'s readers were
frequently told that there could be no question of abandoning
Indochina.[6] It can, of course, be claimed that Schumann's opinions
were unimportant because he was not a member of the Government at
this time. Schumann has been appropriately described as 'the
drum-major' of the MRP,[7] the man who whipped up party spirit, but
not a man of prime importance either in the MRP hierarchy or in MRP
policy-making. Although this is doubtless a fair comment on
Schumann's political career as a whole, his influence in the immediate
post-war period was greater than at any other time in the Fourth
Republic. He was President of MRP and editor of *L'Aube,* and even if
his influence vis-à-vis the Government was small, his importance
within the party was considerable. Certainly his views on colonial
policy seem to have been a true reflection of MRP's attitude at this
time, as, for example, they were not five years later when he became

Minister of State with special responsibility for Tunisia and Morocco.

Christian Democratic politicians were later to claim that they adopted an inflexible attitude towards Ho Chi Minh from the start on account of his Communism. In late 1946 - early 1947, however, they made little of Ho Chi Minh's Communism, perhaps partly for the tactical reason that they were still colleagues of the Communists in government. One searches in vain in the Christian Democratic newspaper, *L'Aube*, for references to the ideological conflict with Ho Chi Minh, whilst in the National Assembly debate of 27 January 1947, no-one in any party attacked Ho Chi Minh as a Communist. In retrospect anti-Communism seemed a suitable motive for the MRP's rejection of a policy of negotiations. The Christian Democrats could maintain that they had always been fighting a crusade against an agent of the Kremlin, and that their motives and policies had always been consistent. In reality, it was their nationalism which largely conditioned their policy at this stage. They were determined to get rid of Ho Chi Minh because he threatened the integrity of the French Union.[8]

MRP intransigence continued to prosper in late 1946 - early 1947, as it had done before, chiefly because political circumstances favoured any group or party which had a consistent policy. Léon Blum's all-Socialist caretaker government of 13 December 1946 - 16 January 1947 was in no position to initiate new policies in spite of Blum's liberal statements about Indochina. Sandwiched between Bidault's government with its nine MRP ministers and Ramadier's with its five MRP ministers, it was inevitable that the policies laid down by Bidault, who had been Prime Minister for almost six months, continued under Blum. Ho Chi Minh was perhaps only being realistic when he decided not to postpone the *coup* of 19 December; doubtless he understood the limitations of Blum's position. The MRP slogan of 'Bidault sans Thorez' resulted in Blum becoming interim Prime Minister, but in practice 'Blum sans Thorez' meant Bidault. It was thus that a government whose leader wanted to negotiate with Ho Chi Minh sent Moutet a telegram at the end of December telling him not to establish any direct contacts with Ho Chi Minh.[9]

Another political circumstance which favoured French inflexibility was the investiture of Paul Ramadier as Prime Minister on 21 January 1947. Like many Socialists, Ramadier proved more conservative in power than in opposition. He had previously spoken in favour of peace and negotiations, but his investiture speech did not augur well when compared with Blum's liberal declaration of the previous month. In fact it struck a new note:

No doubt France will find herself negotiating in due course with representatives of the Vietnamese people who speak the language of reason. In these circumstances, and if it is the will of the Vietnamese people, she will be prepared to accept the reunification of the three Annamite territories and to endorse the independence of Vietnam within the framework of the French Union.[10]

Whereas Blum had talked about making peace with those *against* whom France was fighting, i.e. the Viet Minh, Ramadier spoke merely of negotiations with 'representatives of the Vietnamese people'. The idea of negotiating with those against whom France was *not* fighting had been canvassed in the Assembly for the first time. Ramadier's speech was reminiscent of a statement made by d'Argenlieu earlier in the month:

> Henceforth it is impossible for us to negotiate with Ho Chi Minh. Instead we will look for other representatives, who no doubt will also be nationalists, but the Viet Minh are now disqualified owing to their contemptible behaviour.[11]

These words clearly foreshadowed the Bao Dai policy, on which successive French Governments were to pin so much faith.

Moutet Continues to Vacillate

The one Frenchman who might have influenced the Government towards a more conciliatory attitude was Marius Moutet, the Minister of Overseas France, who visited Indochina for a fortnight in late 1946 - early 1947. But Moutet was a weak man who talked about peace whilst preparing war. In a speech in Phnom Penh (29 December 1946) he said that negotiations with Ho Chi Minh were not *a priori* excluded: 'If he has any propositions to make, they will be examined with care.'[12] But a few days later he stated that negotiations with those responsible for the *coup* of 19 December were out of the question.[13] And when he was in Indochina Moutet made no attempt to contact Ho Chi Minh. In fact he seems to have tried to avoid him, spending only thirty hours (of his fourteen day visit) in Hanoi at a time when Ho was only about twelve miles from the city. On 2 January Ho sent a message to Moutet proposing an interview in Hanoi.[14] Moutet did not reply. He later said he did not believe Ho's proposal was genuine: indeed it was not known whether Ho was dead or alive at the time.[15] But if Moutet had really wanted negotiations, he should have at least taken the trouble to test Ho's sincerity — and existence — by agreeing to meet him. The next day the Viet Minh accused Moutet of being unwilling to negotiate, and on 11 January announced 'the total mobilisation of the country's forces to obtain independence'.[16] The French Government had committed what Leclerc considered the supreme folly: the Viet Minh had been driven into the jungle, and their first tentative peace offer had been summarily rejected, or at least completely ignored, which amounted to the same thing.

As in the case of 1946, it is very difficult to assess how far Moutet was influenced by the MRP and other conservatives. Moutet maintained that he had been anti-Communist since the 1920 Socialist Congress at Tours, when the left wing of the party broke away to found the French Communist Party: it did not require the MRP to make him an anti-Communist. Moreover, he had no wish to negotiate with an unrepresentative organisation, and in his view the Viet Minh represented no more than 10 per cent of the Vietnamese people in 1946-7.[17] Even if one accepts these statements of Moutet, it is likely that he was more influenced by the Right than he realised (or admitted). Moutet was not a strong personality. He never showed any initiative himself after the abortive *modus vivendi* of September 1946, but he remained under constant pressure from more determined men such as Bidault and d'Argenlieu (the latter was in effect General de Gaulle's spokesman). In these circumstances he was almost certainly influenced by their inflexibility. Like Ernest Bevin, Moutet was a strongly anti-Communist Social Democrat, but unlike Bevin he was not a man of great character. Thus, what seems to have happened to Moutet is that he was propelled by the Christian Democrats and other colonial conservatives in the direction in which he wanted to go anyway: their role was to prevent him getting side-tracked at any stage. And they were as successful in carrying out this role in late 1946 - early 1947 as they had been at the time of Dalat and Fontainebleau.

Bollaert's First Six Months as High Commissioner: the Last Chance for Negotiations with Ho Chi Minh

Ho Chi Minh's initial peace moves had been rejected, but all chance of a political solution to Vietnam's problems had not disappeared. In the spring of 1947 two factors gave grounds for optimism – the appointment of Emile Bollaert as High Commissioner in place of Thierry d'Argenlieu and the parliamentary debate on Indochina in March. The MRP leaders continued to use their influence against negotiations with Ho Chi Minh, whilst not excluding negotiations with others, but it was not yet certain that they would get their way. The Government, after all, was still tripartite in early 1947 with nine Socialist, five Communist and five MRP ministers, although the Communists were soon to be evicted and replaced by more Socialists, Christian Democrats, and Radicals (in May).

Bollaert's appointment was essentially a victory for the more conciliatory members of the Government, for he was a civilian and he was given instructions to prepare for negotiations. Bollaert had been a distinguished prefect in the Third Republic, and he had been a close friend of Jean Moulin's in the Resistance. When the latter, who was President of the National Resistance Council, was arrested and executed in 1943, Bollaert too was arrested but survived the war in a concentration camp. He was a member of the Radical Party but had never been active in politics. He had no colonial connections and was a *laïc*. He thus seemed an ideal choice as a negotiator — a man of proven administrative ability without any particular military, colonial or religious axes to grind.

The instructions given to Bollaert were 'rather broad'.[18] His first duty was simply to inform himself about the situation in Indochina, to make a tour of inspection of the military areas, and to find out about the aims of the various Vietnamese political groups. He was to realise the integration of the Indochinese states within the French Union in accordance with the Constitution of 27 October 1946, but he could make contacts with any Vietnamese leaders who would treat with France on this basis. Thus, no group was excluded *a priori* from discussions, evidence that the Socialist-Communist group within the Government had overcome the MRP's opposition to *any* negotiations with the Viet Minh.

If Bollaert wished to understand further the climate of Government opinion he had an opportunity to study the views expressed in the March 1947 debate on Indochina, which took place in the National Assembly ten days after his appointment as High Commissioner. In this debate the Communist, Socialist and MRP attitudes were clearly shown. From them Bollaert could try to deduce what was the overall position of the Government. In a major speech the *Progressiste* Pierre Cot explained what was in essence the Communist line — a firm policy of law and order combined with negotiations with Ho Chi Minh. Cot began his speech with some remarks which seem strange when compared with Communist opinions expressed in later years:

> none of us, it must be emphasised, is thinking of a policy of abandonment. France has a task and mission to fulfil in Indochina. And it is necessary to make this clear in order to discourage Vietnamese extremists and foreign manipulators.[19]

Nevertheless, France could not afford to pursue outdated colonial policies, argued Cot. She must progress 'beyond colonialism'. She must try to show understanding towards her partners in the French Union — in particular towards Ho Chi Minh's government, which,

42

although it had all the faults of youthfulness, was, like France's own Government, the product of difficult times, but was nevertheless the genuine Government of Vietnam, and therefore the Government with which France must negotiate. He wondered whether in all future disputes between member-states of the French Union and the Metropole, the latter would automatically be declared right. He hoped not, emphasising that in the case of Vietnam there had been faults on both sides, and therefore the only answer was for each side to make concessions to the other's point of view and to work out a solution by negotiation. Above all the negotiation must be with Ho's Government, the Government which France herself had recognised and therefore the legal Government of Vietnam; this legality was the vital point, not the question of whether or not Ho was a Communist.

Ramadier declared that the Socialist position had not changed since his statement of 21 January, i.e. the Socialists supported the Government's declared objective, which was to negotiate with 'qualified Vietnamese representatives' (but who were they?), to unite the three Vietnamese territories if that was what the people wanted, and to grant 'independence within the framework of the French Union'.[20] Marius Moutet, as might have been expected, adopted a less flexible attitude, emphasising that 'France must remain in Indochina'. She had a right to be there as a result of the agreements freely entered into by both sides. She would not pursue a policy of conquest, but equally she would not concede to violence. So far Moutet's statements were in line with those of Pierre Cot, but when he started to talk of the Viet Minh he swung over to the MRP view. He doubted whether the Viet Minh had ever really wanted to apply the agreements of 1946. Ho Chi Minh had given no indication that he regarded the 6 March Agreement as more than an armistice. At Dalat and Fontainebleau the Viet Minh delegations had shown their unwillingness to reach a peaceful agreement. Moreover, as 1946 had gone on, the Viet Minh Government had changed its nature: at the time of the March Agreement it had been a coalition of Nationalists, Communists, Catholics, and Buddhists, but by late 1946 all except the Communists had been eliminated — 'there is no doubt about this; I could give you the names of all those who have been evicted from the government'.[21] (This statement was in fact only partially accurate, as the Viet Minh claimed that twenty of the twenty-six members of their government at this time were non-Communists. There is no reason to accept this claim at face value — a majority of the non-Communists were undoubtedly Communists masquerading under other names. At the same time Moutet's claim that *all* twenty-six were Communists also appears to have been an exaggeration. Probably six to eight members of the provisional government were not members of the Communist party).[22]

Moutet went on to say that, in any case, 'Vietnam is only part of Indochina, and the Viet Minh are only a tiny part of Vietnam'. As regards the three territories of Vietnam, he was not opposed to their being united if this was the will of the people. Nor was he averse to negotiations, but he warned that France would not negotiate with those whose sole aim was to throw her out of Indochina, i.e. the Viet Minh.

The MRP position was outlined by Maurice Schumann in his usual forceful manner.[23] He quoted Tran Huy Lieu, the Viet Minh Propaganda Minister, as saying that France was so split internally that she was no longer interested in her overseas territories. Anyone who believed such a statement, Schumann said, was labouring under a grave delusion. France was determined to build the French Union on the basis of justice and liberty, but Ho Chi Minh's 'government' had been incapable of guaranteeing justice or liberty; it had allowed the murder of its own people, the Annamites, before 19 December; it had broken both the 6 March 1946 Agreement and the September *modus vivendi*; it had then been responsible for the premeditated attack of 19 December; in short, it was not a 'government' which could be trusted; it was France's duty to protect the Vietnamese from themselves and to bestow upon them the benefits of civilisation; France should negotiate with 'suitable Vietnamese representatives' but not with Ho Chi Minh; and the three parts of Vietnam should certainly be reunited if that was the wish of the people, but at the same time France had a duty to protect the various ethnic minorities.

The March debate, the only full one on Indochina in 1947, ended with a vote decisively supporting the Government's policy by 421-0 with 181 abstentions. As part of an agreed compromise the Communist ministers voted with the Government, but the Communist deputies abstained. The debate had made it clear that there was a major division within the Government between the Communists, who now wanted to negotiate exclusively with Ho Chi Minh's Government, and the Christian Democrats, who were willing to negotiate with anyone except Ho Chi Minh. The Socialists held the middle ground. The majority of the party still favoured negotiations with Ho Chi Minh, the National Council of the SFIO demanding negotiations with 'all those qualified to represent Vietnam, including the Viet Minh'.[24] But the party leadership was less certain about the policy it should adopt. Moutet told Bollaert that he was not opposed to negotiations with the Viet Minh, but, like Ramadier, he was averse to negotiating exclusively with them.[25] According to Bollaert, Ramadier's attitude towards Ho Chi Minh hardened during 1947, largely, he thought, because of the conservative influence of his son, Jean-Paul Ramadier, a former Indochina administrator and later Governor-General of French West

Africa (1948-51).[26] Even if the Socialist leaders had been united in their desire to negotiate with the Viet Minh, it is by no means certain that they could have advocated such a policy openly, for they had the responsibility of holding the Government together. The two left-wing parties were too weak to govern without the MRP. Concessions, therefore, had to be made to the MRP's policy of opposition to negotiations with Ho Chi Minh. This was the price for continued governmental solidarity. Moreover, by the spring of 1947 the MRP wanted to get the Communists out of the Government, and the Communists half wanted to go. This strengthened the position of the MRP vis-à-vis the Socialists, because if the Communists were to go, the Socialists would have to remain in the Government with the MRP or risk the disintegration of the republican system. In these circumstances the Socialist leaders were inevitably more susceptible to MRP pressure than were the rank and file.

Hence, Bollaert left for Indochina with instructions to prepare the way for negotiations, but he was not told with whom he was to negotiate.[27] Ho Chi Minh's government was not excluded *a priori,* but there was no real encouragement for Bollaert to approach the Viet Minh. As it happened, this did not matter, because Ho Chi Minh, sensing the new atmosphere engendered by Bollaert's appointment, made the initial approaches, as he had done four months earlier when Moutet visited Indochina. At the end of April Bollaert received a communication from Ho Chi Minh proposing negotiations. It was up to France to make a constructive response. It must be stressed, however, that Bollaert's actions and the progress of the 'negotiations' during the next few months were almost as dependent on party attitudes in France as on the realities of the situation in Vietnam. As Ho Chi Minh put it: 'The key to the problem of Indochina is to be found in the domestic political situation in France'.[28] After the Communists had been evicted from the French Government (5 May 1947) the Christian Democrats replaced the Socialists as the main party in the coalition, and the Christian Democrats were both of their own volition and on account of Gaullist pressure averse to making concessions in the colonies.[29] Bollaert could analyse the political situation in Indochina and make recommendations, but no compromise solution could be expected unless the MRP leaders could be persuaded to change their views. That no agreement was reached with Ho Chi Minh in the summer of 1947 was only partly the fault of the Christian Democrats, but their inflexibility was one essential factor in ensuring the final breakdown of contacts with the Viet Minh government, who, it must be emphasised, also showed little interest in compromising.

Bollaert's Failure

The peace contacts of the summer and autumn of 1947 may be conveniently divided into three phases. The first began soon after the March debate on Indochina and ended with Paul Mus's abortive mission to Ho Chi Minh (May). The second occurred in June-July when further messages were exchanged between Bollaert and Ho Chi Minh, but even after these produced no concrete results there was still a chance that a negotiated peace might be achieved, for Bollaert and Ho Chi Minh made a third and final attempt to work out the basis of an agreement in September.

After the March 1947 debate Paul Ramadier, the Prime Minister, had declared that 'The Indochina problem will not be solved by force. There must be a political solution',[30] (20 March). Three days later Ho Chi Minh responded to Ramadier's declaration by announcing that if the French Government would recognise 'the unity and independence of Vietnam', all other problems could easily be solved by negotiation.[31] Bollaert arrived in Saigon on 1 April and declared that he would consider any request for an armistice.[32] Ho Chi Minh replied with a secret telegram on 19 April, in which he declared his readiness to negotiate: 'In order to demonstrate Vietnam's attachment to peace and its friendship towards the people of France, the Government of Vietnam (i.e. that of Ho Chi Minh) proposes to the Government of France the immediate cessation of hostilities and the opening of negotiations in order to produce a peaceful settlement to the present conflict'.[33] Bollaert proposed to the French Government that armistice negotiations should be opened with Ho Chi Minh on the basis of five conditions: (1) the surrender within two weeks of 'a considerable quantity of war material'; (2) the immediate cessation of acts of war and terrorism; (3) the immediate freeing of prisoners-of-war; (4) the handing-over of French and Japanese army deserters; (5) complete freedom of movement throughout the country. Ramadier approved these terms on 29 April, but told Bollaert that he must define the amount of war material and avoid handing over Viet Minh prisoners until there was definite evidence that the armistice was being applied. After consulting General Valluy, Bollaert proposed that 180 heavy machine-guns, 675 light machine-guns, 1,000 sten guns, 30,000 rifles and 4 million rounds of ammunition be handed over. Paul Mus warned the national defence council in Saigon that these terms would be unacceptable to Ho Chi Minh, to which General Valluy replied 'I hope so'.[34] The military clearly preferred guns to negotiations, and they were supported by Paul Coste-Floret, the MRP Minister of War, who was then paying a visit to Indochina. He found the soldiers confident and was won over by their proposal for a big offensive against the Viet

Minh in the autumn. Hence Coste-Floret advised General Valluy to 'do all he could to persuade Bollaert not to negotiate with Ho Chi Minh'.[35] Coste-Floret later said he did not recollect making this statement, but Devillers remains confident that his source for the statement (a French civil servant) was completely reliable.[36] And Louis Jacquinot, then Conservative Minister for the Navy, recalled that Coste-Floret returned from Indochina in May 1947 convinced that a military victory over the Viet Minh would be achieved by the autumn.[37] Certainly Coste-Floret exuded confidence when he arrived back in Paris. He told the press that 'There is no longer a military problem in Indochina. No French garrison is surrounded. All the roads are clear. All the towns of any size are under our control'.[38] Not for the last time in the long history of the war in Indochina had a politician been convinced by the generals that military victory was just round the corner.

Paul Mus was later to accuse Coste-Floret of blindness to the *political* nature of the problem in Vietnam.[39] Instead of trying to understand the growth of Vietnamese nationalism, he simply listened to the 'technicians', i.e. the soldiers and administrators, who told him respectively that Ho's army had no weapons and Ho's government no administrative experience. Coste-Floret's famous statement of 14 May 1947 ('there is no longer a military problem in Indochina') was more or less true from a *technical* point of view but showed no understanding of the political nature of the *levée en masse*. General Valluy might be expected to do no more than study the logistics of the problem. There was no excuse for Coste-Floret, the politician, ignoring its political aspects. When Ho Chi Minh rejected Bollaert's very tough armistice terms with the words: 'There is no place for cowards in the French Union; I should be one if I accepted these conditions', the responsibility was as much Coste-Floret's as Bollaert's or Valluy's.

In Bollaert's opinion the Mus mission failed partly through its leader's inability to get counter-proposals from Ho Chi Minh,[40] but this was an unreasonable criticism, because it was Ho who had made the first specific proposals on 19 April. It was up to France to make counter-proposals: she did this, but in such a way that they were almost inevitably rejected. However, Bollaert himself had still not given up all hope of fulfilling the peace-making role to which he had been appointed, and Ho Chi Minh's actions of June and July seemed to indicate that he might still be interested in a political solution. On 19 June he sent a telegram to Bollaert expressing his desire 'to co-operate closely with the French people within the framework of the French Union',[41] and a month later he reorganised his cabinet in an attempt to show his moderation. It now ostensibly consisted of three Marxists (previously there had been six), four Socialists, four Democrats, three Catholics, two Nationalists, two ex-Mandarins, one Buddhist and eight Independents. Vo Nguyen Giap, a fanatical Francophobe and outspoken Communist, was dropped, whilst Vinh Thuy (the ex-Emperor Bao Dai) was even asked to rejoin the government.[42] The French, of course, were justified in regarding these changes with scepticism, for over the years Ho Chi Minh had shown no compunction about disguising the essentially Communist nature of all his governments. However, the fact that the changes were announced at all at least suggested that Ho Chi Minh had not given up all hope of a negotiated solution.

Bollaert too continued to press for peace. On 22 July he replied to Ho's moves of 19 June and 19 July by telling the press that as soon as the guerrilla fighting had stopped France would negotiate with 'all parties and groups — except the irreconcilable enemies of reason — grouped together under the banner of patriotism . . . Colonialism is dead and France has no wish to revive it'.[43] Bollaert wanted France to take a bold initiative and pronounce the word 'independence', especially in the light of the experiences of India, Burma and the Philippines.[44] He wanted to make a major speech on 15 August, the day on which India was to receive independence. He proposed to the French Government that he should declare (over the radio) conditional independence and an immediate cease-fire. To put the latter into effect hostages would be returned by both sides and joint control over arms dumps would be established; as a gauge of France's goodwill 30,000 men of the Expeditionary Corps would embark for home as soon as possible. He wanted all hostages to be handed over by 1 September, and if peace reigned thereafter, independence would be declared on 1 November.

If Bollaert hoped to achieve peace by such means, he was soon to be disillusioned by the combined efforts of General Valluy and those members of the French Government who were opposed to negotiating with Ho Chi Minh. On 10 August Valluy flew to Paris to warn the Government of what was afoot. On 12 August Bollaert was recalled, and four days later a special cabinet meeting was held at the Elysée under President Auriol to discuss Bollaert's proposed speech. Seven ministers were present: Ramadier (Prime Minister); Teitgen and Delbos (Deputy Prime Ministers); Bidault (Foreign Affairs); Moutet (Overseas France); Coste-Floret (War); and Jacquinot (Navy). Of these seven, three were Christian Democrats, Bidault, Teitgen and Coste-Floret, and two supported their colonial policy, the Conservative Jacquinot and the Radical Delbos; Ramadier and Moutet were Socialists, but were not representative of militant opinion in the SFIO in their attitude to Indochina. General Valluy and High Commissioner Bollaert also attended the meeting.

The result was almost a foregone conclusion owing to the combined effect of French internal political developments since May 1947 and the conservatism of the majority of the members of this special cabinet. Since the departure of the Communists from the French Government (5 May), the axis of power within the Government had moved to the Right, the MRP now being the fulcrum which the Socialists had been in previous tripartite governments. Moreover, the announcement of the Marshall Plan (5 June), with its promise of economic aid, helped to stiffen the anti-Communist attitude of the French Government. Bidault had visited the U.S.A. to discuss the details of the Marshall Plan, and later announced that Marshall Aid would make it possible for France 'to avoid the abandoment of French positions'.[45] In the Government's eyes (although not in America's at this time), this doubtless included Indochina.

At the special cabinet meeting none of the ministers gave positive support to Bollaert's views, although Auriol apparently favoured the pronouncement of the word 'independence'. Bollaert could not recall in detail anything that Ramadier, Moutet or Coste-Floret said at this meeting, although he remembered that Bidault was firmly against using the word 'independence' on the grounds that Indochina was like 'a link in a chain':[46] if one link were broken, the whole French Union would gradually fall to pieces. Teitgen agreed with Bidault, emphasising the possible repercussions in North Africa. Ramadier and Moutet seem to have been persuaded by these arguments. By the end of the day Bollaert's proposed speech offering an armistice and 'independence' (even although 'independence' excluding the idea of secession) had been analysed, discussed and overthrown, and the major reason for this decision seems to have been the attitude of the MRP Ministers. At the same time, Bollaert was doubtless right to point out that the MRP Ministers really only reflected the opinion of the majority of the French deputies at this time.[47] Any policy which might have been construed as the abandonment of Indochina would have been rejected by the National Assembly in 1947, if not by an overwhelming majority, at least by a decisive one.

Bollaert returned to Indochina on 29 August, and on 10 September made his long-awaited speech at Hadong. He did not offer an armistice and he did not use the French word 'indépendance' (although he spoke in French); instead he used a Vietnamese word, 'Doc Lap', which does in fact mean independence. However, this 'independence' was to be accompanied by various limitations, in particular by those imposed by membership of the French Union, i.e. Vietnam was to have neither an independent army nor independent diplomacy, limitations which Ho Chi Minh's Foreign Minister, Giam, immediately declared to be contrary to genuine liberty and independence. Bollaert went on to say that the three territories of Vietnam could be unified if this was what

49

the people wanted, but in the meantime each should be temporarily run by a Commissioner responsible to the High Commissioner. Bollaert took a firm position by declaring that his proposals must be accepted *en bloc*. He finished by appealing to 'all the political and cultural groups within Vietnam' to respond to his initiative.[48] In theory, Ho Chi Minh was not excluded by the Hadong appeal; in practice he could hardly have been expected to accept terms he had refused a year ago at Fontainebleau. Although the Hadong speech seems to have made some impression on the Vietnamese non-Communist nationalists, it also left the French *colons* believing that there had been no change in the Government's policy. The speech thus defeated its own ends by attempting to please both sides and satisfying neither.

Meanwhile, the Christian Democratic view of the Hadong speech was summed up by Maurice Schumann in *L'Aube*. In a leading article he spoke of the generosity of France's proposals, contrasting 'French peace' with 'Indian chaos': since the so-called 'independence' of India, 50,000 had died in racial conflicts, but if France stayed on in Indochina she would create genuine 'democracy' and 'freedom' such as India had never known. The Indochinese States would in due course aspire both to internal autonomy and security, but neither would be possible without continued 'French presence'; France had no right to abandon her friends in Indochina in the way that the British had done in India.[49] No doubt much of this article was journalistic hyperbole, but Schumann was expressing in a rather emotive manner what most members of the French Right and Centre believed, namely that the French Union was worth building whatever the indigenous populations might think about it.

In spite of this unpromising situation, Ho Chi Minh did respond, albeit indirectly, to Bollaert's 'peace contacts'. In September a secret telegram was sent to the French Government via the French embassy in Bangkok. On this occasion Ho Chi Minh sent specific bases for negotiation:

(1) Political conditions: the unity of the three Vietnamese territories and independence within the framework of the French Union. . .

(2) Military conditions: the maintenance of a small Vietnamese national army with French instructors. . . No French garrisons in the interior, but defence bases at Lao Kay, Langson, Hongay, Tourane, Camranh and Cap St Jacques, with freedom of movement between them.

(3) Diplomatic representation: Vietnam to align itself with France within the framework of the French Union, but to

have its own representation in China, Siam and other
countries close to Vietnam.[50]

These conditions were very similar to those later accepted by the
French Government in the Bollaert-Bao Dai secret protocol signed at
Along Bay on 7 December 1947, but coming from a 'rebel', who was
also a Communist, they were almost inevitably rejected. Increasingly
in fact the Vietnam issue was producing polarisation between French
Communists and non-Communists. Meanwhile, General Valluy was
preparing his October offensive; Paris had opted for a quick campaign
to crush the Communist-led Viet Minh. An agreement would then
be made with Bao Dai and the non-Communist nationalists. No reply
was ever sent to Ho Chi Minh's proposals.
   Thus the 1947 probes for peace came to nothing, in large measure
as a result of MRP inflexibility. The Christian Democrats had succeeded
in preventing negotiations with Ho Chi Minh for a variety of reasons.
In Ramadier's Government (prior to May 1947) the Communist-
Socialist group which favoured negotiations with the Viet Minh had had
a slight majority over the MRP-Socialist group which opposed this
course of action, but in order to avoid a split within the Government
Ramadier made sure that the instructions given to Moutet, and later to
Bollaert, were imprecise. Certainly Bollaert offered negotiations, thus
satisfying all groups within the Government, but so long as he was not
specifically told to arrange negotiations with the Viet Minh, the MRP
and the Right generally could continue to exert pressure to prevent this
happening. In the first phase of the Bollaert-Ho Chi Minh contacts
Valluy and Coste-Floret had succeeded in ensuring that the peace terms
offered to the Viet Minh were unacceptable. From this point onwards
the Christian Democrats were in a much stronger position owing to the
eviction of the Communists from the French Government (5 May), but
it still took a determined effort by the MRP and Valluy in August to
make quite sure that Bollaert's Hadong speech should not give Ho Chi
Minh a chance to talk and thus perhaps to avoid the military defeat
which was being prepared for him. After the special cabinet meeting on
16 August 1947, it was almost inevitable that Ho Chi Minh's third
peace offer (in September) should be rejected. As in 1946, the
Christian Democrats were helped by French internal political
developments, because the social and economic crisis through which
France was passing in late 1947 seemed to demand strong, and firmly
anti-Communist, government. The major strikes of June and
September had genuine economic causes and were not initially
Communist-inspired; but by the end of October and throughout
November the Communists were trying to foment industrial unrest
and create a 'revolutionary' situation. The result was that all those

opposed to Communism rallied in support of those members of the Government who showed their determination not to be browbeaten by the extreme Left. It was in these circumstances that Robert Schuman of the MRP became Prime Minister on 24 November, Ramadier having resigned on 19 November after MRP criticism of his weakness in dealing with Communist agitation during the social crisis. The Government thus swung further to the Right, although ironically this was not the intention of the Socialist party Secretary Guy Mollet, who actually engineered Ramadier's downfall. Moreover, the triumph of the Gaullist RPF in the municipal elections of October indicated that a majority of Frenchmen supported a policy of strong resistance to Communist pressure.[51] Consequently the Government seemed to have a mandate to stand firm against the Communists both at home and abroad. It was therefore not surprising that the Socialist Party congress motion calling for further negotiations with Ho Chi Minh (September 1947) was ignored by the Government. Moreover, the apparently successful crushing of the Madagascar nationalist revolt, which had broken out in March, seemed to reinforce the case for standing firm in Vietnam.[52] Strong government appeared to be essential if the Metropole and the French Union were to avoid destruction from within.

The opponents of colonial concessions thus got their way in 1946-7, partly because the Christian Democratic and Gaullist leaders had a decisive and consistent policy, whilst others, particularly the Socialists, vacillated, but above all because of the political circumstances of the time. The divisions within the tripartite governments of 1946-7, the departure of the Communists from the Government (May 1947), the strikes of June-November 1947, and the apparently successful suppression of the Madagascar revolt, were all factors which combined to ensure that the policy of opposing concessions in the colonies triumphed, a policy which was appropriately described by Georges Bidault in the National Assembly in August 1947 with the remark that, 'there can be no concessions when it is a question of France, of its colours, of its presence, and of its destiny'.[53]

NOTES

1. *Le Populaire,* 24 November; 1946; see above p.30.
2. *Journal Officiel* (Assemblée Nationale), 23 December 1946.
3. Interview with Moutet, 18 October 1966.
4. Interview with Devillers, 4 December 1967.
5. *L'Aube,* 14 December 1946.
6. e.g. *L'Aube,* 21 and 24 December 1946.

7. Interview with Le Brun-Kéris, 14 October 1966.
8. For a full discussion of party motives, see below, Chapter 9, pp.133-46.
9. Interview with Moutet, 18 October 1966.
10. *Journal Officiel* (Assemblée Nationale), 21 January 1947.
11. *France-Soir,* 2 January 1947.
12. *Le Monde,* 1 January 1947.
13. *Le Monde,* 5/6 January 1947.
14. ibid.
15. Interview with Moutet, 18 October 1966.
16. Quoted, Devillers, p.365.
17. Interview with Moutet, 18 October 1966.
18. Interview with Bollaert, 29 October 1966.
19. *Journal Officiel* (Assemblée Nationale), 11 March 1947.
20. ibid.,18 March 1947.
21. ibid.,11 March 1947.
22. Devillers, p.401.
23. *Journal Officiel* (Assemblée Nationale), 11 March 1947.
24. *Le Monde,* 21 March 1947.
25. Interview with Bollaert, 29 October 1966.
26. ibid.
27. ibid.
28. Quoted, Devillers, p.371, n.18.
29. Interview with Bollaert, 29 October 1966; on Gaullist pressure see below, pp.140-3.
30. *Le Monde,* 20 March 1947.
31. *L'Express,* 19 December 1953.
32. *Le Monde,* 4 April 1947.
33. *L'Express,* 19 December 1953.
34. Paul Mus in *L'Observateur,* 31 December 1953; and see also Jean Lacouture in *Le Monde,* 11 January 1967.
35. Devillers, p.387, n.12.
36. Interview with Devillers, 12 January 1967.
37. Interview with Jacquinot, 12 January 1967.
38. Press conference of 14 May 1947; quoted in *Année Politique,* 1947, p.305.
39. *L'Observateur,* 24 December 1953.
40. Interview with Bollaert, 29 October 1966.
41. Quoted *L'Express,* 19 December 1953.
42. Devillers, p.400.
43. *Le Monde,* 24 July 1947.
44. Interview with Bollaert, 19 October 1966.
45. *L'Aube,* 12 October 1947.
46. Interview with Bollaert, 29 October 1966.
47. ibid.
48. For Hadong speech in full, see *Année Politique* 1947, pp.360-2.
49. *L'Aube,* 22 September 1947.
50. *L'Express,* 19 December 1953.
51. RPF coalition lists won 38 per cent of votes cast in the municipal elections of October 1947, gaining control of Bordeaux, Marseilles, Strasbourg, Rennes, and other large towns.
52. See for example, *L'Aube,* 12 June 1947.
53. *Journal Officiel* (Assemblée Nationale), debate on Algeria, 27 August 1947.

4. THE BAO DAI 'SOLUTION': COSTE-FLORET'S PERIOD AS MINISTER OF OVERSEAS FRANCE

The so-called Bao Dai 'solution' was the brainchild of Admiral d'Argenlieu and Léon Pignon (who succeeded Bollaert as High Commissioner in October 1948), but it was principally the Christian Democrats who adopted it and tried to make it work, firstly under Paul Coste-Floret, who was responsible for Indochina from November 1947 - October 1949, and then his successor, Jean Letourneau, from October 1949 - June 1953.

The Christian Democrats had considerable difficulty in implementing the Bao Dai 'solution', and ultimately their policy failed. The Conservatives and Gaullists contended that too much had been conceded to Bao Dai; the Socialists, after toying with the idea of some kind of joint Bao Dai — Ho Chi Minh government, came ultimately, if hesitantly, to advocate direct negotiations with Ho Chi Minh; meanwhile the Communists continued their barrage in favour of conceding everything to Ho Chi Minh. To add to the French Government's difficulties, the ex-Emperor Bao Dai was not particularly well equipped to play the awkward role allotted to him as a nationalist — but not too nationalist — *deus ex machina.*

Those who knew Bao Dai were broadly in agreement that he was an intelligent and patriotic man, but lacking self-confidence, consistency and powers of leadership. Bollaert refused to continue as High Commissioner after the autumn of 1948 because he found Bao Dai so hopelessly inconsistent.[1] His successor, Pignon, at first a strong supporter of the Bao Dai 'solution', described Bao Dai as 'always very nervous and diffident'.[2] Tran Van Huu, one of Bao Dai's Prime Ministers, also emphasised the ex-Emperor's diffidence.[3] At the same time the extreme difficulty of the task facing Bao Dai can hardly be overstressed. He took over the government of a country wracked by civil war. He could not survive without French support, and yet he had to project an image of himself as an independent, nationalist ruler who could offer more to his fellow-countrymen than Ho Chi Minh. More-over, by 1949 Ho Chi Minh had the advantage of a three-year head-start, and the average Vietnamese peasant probably knew little of Ho's fundamental commitment to Communism, or if he did know anything about it, had little understanding of its long-term implications. The well-meaning but diffident Bao Dai was therefore faced with a daunting task.

Perhaps one reason for Bai Dai's lack of self-confidence was that he was not strictly speaking a member of the Annamite royal family. Born in 1913, he was adopted into the royal family a few years later owing to the infertility of the Emperor Khai Dinh. Bao Dai succeeded his 'father' in 1925 at the age of twelve.[4] Brought up in France, he returned to Vietnam in 1932 and soon showed that he had some sympathy for the nationalist movement which was already stirring in the 1930s. However, he preferred a good salary, hunting and gambling to conflicts with the French administration. During the war he supported first the Vichy régime of Admiral Decoux, and then the Japanese concept of 'Greater Asia' (after the Japanese *coup* of 9 March 1945). With the Viet Minh revolution of August 1945 he changed tack again, abdicating his imperial throne and becoming an adviser to Ho Chi Minh as plain Mr Vinh Thuy. Sent on a political mission to China he abandoned his task and made his way to Hong Kong. It was whilst he was there that he was first approached by the French early in 1947. He eventually returned to Vietnam as Head of State in April 1949, a month after his country had been granted a significant degree of independence by the Elysée Agreement.

Léon Pignon outlined the background to, and concept of, the so-called Bao Dai 'soultion' as early as January 1947:

> One fact is certain: the impossibility of negotiating further with Ho Chi Minh. We now know clearly that Ho Chi Minh's Government has only one objective: to obtain the independence of Vietnam and to prevent by all means the return of France.

> . . . Nevertheless, nationalism is an important force amongst the Annamite population, and we must take account of this factor. We must aim to detach the mass of Viet Minh supporters from Ho Chi Minh by showing that we are not against the nationalist idea. . .[5]

Pignon did not refer specifically to Bai Dai in this report, but the Bao Dai 'solution' was there in embryo. Nationalism was an established fact; Ho Chi Minh was an enemy (but still, it should be noted, there was no reference to Ho's Communism, only to his extremism); therefore a new, more pliable nationalist must be found, who would accept a combination of 'independence' and French presence, and at the same time win over the Vietnamese people to this compromise solution.

The Implementation of the Bao Dai 'Solution'

The Bao Dai 'solution' *might* have worked if it had been applied with decision, speed and generosity.[6] But it was not. The French Government took three years to 'apply' it. Bao Dai was first mentioned as a possible head of government in January 1947. It was not until

January 1950 that the French National Assembly finally ratified the various agreements concluded with Vietnam, Cambodia and Laos during 1949. Even then the details of France's relationship with the new Associated States had not been fully worked out; this was not finally achieved until the Pau Conference of May-November 1950, and this in turn did not produce a lasting solution because the Pau Agreements were regarded as unsatisfactory by all three Associated States, but especially by Vietnam.[7] Looking back, it is clear that 1948 was a crucial year in the history of post-war Indochina. The Chinese Communists did not reach the Tonkin frontier and start helping the Viet Minh until 1949. The United States did not begin to send aid and influence French policy until 1950. In 1948 France still held the political and military initiative. She could have negotiated either with Ho Chi Minh or with Bao Dai. To all intents and purposes she did neither. It is true that under Coste-Floret she began to implement the Bao Dai 'solution', but she did it in such a dilatory, backhanded manner that the 'solution' was discredited before it was properly implemented. This played into the hands of Ho Chi Minh. It also led to increased opposition to the MRP's Indochina policy both from within the MRP and from the parties to its Right and Left.

Probably the main reason for the slow implementation of the Bao Dai 'solution' was that it was not so much a policy worked out by the French Government as a solution forced upon it by developments in Vietnam. Although it is true that Coste-Floret was 'the chief architect of the Bao Dai solution',[8] it is clear that the 'solution' as finally worked out had little to do with Coste-Floret's original aim. There is no reason to dispute Bollaert's contention that the French Government came round to the Bao Dai 'solution' only because of the failure of the October 1947 offensive against the Viet Minh.[9] The military solution having failed, it became necessary to evolve a political one, and the only politicians with whom France could negotiate were as nationalistic as Ho Chi Minh: they too demanded unity and independence.

Bao Dai was adopted as the only man who seemed capable of rallying the Vietnamese nationalists whilst remaining susceptible to French influence. Here Coste-Floret made a double miscalculation, for Bao Dai did not have the charisma to rally a majority of the Vietnamese people, nor was he willing to remain a French puppet. It was because he represented no-one that Bao Dai always tried to push his terms beyond Ho Chi Minh's. At this game the French stood to lose, because the French Ministers chiefly responsible for Indochina — Schuman, Bidault and Coste-Floret — kept on insisting that Bao Dai should return to Vietnam and that the 'independence' protocols would be liberally interpreted after his return, whilst Bao Dai, knowing the feebleness of his own position, kept on refusing to return until the French Government agreed to grant a greater measure of independence than had been originally envisaged by it. It was thus that Bao Dai did not finally return to Vietnam until April 1949, and that the Bao Dai 'solution' got out of control before it began to be implemented.

Various contacts had been made with Bao Dai during the summer of 1947, but it was only after the formation of Robert Schuman's Government in November that Bollaert received instructions to make a definite agreement with the ex-Emperor.[10] The result was the Along Bay protocol of December 1947, signed by Bao Dai and Bollaert. This protocol mentioned the word 'independence', but, like the Hadong offer, it was so hedged around with conditions that Bao Dai's friends told him that he had been duped by Bollaert. From this point on Bao Dai seems to have had a personal distrust for Bollaert. He made up his mind not to return to Vietnam nor to sign any more agreements with the French Government, unless he was sure that such agreements would definitely lead to unity and independence for Vietnam.[11] It was for this reason that 1948 provided the unsavoury spectacle of Bollaert or his colleagues trying to pin down Bao Dai in Geneva, Cannes, Paris or Hong Kong.

The determination of Coste-Floret and Bollaert did not go unrewarded, for on 26 March 1948 Bao Dai took an important step by agreeing to form a provisional government, whose chief objectives were to be the achievement of Vietnamese unity and the negotiation of a *modus vivendi,* but not a full treaty, with France. Bao Dai chose General Xuan as head of this government. Xuan, a former *Polytecnicien,* was known to favour contacts with the Viet Minh with a view to forming some sort of national government after unity had been achieved. It was thus not surprising that the Schuman Government decided on 27 May only to 'take note' of the government formed by Xuan, i.e. a very cool reception was given to the man who had condemned the Along Bay protocol and who was known to favour a negotiated solution. The Bao Dai 'solution' took a further step forward with the signature of a *modus vivendi* at Along Bay in June 1948. This second Along Bay agreement was similar to the December 1947 protocol, but Xuan agreed to sign it, together with Bao Dai and Bollaert, on the grounds that it was only a statement of intent rather than a full agreement. France 'solemnly recognised Vietnam's right to unity and independence'. On her side, Vietnam proclaimed her membership of the French Union as an Associated State, . . . and pledged herself 'to respect the rights of French nationals in Vietnam'.[12] In spite of its brevity (details concerning France's military, economic and legal rights in Vietnam were to be worked out later), the Along Bay *modus vivendi* of 1948 was an important document, for the word 'independence' had at last been officially pronounced, even if it had not been spelt out with sufficient clarity to persuade Bao Dai to return to Vietnam. In particular, there was still no reference to an independent army or independent diplomacy, both of which Bao Dai, no less than Ho Chi Minh, regarded as essential. Bao Dai was determined to extract both from the French Government before returning to Vietnam. Moreover, he was quite willing to wait indefinitely, whereas the French Government could not afford to wait, especially as a Communist victory in China became increasingly probable in early 1949.

With the Elysée Agreement of 8 March 1949 Bao Dai gained a sufficient degree of independence to satisfy him in the short term. France recognised the 'independence' of Vietnam and provisionally agreed to its unity (this was finally achieved after a special Cochinchinese assembly voted in favour of it in April 1949). However, Vietnamese independence was still restricted, because initially Vietnam was to have direct diplomatic relations only with Siam, the Vatican and China. A national army was conceded, but at the same time the French army was to have complete freedom of movement throughout Indochina. The principle of internal sovereignty was accepted, although here again there were certain limitations: special courts to try French citizens were to continue; and the Associated States (i.e. Vietnam, Cambodia and Laos) were to remain within the franc zone. It was also decided that a further conference should work out the various details of the relationship between the Associated States and France.

Finally, on 30 December 1949 France signed a series of Conventions handing over control of most internal matters to the three Associated States of Indochina. Léon Pignon afterwards declared: 'A new policy, which should be regarded as definitive, has begun', but it was not the solution originally envisaged by Coste-Floret. France had conceded more than she had intended, but less than the Vietnamese nationalists wanted. The 'solution' was being criticised by French Conservatives and Gaullists as a sell-out, whilst the Socialists considered both that France had conceded too little and that the concessions had been made to the wrong man (they would have preferred Xuan to Bao Dai). The Communists meanwhile continued to support all the demands of Ho Chi Minh. In these circumstances it was not surprising that the Bao Dai 'solution' produced internal tensions within the MRP, the most important advocate of the 'solution', and between the MRP and the SF10, the other major government party. These differences of opinion were soon to reach their culmination in the Generals' Affair.[14]

Criticisms of the Bao Dai 'Solution'.

Paul Coste-Floret was not really a member of the conservative wing of the Christian Democratic party. Robert Buron described him as 'a liberal except when in office',[15] and Bollaert considered him to be less intransigent than Bidault or Maurice Schumann.[16] Nevertheless, Coste-Floret came under fire from a few Christian Democrats, a considerable number of Socialists, and of course all the Communists, for his apparently inflexible commitment to Bao Dai, the corollary of which was his refusal to contact Ho Chi Minh or even to use General Xuan as a mediator. However, the most important, if not the most vociferous, criticism of Coste-Floret came from the Right, i.e. from the Gaullists and Conservatives (including those in MRP), who considered that too much had been conceded to Bao Dai. Indeed, it is difficult to disagree with Devillers' view that the conservatives of all parties were primarily responsible for ruining whatever chance of success the Bao Dai policy might have had if it had been implemented generously and decisively in 1948.[17]

The most important right-wing critic was Georges Bidault. He judged the concessions made by Bollaert at Along Bay in December 1947 and June 1948 to have been dangerous simply because the word 'independence' had been pronounced, and throughout the various negotiations with Bao Dai he remained firmly against Vietnam receiving diplomatic independence.[18] In this last matter he was supported by Robert Schuman, who later showed some signs of liberalism over North Africa, but who — at least until 1950 — favoured a single diplomatic voice for the French Union. The effect of this right-wing pressure against diplomatic concessions can be seen in the Elysée Agreement of 1949.[19]

Closely connected with this refusal to concede diplomatic independence were the persistent right-wing demands for 'solidarity within the French Union' and increased military effort in Vietnam. What one might call the 'Bidault line' was regularly supported by *Carrefour,* the influential Gaullist newspaper widely read by conservatives of all parties. In January 1949, for example, *Carrefour* argued that France was right to implement the Bao Dai policy, but that she must maintain her important influence in Indochina, where she had succeeded in imbuing the natives with French culture and values in a way which the British had never done in Malaya.[20] On various other occasions *Carrefour* emphasised that Bao Dai should derive his authority solely from France.[21]

If Bao Dai were to succeed as a French protégé, clearly a greater effort to annihilate the Viet Minh was necessary. The chief advocates of *la guerre à outrance* were Christian Democrats like Maurice Schumann and André-Francois Mercier, strongly supported by Gaullists like Louis Terrenoire and Jean-Paul Palewski. In 1948, for example, Schumann argued that France should strengthen her forces in Indochina to maintain 'la paix française',[22] and in 1949 Mercier told the National Assembly that, as Indochina was an integral part of the French Union, conscripts should be sent there to defend what was in effect French territory.[23]

The intransigence of the Conservatives was aided by the widening gulf between Catholics and Communists in the late 1940s. The Pope excommunicated all Catholics who had dealings with Communists on

15 July 1949, a pronouncement which strengthened the influence of the hard-liners in the Christian Democratic and Gaullist parties, both of which relied heavily on Catholic votes. It was convenient for them to be able to equate anti-Communism with the preservation of the French Union. Conversely it became more difficult for a liberal newspaper like *Témoignage Chrétien* to be critical of Indochina policy without risking censure from the Catholic hierarchy. It is hard to assess the precise effect of this right-wing pressure, but it undoubtedly had an important influence in delaying the implementation of the Bao Dai 'solution'.[24] Coste-Floret, for example, had no sooner authorised Bollaert to sign the Along Bay Agreement of June 1948, than he reassured the National Assembly that Vietnam's 'independence' would be strictly limited and that Vietnam would only be united if this was the 'democratic wish' of all the Vietnamese people. He went on to describe the Along Bay Agreement as 'a preliminary document'.[25]

If Coste-Floret really intended to implement the Bao Dai policy in a generous manner, a speech such as this must have given a strange impression to the Vietnamese nationalists. The speech was in fact clearly designed to satisfy the politicians of the Right at a time when the Schuman Government was near to collapse, and to reassure the French administrators in Indochina that nothing had really changed. But it was a major tactical blunder, for Bao Dai refused to return to Vietnam without a definite promise about Vietnamese unity, and each day he was absent his prestige declined and that of Ho Chi Minh increased. And so throughout the winter of 1948-9 the haggling between Bao Dai and France went on, with the French Government being pressed by the Communists and some Socialists to negotiate with Ho Chi Minh, and by the Right to negotiate with Bao Dai, but to concede the minimum to him. These right-wing pressures were articulated above all by Gaullist-orientated MRP conservatives, whose tactics helped to whittle away weeks and months which were vital to the possible success of the Bao Dai 'solution'.

Although the Christian Democratic right-wingers were a minority within the party, they were remarkably successful in making their point of view prevail. Besides international factors favouring their policy, such as the growing bitterness of the Cold War and the inflexible anti-Communism of Pius XII, various internal factors also worked on their behalf. Most Christian Democrats were not particularly interested in Indochina until the Chinese Communists came to power, when the forgotten colonial war suddenly became a front-line battlefield in the war against world Communism. At the same time Georges Bidault continued to be a man of great prestige within the MRP because of his war record; indeed his prestige was such that he could always count on the loyalty of party members even when they were far from happy about the details of his policy, and this loyalty continued until the late 1950s when the Christian Democrats at last became aware of the folly of Bidault's colonial intransigence over Algeria. But in the late 1940s and early 1950s the building of the French Union was still seen as a patriotic duty, and the Christian Democrats, whose party had emerged from the Resistance, were particularly sensitive about right-wing comments on their 'declining' patriotism. Moreover, from late 1947 the increasingly powerful Gaullist RPF contributed to the strength of the MRP conservatives, because the Christian Democrats were fully aware that they could only criticise the RPF for its intransigence at the risk of losing more of their own conservative, Catholic electorate to the Gaullists. It was thus possible for a relatively small group of right-wing Christian Democrats to join with the Gaullists and other conservatives in slowing up the implementation of the Bao Dai policy to such an extent that its potential success was quickly jeopardised. Ironically it was the strongly anti-Communist French nationalists who torpedoed the possibility of a nationalist solution in Vietnam, and thus in the final analysis they helped the Communist Ho Chi Minh to attain power.

Criticisms from the liberal wing of the MRP and from the Socialists were more numerous, but much less effective, than those from the Right. This was partly because the Left lacked a clearcut policy (apart from the Communists), and partly because the Left (again excluding the Communists) was divided. The main left-wing criticisms were directed against Bao Dai. In particular it was suggested that a solution to the Indochina problem might be found either if a more vigorous leader, such as General Xuan, were appointed to rally the nationalists, or if some sort of entente could be arranged between Xuan, Bao Dai and Ho Chi Minh. However, it soon became apparent that Xuan commanded even less support in Vietnam than Bao Dai, and that sooner or later negotiations would have to be opened with Ho Chi Minh. The only alternative would have been an all-out war against the Communists. By the early 1950s most Socialists, those Radicals who supported Pierre Mendès-France, and a small number of Christian Democrats had come to the conclusion that negotiations with Ho Chi Minh were preferable to *une guerre à outrance* against the Viet Minh. But first they toyed with the idea of the Xuan 'solution'.

This 'solution' was basically a Socialist idea,[26] but it was supported by a small number of MRP left-wingers. The Xuan 'solution' envisaged as a first step the formation of a Vietnamese confederation, with Ho Chi Minh controlling Tonkin, Bao Dai Annam, and Xuan Cochinchina. Later, the Socialists hoped, a single Vietnamese government might be formed under Xuan, who had been a member of the SF10 when he lived in France. Whether the Xuan 'solution' was feasible at all is doubtful. Philippe Devillers thinks it *might* possibly have worked if

Xuan had acted more tactfully, and if he had been supported by the French Government; but in practice Xuan was little more than a pawn in the MRP-Socialist dispute over Indochina policy.[27] Bollaert said that he favoured the idea of employing Xuan as a mediator between the Catholics (represented by Bao Dai) and the Communists (represented by Ho Chi Minh), and he thought that Coste-Floret might have been willing to support such a policy but for the men to his Right.[28] The Schuman Government certainly showed no enthusiasm for Xuan, and Louis Caput, a Socialist deputy who was in contact with both Ho Chi Minh and Xuan, was instructed to make no further approaches to either in June 1948. Even if the French Government had supported Xuan there is no certainty that he would have succeeded. Pignon, for example, said that by the time the Xuan idea was in vogue (1947-8), it was already too late to consider an entente between Bao Dai and Ho Chi Minh: this was simply not practical politics after the Viet Minh *coup* of December 1946. In any case, 'no one took Xuan seriously'.[29] It is quite clear that Xuan lacked support in Vietnamese, as well as in French, circles. Both Tran Van Huu and Nguyen Van Tam pointed out that Xuan had spent most of his life in France and was virtually unknown in Vietnam until his arrival there in November 1947.[30] Thus, by early 1949 the Xuan idea, supported by a considerable number of Socialists and a small number of Christian Democrats, had fallen by the wayside, partly owing to Ho Chi Minh's total rejection of the idea, partly owing to Bao Dai's lack of interest in it, but principally because the French Government understandably refused to commit itself to a personality who was such an unknown quantity. To have put all its eggs in the Xuan basket would have been a very foolhardy step.

After the collapse of the Xuan idea there were really only two alternatives: support for the Bao Dai policy or advocacy of a direct approach to Ho Chi Minh. The Communists alone were unwavering proponents of the second alternative. Over the years they received spasmodic support from Radicals like Mendès-France, Socialists like Alain Savary, and Christian Democrats like André Denis. These were the politicians whom Léo Hamon once described as *la gauche dure* (with specific reference to their Indochina policy).[31] *La gauche molle,* i.e. most Radicals and Socialists and progressive Christian Democrats, on the other hand opted, albeit reluctantly, for the first alternative. They did so, not on account of any real enthusiasm for Bao Dai, but because they were still not prepared to consider direct negotiations with the Communist-led Viet Minh. In the early 1950s the shortcomings of the Bao Dai 'solution' had not become fully apparent, and the vast majority of Christian Democrats, Radicals and Socialists were far too anti-Communist to advocate negotiations with Ho Chi Minh until military defeats forced them to consider this alternative seriously. In the meantime the Christian Democrats proceeded to tighten their grip on Indochina policy: this was the chief significance of the Generals' Affair of 1949-50.

NOTES

1. Interview with Bollaert, 29 October 1966.
2. Interview with Pignon, 1 December 1966.
3. Interview with Huu, 3 December 1966.
4. It should be mentioned that scholars of Vietnam have expressed differing views about the parentage of Bao Dai. Devillers and Lacouture accept that he was adopted into the royal family, whereas Honey contends that there is no convincing evidence that he was not the natural son of Khai Dinh.
5. *Note d'Orientation de Léon Pignon,* 4 January 1947.
6. This is the strongly-held view of Nguyen De, Bao Dai's *chef de cabinet* from 1950-4; interview with De, 1 May 1974.
7. Interview with Tran Van Huu, Bao Dai's Prime Minister, 1950-2; 3 December 1966.
8. Jean Rous in *Les Temps Modernes,* July 1954, p.29.
9. Interview with Bollaert, 29 October 1966.
10. Interview with Bollaert, 29 October 1966.
11. Interview with Nguyen De, 1 May 1974.
12. *Journal Officiel* (Assemblée Nationale), 8 June 1948.
13. *Le Monde,* 31 December 1949.
14. See below, Chapter 5, pp.64-78.
15. Interview with Buron, 23 December 1966.
16. Interview with Bollaert, 29 October 1966.
17. Interview with Devillers, 21 December 1966.
18. Interview with Bollaert, 29 October 1966.
19. Above, p.58.
20. *Carrefour,* 19 January 1949.
21. e.g. *Carrefour,* 17 August 1948; 24 August 1948; 31 August, 1949.
22. *L'Aube,* 4 March 1948.
23. *Journal Officiel* (Assemblée Nationale), 10 March 1949.
24. Interview with Devillers, 21 December 1966.
25. *Journal Officiel* (Assemblée Nationale), 8 June 1948.
26. See, for example, *Le Populaire,* 26 November 1947.
27. Interview with Devillers, 21 December 1966.
28. Interview with Bollaert, 29 October 1966.
29. Interview with Pignon, 1 December 1966.
30. Interview with Huu, 3 December 1966, and Tam, 23 December 1966.
31. Interview with Hamon, 1 December 1966.

5.   THE GENERALS' AFFAIR

The Generals' Affair coincided with the period of uncertainty which
followed Coste-Floret's Bao Dai 'solution' and preceded Letourneau's
modified version of the same 'solution'. It occurred whilst Coste-Floret
was still Minister of Overseas France, but became an open scandal during
the early months of Letourneau's tenure of the same office. It was
important not only as a sign of the Government's indecision about
Indochina but also as an open demonstration of the underlying disagreements between the Socialists and Christian Democrats over Indochina
policy. Up to the time of the Generals' Affair, the MRP and Socialists
had been jointly responsible for Indochina. After it Indochina was
almost entirely the prerogative of MRP (and of René Pleven), with the
exception of the Socialist Jules Moch's period as Minister of Defence,
July 1950 - July 1951. From the point of view of Christian Democratic
internal politics, the Generals' Affair also marked a watershed. It ended
the period of mild criticism of Indochina policy by the party's moderate
liberals, who mostly rallied to their leaders in this conflict with the
Socialists and remained loyal to them as the war in Indochina took on
an increasingly anti-Communist complexion. The small group of left-
wingers in the party, on the other hand, came increasingly to favour
a negotiated settlement, gradually aligning themselves with the
followers of Mendès-France in opposition to the war.

The Generals' Affair may be regarded as the third, and most serious,
phase of MRP-Socialist rivalry over Indochina. During Moutet's period
as Minister for Overseas France (January 1946 - November 1947) there
had been a strong undercurrent within the Socialist Party against the
policy of Moutet. The SF10, like the MRP, was a party without vested
interests in the old Empire. The vast majority of Socialists favoured
the development of a federal French Union, with full internal autonomy
for the more advanced territories. The dissension within the party was
over the pace at which the French Union should evolve. Sainteny's
comment about the MRP could equally well have been applied to the
SF10: 'Basically it was not a colonialist party, but there were all too
few within it who saw the need for rapid progress'.[1] By pre-war
standards Moutet was perhaps a liberal colonial minister, but he showed
his incomprehension of the need to act quickly in the post-war situation,
when he said in an interview that he had been opposed to pronouncing
the word independence for any French territory in 1946-7 because
none was ready for it.[2] In practice, this attitude led all too easily to the

need to use force. There were, however, many Socialists who were more flexible than Moutet. Typical of them was André Philip, chairman of the Socialist parliamentary group and of the committee responsible for the second draft of the 1946 Constitution. Philip favoured Ferhat Abbas's egalitarian proposals for a confederal French Union and was opposed to Bidault's 'progressive federalism', which was supported by Moutet.[3] Léon Blum also emphasised the importance of interpreting the Constitution in a liberal manner. Before the Viet Minh *coup* of December 1946 he advocated the rapid granting of independence to Vietnam,[4] and in August 1947 he said that the French Government should negotiate with 'all the authentic and qualified representatives of the Vietnamese people, including Ho Chi Minh'.[5] But when in office in December 1946 - January 1947 Blum committed, or allowed the commission of, a series of blunders which let the war continue at a time when peace proposals might well have received a favourable response from Ho Chi Minh.[6] The Socialist militants showed their anxiety about the Government's Indochina policy by demanding negotiations with the Viet Minh at their congresses of 1947 and 1948, (as well as later, i.e. in the early 1950s). Unlike the MRP militants, who were *au fond* perhaps no less liberal, the Socialists never had any qualms about challenging the policies of their leaders, of whom Paul Ramadier and Marius Moutet were the two most directly concerned with Indochina up to 1948.

The Christian Democrats, supported by most of the Socialist Ministers and a small majority of Socialist parliamentarians, won the first round of their conflict with the SFIO when the Viet Minh peace offers of the spring and autumn of 1947 were rejected. The majority of Socialist parliamentarians (unlike the militants) were at first prepared to give Coste-Floret the benefit of the doubt over his Bao Dai policy, but the party as a whole became increasingly uneasy about the character of Bao Dai, the rigid structure of the French Union, and the failure to negotiate with Ho Chi Minh. In a debate in the National Assembly in early 1949 the Socialist Paul Rivet blamed the French Government for the failure of the Conference of Fontainebleau and for the outbreak of war three months later at Haiphong. He emphasised that since the beginning of the war the Socialists had not hidden their desire for a renewal of contact with Ho Chi Minh as the sole means to end the conflict. After the return of peace it would be possible for France to maintain her special economic and cultural links with Indochina, even with a Vietnam governed by Ho Chi Minh.[7] Gaston Defferre compared the careers of Ho Chi Minh and Bao Dai, greatly to the disadvantage of the latter. Not only was Bao Dai a man of feeble character, incapable of rallying the Vietnamese, he was also a man without any official position in Vietnam: even the Elysée Agreement had not made it clear whether Bao Dai was supposed to be Emperor, Head of State or Head of Government, and Coste-Floret's statement that Bao Dai was to be only 'provisional' head of state until his return to Vietnam had done nothing to clarify the legal muddle.[8] Like Rivet, Defferre emphasised that the Socialists had always favoured negotiations with all sections of Vietnamese opinion, including the Viet Minh, but he also criticised the whole structure of the French Union, arguing that real independence was impossible within it; he wanted to see the French Union develop in the same way as the British Commonwealth:

> The people of the British dominions do not regard dominion status as an imperfect form of independence: on the contrary dominion status means independence with something extra. It means independence together with membership of a worldwide free association, which is characterised by mutual confidence and the complete autonomy of each member.[9]

Although Defferre laid great emphasis on changes within the structure of the French Union, the essential part of his speech, as of Rivet's, was his demand for negotiations with Ho Chi Minh and his condemnation of the Bao Dai policy.

The MRP spokesmen, on the other hand, made it quite clear that they were opposed to the revival of negotiations with Ho Chi Minh. Paul Coste-Floret denounced Ho Chi Minh as the man who had violated the March 1946 Agreement and the September *modus vivendi*, and who had then been responsible for the treacherous attack of 19 December 1946.[10] Jean-Jacques Juglas said that MRP certainly favoured a unified and independent Vietnam within the French Union, but on condition that Vietnam was not run by Ho Chi Minh, a self-confessed Communist; the Elysée Agreement ensured the unity, independence *and* liberty of Vietnam.[11] Coste-Floret explained in detail the effect of the Elysée Agreement, emphasising, on the one hand, Vietnam's new 'independence', on the other, the continuation of France's economic, cultural and military presence in Indochina; he suggested that now that Cochinchina had been legally united with Tonkin and Annam and that Bao Dai was returning as legal sovereign, all support for Ho Chi Minh would wither away. At the same time, he betrayed some anxiety about his policy by emphasising that the French Government had made every effort to make peace first with Ho Chi Minh: it was only after the failure of the Mus mission (May 1947) and of Bollaert's Hadong appeal (September 1947) 'that we turned to His Majesty Bao Dai'.[12]

The Generals' Affair developed out of the latent differences between the Christian Democrats and Socialists over Indochina, which had been apparent for three years, but which were not exposed in all their bitterness until the March 1949 debate and subsequently in the Affair itself. The Generals' Affair began in 1949, but it was during 1950 that it became headline news, making a profound impression on the parliamentary life of the Fourth Republic. For several months the Assembly tried to expose the *affairistes,* and there seemed a real possibility that the attempt to pinpoint ministerial responsibility might succeed, but, in the last analysis, ministerial and governmental solidarity prevented this. The Generals' Affair seriously divided, but did not break, the parliamentary majority: in particular it led to an open clash between the Christian Democrats and the Socialists, but even this clash did not destroy the Government, whose members were determined (in spite of their differences) to defend the Fourth Republic against its enemies (i.e. the Gaullists and Communists). Thus, although the quarrel between the two main parties of government (MRP and SF10) was serious, it was not so serious that either was prepared to let the Gaullists or Communists gain any real advantage from it. In the end no Minister was impeached, and the Assembly showed its inability to probe into the secrets of the Queuille Cabinet, secrets jealously guarded by its successors, the Bidault and Pleven Cabinets.

The facts of the Affair occurred during Henry Queuille's first Ministry (September 1948 - October 1949). Under the premiership of a Radical, the Christian Democrats and Socialists held the chief posts in the Government. The Christian Democrats had Bidault at the Ministry of Foreign Affairs and Coste-Floret at the Ministry of Overseas France; the Socialists had Moch at the Interior and Ramadier at Defence. These were the four Ministers most directly concerned with Indochina, on which, as has been seen, there was considerable disagreement between the two parties. In April 1949 the Minister of National Defence, Ramadier, appointed General Revers, Chief of the General Staff, to make a tour of inspection in Indochina. Revers was to examine the military situation and to make his recommendations in the light of the probability of a Communist victory in China. The appointment of Revers was approved by Coste-Floret.

Revers spent six weeks in Indochina during May and June, accompanied by Colonel Fourcaud, an important member of SDECE.[14] Roger Peyré, later a key figure in the Affair, was also in Indochina at this time on a 'private' visit. The Delahoutre Report described Peyré as 'any man's agent.'[15] He was certainly a man whose chief interests in life were money and intrigue. He had been in the white slave trade before the Second World War, worked for the French *milice* and Gestapo during the War, and spent five weeks in Fresnes gaol at the end of 1945. After his release he became friendly with General Revers, who, in recommending him for the Legion of Honour, described him as 'an excellent Frenchman, who rendered great service to the Resistance'.[16]

Peyré was friendly with General Xuan, and was well known in the Socialist circles which favoured greater influence for Xuan in Vietnam. He was also engaged in the piastres traffic, and had part-time jobs with both the SDECE and the American OSS. But his most important contact was his friendship with Revers - the familiarity of their relationship being shown by several letters quoted in the Delahoutre Report.[17] It was through Revers that Peyré met General Mast, the former Resident-General in Tunisia and the man whom Peyré hoped would be appointed High Commissioner in Indochina, not because Peyré had any real interest in politics but so that he could increase his financial influence in Indochina; he told his friend Morand that 'the appointment of General Mast would suit me very well'.[18] He seems to have hoped that he would gain control of the Indochinese Exchange Office; he promised to have another friend, Pini, appointed Director.[19] Peyré's main object was clearly to make capital out of MRP-Socialist disagreements over Indochina, but he was sufficiently aware of the political aims of Revers, Mast and their Socialist friends to say to Pini in 1949: 'There is only one solution: to negotiate with Ho Chi Minh'.[20]

The essence of the Affair, as far as Revers was concerned, was that Bao Dai should be reduced to the status of constitutional monarch, with General Xuan as Prime Minister and General Mast as High Commissioner.[21] The next stage would be a negotiated compromise with Ho Chi Minh. Revers himself was 'a left-wing General . . . He was a freemason. He had Socialist and Radical friends who would do nothing to save him and ideas about Indochina which were to destroy him. His Report was a condemnation of the policies being pursued at that time, of High Commissioner Pignon, and of the whole entourage of Bao Dai'.[22] The first and longer part of the Report dealt with the military situation.[23] It advocated immediate withdrawal from the fortress towns on the Chinese frontier, which would be dangerously threatened when the Chinese Communists reached the frontier, assuming the Chinese decided to aid the Viet Minh. Revers claimed that the fortresses were strategically unimportant and were already tying down troops badly needed in the Tonkin Delta; he then referred to an operation he had watched there, which, although efficiently carried out, had achieved little owing to a lack of troops to consolidate gains.[24] If the French withdrew to the Delta they would be able to prevent the enemy from obtaining rice, coal or iron (he pointed out that some Hongay factories were still in Viet Minh hands). With the Delta securely held, other clearing operations could begin. Coste-Floret later claimed that he agreed with Revers' military conclusions and would have carried them out if he had remained as Minister after October 1949; he could not explain why the Government failed to carry out the military recommendations, but suggested that it was perhaps the fault of Letourneau, 'a young and inexperienced Minister at that time'.[25]

The part of the Report which caused all the trouble was the political section. It contained direct criticisms of the policies being pursued by the MRP Ministers and of the men appointed by them. In particular it maintained that the Associated States must be granted more than pseudo-independence. Proper independence entailed ' a national government, a national administration, and a national army'; meanwhile, there was no government worthy of the name, only 'a Head of State, Bao Dai', and he had attracted the support of virtually no-one. General Revers quoted with approval the remark of a Vietnamese Colonel who had told him that, 'if Bao Dai does not change his advisers and show himself in the rice paddies as a sovereign fighting for his country, he might as well be swept aside with the clique of politicians who surround him'. If Bao Dai's Government were to be viable, it was essential that he should have a prime minister capable of rallying the country, such as General Xuan. Pignon should also be replaced so that 'Vietnamisation' of the administration could take place.[26]

Coste-Floret could hardly have been expected to submit to such overt criticism of his policies. Hence, in August 1949 he went to Indochina to study the situation for himself. Returning to Paris on 26 August, he drew up his Report of 13 September. Like the Revers Report, it was divided into military and political sections. In view of the bitterness of the quarrel which was later to develop between Coste-Floret and Revers, it is interesting to note that Coste-Floret endorsed many of Revers' proposals, political as well as military. He agreed that the recent developments in China constituted a threat to the frontier fortresses, which ought to be evacuated, as they were dangerously isolated and strategically unimportant compared with the Delta itself. In the political part of the Report Bao Dai himself was praised, but Coste-Floret was critical of the bad influence of some of the ex-Emperor's close friends, Prince Buu Loc being mentioned by name. Clearly thinking of Revers' criticisms, Coste-Floret emphasised that Bao Dai's Government needed strengthening. He mentioned Ngo Dinh Diem and General Xuan as two personalities of prime political importance, either of whom would have made a suitable Head of Government. But Diem had refused to form a government, despite Coste-Floret's own efforts to persuade him to do so, and Xuan was no longer trusted by Bao Dai. As it appeared to be impossible to get a first-class man to form a government, and yet it remained essential for the Bao Dai Government to play its role with more determination, Coste-Floret suggested that three special Governors, responsible directly to Bao Dai, be appointed for Tonkin, Annam and Cochinchina. These men should be given wide powers to galvanise the administration into action and, in particular, to promote social reforms, which would help to rally the people to Bao Dai.[27] Although the Report was naturally optimistic about the outcome of the Bao Dai solution, Coste-Floret later said privately that after this visit to Indochina he felt rather sceptical about Bao Dai's ability to carry out the role assigned to him.[28]

On the day of his return to Paris (26 August) Coste-Floret heard from Pignon that parts of the Revers Report had been broadcast by the Viet Minh radio.[29] Coste-Floret at once told the Prime Minister, who in turn summoned Ramadier, the Minister of Defence, because it appeared that there had been a leakage of defence secrets, but, owing to a lack of evidence, no further action was taken at this stage. On 18 September a fight, 'fortuitous or not'[30](Fauvet's reservation), between a French soldier and two Vietnamese on a bus outside the Gare de Lyon, led to the discovery of some copies of extracts from the Revers Report in the brief-case of one of the Vietnamese, Do Dai Phuoc, a student leader and well-known Viet Minh sympathiser. Phuoc was also carrying a list of Vietnamese living in Paris. One of the men on this list, Van Co, a wealthy associate of General Xuan and of Bao Dai, confessed that he got the Report from Roger Peyré, the double agent who was a close friend of Generals Revers and Mast. The Delahoutre Commission later concluded that Peyré borrowed the copy of the Report given by Revers to Mast and roneotyped it before returning it.[31] Summoned before Ramadier, the two Generals gave their word of honour that they had received no money. After a meeting with Queuille and Moch on 23 September Ramadier expressed the opinion that defence secrets had not been divulged, because the extracts of the Report so far broadcast by the Viet Minh were from the political section. On 24 September the Affair was 'closed' by an *ordonnance de non-lieu* (a verdict of no true bill, throwing out the accusation). Documents seized in the course of the inquiry had to be returned and the prisoners released. On 27 September Coste-Floret protested to the Prime Minister against the issue of the *non-lieu* and against 'corruption' in certain Socialist circles; he was particularly indignant, not without justification, that he had not been summoned to the Cabinet meeting of 23 September which had decided on the *non-lieu.*[32] He went on to protest against the 'plotting' of Revers, Mast and their Socialist friends, notably their attempts to get Pignon replaced by Mast. Throughout this 'plotting' Mast had been aided by Roger Peyré, 'the business acquaintance and political agent of General Revers'.[33] Coste-Floret also hinted that the Socialist party (whose electoral funds were known to be low) was receiving money for its support of the Mast 'candidature'. In the conclusion of his letter Coste-Floret again attacked Revers by name and the Socialists by implication: 'All these leakages go back directly or indirectly to the entourage of General Revers and have as their objective the promotion of the campaign in favour of General Mast being pursued by certain parliamentarians'.[34] A few days later the Queuille Government fell (5 October), and Coste-Floret's accusations were left unanswered. The rumours of the Affair had so far not reached parliamentary or public opinion.

During the third parliamentary session of 1949 the Bidault Government continued to guard the secret, but in the background the Affair smouldered on. At the beginning of October General Mast was relieved of his post as Director of the *Institut des Hautes Etudes de Défense Nationale*; on 30 November Roger Peyre left with his family for Brazil; on 7 December the Government replaced General Revers with General Blanc as Chief of Staff. On 26 December the American weekly, *Time,* published an article (despite the intervention of the French ambassador in Washington) criticising General Revers, and at the beginning of January 1950 *Carrefour* began to talk of the leakage of the Revers Report; finally, on 12 January *Le Monde* asked 'Is there a Revers-Mast Affair?' With attacks being made on the Ministers of Defence and the Interior, the Bidault Cabinet could no longer guard the secret.

At last, on 17 January 1950, four months after the discovery of the Affair, Bidault told the National Assembly about it. But he did so very summarily. He described briefly the careers of the main personalities involved – Revers, Mast, Peyré; he admitted that the last-named was a suspect character, but denied that Revers had taken any money from Peyré, whilst conceding that Peyré had received almost 3 million francs from the Vietnamese Van Co 'for supporting the candidature of General Mast for the post of High Commissioner'.[35] He denied that there had been a leakage of defence secrets, because the extracts from the Report which had reached the Viet Minh did not contain the military appendices. Having revealed almost nothing that had not already been published in *Carrefour* and *Le Monde,* Bidault asked the deputies not to make an unnecessary scandal of the Affair, and to trust the Government to take care of defence matters. However, he counted without the reaction of the extreme Left. He was forced to agree to an immediate debate (an interpellation debate) because the Socialists, affronted at the attacks on their Ministers, supported the Communist Jacques Duclos in his demand for an immediate debate. The upshot was that the Assembly passed a motion to set up a Commission of Inquiry into the Affair. The Commission was quickly established with Michelet (Gaullist) as President and Delahoutre (MRP) as *rapporteur,* and by the end of January 'it was giving every sign that it intended to make a thorough investigation of the Affair'.[36]

71

During February the Commission heard Queuille, Ramadier, Moch, Coste-Floret and General Revers, as well as a number of less important civil servants and soldiers. The Commission's inquiries were supposed to be secret, but in fact they were well publicised in the Communist press owing to Kriegel-Valrimont's presence on the Commission. It was for this reason that Colonel Morand, a former member of SDECE, was given a private hearing by three members of the Commission, Michelet, Anxionnaz and Chamant; this private hearing, revealed by the Socialist Arnal on 17 March, aroused the indignation of the Socialists and to some extent compromised the value of the findings of the Commission. These were further compromised, when on 29 March the Commission learned that one of its members, Castellani, the Gaullist deputy for Madagascar, had been a close friend of Peyré's. Castellani naturally had to resign from the Commission.

In April a preliminary report was produced by the Delahoutre Commission. The majority of the members of the Commission wanted to retain this preliminary report for private use during the remainder of the inquiry,[37] but the National Assembly decided that it should be debated. The Socialists were impatient to get an acquittal for Ramadier, and on this occasion were supported by the Christian Democrats who wanted to avoid the disintegration of the parliamentary majority. In the debate of 4-5 May 1950, the Communists, whose chief spokesman was Kriegel-Valrimont, demanded that Ramadier be sent before the High Court (i.e. impeached) for his 'treason' in concealing the Affair. The extreme Right, led by Frédéric-Dupont, maintained that 'the Socialists have been protecting Viet Minh agents', because Ramadier had released Do Dai Phuoc and his friends a week after the Gare de Lyon fight in spite of their being in possession of secret documents.[38] Nevertheless, the majority of deputies agreed with Bidault, the Prime Minister, that Queuille and Ramadier had acted in good faith, and the attempt to proceed to impeachment was rejected by 335-201. Amongst the majority were all the Socialists and Christian Democrats, the SF10 and MRP preferring to close ranks despite their quarrel about Indochina when the Government was threatened by a combined Communist-Gaullist attack. But the latent distrust of many Christian Democrats for Ramadier was shown by a curious incident on the evening of 5 May when the minutes of the first sitting ('le procesverbal de la première séance') were adopted by only 270-255, i.e. in practice Ramadier was acquitted only with reservations. Amongst the 255 were 7 Christian Democrats, whilst 11 more abstained. The rehabilitation of Moch six months later was to be even less clear-cut.

The final Report of the Delahoutre Commission was completed in July 1950 and presented to the National Assembly on 28 November, but between May and November it had been revealed that various documents had been burned by the *Direction de la Surveillance du Territoire* (DST -- the civilian secret police organisation responsible to the Minister of the Interior). In the opinion of many deputies the failure of Jules Moch, the Socialist Minister of the Interior in the Queuille and Bidault Cabinets, to prevent the burning of these documents was treasonable, and a Communist motion demanding the impeachment of Moch was carried by 235-203. The majority required by Article 57 of the Constitution being 286, Moch escaped impeachment, but the vote was a grave blow to his honour, especially as he was still Minister of Defence in Pleven's Government. As the vote of 28 November was secret, it is uncertain how many members of the MRP voted against Moch, but some certainly did. This was shown on 1 December when Pleven asked for a vote of confidence in his Government. The confidence motion specifically referred to 'the courage and integrity of M. Jules Moch', and was carried by 347-184. This public vote of 1 December allowed the majority to consolidate again, with only the Communists voting against the Government, but certain of those who had voted against Moch on 28 November were prepared to say so in public, notably the Christian Democrats Alfred Coste-Floret and Jacques Fonlupt-Esperaber, who claimed that if Moch were innocent he should have had no qualms about appearing before the High Court. Coste-Floret and Fonlupt-Esperaber decided, reasonably enough, that they could not vote against the Pleven Government in a vote of confidence despite their disapproval of Moch's previous conduct, but they demonstrated their continued distrust of the former Minister of the Interior by abstaining, together with one other Christian Democrat, Mme Poinso-Chapuis, on 1 December.[39]

There was at least as much MRP-Socialist bitterness expressed before the Delahoutre Commission itself as in the National Assembly. On 10 February Paul Coste-Floret accused Revers, Mast and the Socialists of deliberately conspiring to obtain the replacement of Bao Dai by General Xuan. He said that the latter was known to be in touch with the Viet Minh, thus hinting that the Socialists were in contact with the enemy: 'This whole plot has been directed against the policy of the Government, against M. Pignon and against Bao Dai'.[40] During the joint hearing of Coste-Floret and General Revers (24 February), the latter accused Coste-Floret of being 'imbued with animosity and bitterness towards me',[41] whilst Coste-Floret retorted that Revers had shown little gratitude to him for getting him promoted full general ('général d'armée') in April 1949. Moreover, Revers' attacks on the Bao Dai policy had done incalculable harm at the very time when that policy appeared to be on the verge of success; Coste-Floret quoted a letter from Pignon of 15 July 1949 to support this last contention.[42] The inquiry also showed the bitterness between the military SDECE, for whom Colonel Fourcaud was chief witness, and the civilian DST, whose principal spokesman was Roger Wybot. The appearances of Moch and Ramadier revealed little that was new and did not exacerbate MRP-Socialist differences further. The main direct clashes were between Coste-Floret and Revers rather than between Coste-Floret and the Socialist Ministers. The Delahoutre Commission concluded that Peyré was responsible for handing a copy of the Revers Report to Van Co, and hence to the Viet Minh; that Revers had lacked discretion, in particular over the friends he had chosen, but that there was no proof that he had accepted money from Peyré or from anyone else; equally, there was no evidence that Mast had been bribed, although 'there is more uncertainty in his case';[43] Ramadier had acted throughout in the national interest, even if rather precipitately in suppressing the Affair with a *non-lieu* in September 1949; however, there was no evidence that he had been offered or had received any money.[44]

One point which the Delahoutre Commission did not discuss and to which no final answer has yet been given is whether the Christian Democrats, or at least Coste-Floret and a few friends, were themselves partially responsible for the Generals' Affair. The hypothesis is that Pignon, probably in collusion with Coste-Floret, either leaked the Revers Report to the Viet Minh, or merely announced that the Viet Minh were broadcasting it; it has apparently never been proved that a Viet Minh radio transmitter did broadcast extracts from the Report on 22 August (although it is known that later in the year extracts were broadcast). The Gare de Lyon fight of 18 September was then framed so that it could be made to look as if certain Socialists, or their friends, were responsible for the leakages. A letter written by Paul Dehème, alias Paul de Méritens, dated 24 September, accusing Revers of receiving money for his participation in the plot to get rid of Pignon, was the next stage in this theoretical MRP conspiracy. Revers himself declared before the Commission that the essence of the Affair was the desire of Coste-Floret, aided by Wybot of the DST, to get rid of him because he did not like the recommendations in his Report, an accusation which Coste-Floret denied on the grounds that his own criticisms of the military and political situation in Indochina were 'even more incisive than those of General Revers'.[45]

The theory that the Christian Democrats may have been responsible, at least in part, for the leakage of the Revers Report, was put forward tentatively by Claude Bourdet in *Les Temps Modernes* in August 1953. Alexander Werth, reading more into Bourdet's suggestions than seems to be warranted, went much further and accused the MRP directly: 'If the Viet Minh got hold of the military part (of the Report), it was not from Revers, but, on the contrary through certain channels close to the MRP, who could not afford to allow the Socialists and Radicals to capture their Indo-China 'fief' and had to wreck the Peyré-Van Co-Mast project at any price.'[46] Werth is doubtless on reasonable ground in asserting that the Generals' Affair was primarily an MRP-Socialist power struggle, but there does not seem to be, as yet, any proof that the Christian Democrats went so far as to use treasonable methods to gain their ends. Coste-Floret rejected the accusation out of hand,[47] and it does seem unlikely that the man who had written the 13 September Report, largely endorsing Revers' recommendations, would have gone so far as to divulge the General's Report to the enemy. Pignon was quite willing to discuss the accusation against him; he said he held nothing against Claude Bourdet or *Les Temps Modernes*, although both had been responsible for 'a great many lies' over the years, but in this case there was clearly no truth in the allegation: if there had been, it would certainly have come to light by 1967, eighteen years after the event.[48]

The Gare de Lyon fight may have been framed, but it is equally possible that it was not; after all the French soldier responsible, Perez, got into trouble with the Pontoise police a year later for provoking a similar street fight. The case against Coste-Floret and the MRP remains 'not proven'. The likelihood is that if the accusation had any real basis, some evidence to support it would have been unearthed by now, given the French passion for backstairs history. Edmond Michelet, who was President of the Delahoutre Commission, said that he still had some doubts about the genuineness of the Gare de Lyon fight, but he was certain that neither Coste-Floret nor Pignon would have acted treasonably, although both had certainly taken full advantage of the Affair to attack their political rivals.[49] In the present state of the evidence there seems to be no reason to disagree with Michelet's conclusion.

The Generals' Affair had far-reaching effects both on the Fourth Republic and on French Indochina policy. Firstly, it widened the distrust between the Army and the politicians of the Fourth Republic. Moreover, the rift which developed between the Army and the Republic in 1949-50 was further widened by the Leakages Affair *(affaire des fuites)* of 1953-4. The two inquiries which followed the latter did not produce conclusive results, but they indicated that military secrets concerning Indochina had been deliberately leaked by two civil servants in the Defence Ministry and inadvertently leaked by Marc Jacquet, the Minister of State responsible for Indochina in Laniel's Government of 1953-4. Professional soldiers drew the conclusion that the politicians of the Fourth Republic were, to say the least, incompetent, if not actually guilty of treason. The seeds of the Army's revolt in Algiers in May 1958, which destroyed the Fourth Republic, were clearly sown at the time of the Generals' Affair.[50] Secondly, the Affair benefited the arch-enemies of the Fourth

Republic, the Communists and Gaullists, by hinting at the corruption of the régime. Thirdly, it was the last great Socialist challenge to the MRP's control of Indochina policy. Although individual Socialists like Alain Savary continued to strive for direct negotiations with Ho Chi Minh, the SF10 as a whole tended to fall in behind the Government after 1951, from which point the war was seen, above all, as part of the world struggle against Communism. The Socialists continued to favour a negotiated solution by 'internationalisation' (i.e. by an international conference), but their criticism of the Bao Dai régime, once so strong, became negligible. The MRP had won a 'victory' over the SF10, but the Christian Democrats had no wish to exploit it to the extent of endangering governmental solidarity. Despite the temporary absence of the Socialists from the Government (February-July 1950), the Christian Democrats could not do without the Socialists until after the General Election of June 1951.[51] A government without the Socialists would have been in constant danger of being overthrown by the combined forces of the extreme Left and extreme Right.

The Generals' Affair also brought about greater unity within the MRP. The moderate liberals, who had thought in terms of General Xuan creating a 'bridge' between Bao Dai and Ho Chi Minh, rallied to their leaders in this battle with the Socialists. And the increasingly anti-Communist complexion of the war after 1950 was enough to keep them loyal to the party line thereafter. The small band of extreme liberals like Léo Hamon and André Denis continued to criticise their party's Indochina policy, but their criticism had little or no effect, partly owing to their increasingly open alignment with the Mendésistes. The chief importance of the Generals' Affair from the MRP's point of view was that it entrenched the party even more decisively behind Bao Dai; previously the Christian Democrats had supported him whilst considering the claims of Xuan; now they were determined to make a political success of Bao Dai alone. Many of Revers' ideas had been sensible — the rapid transfer of the administration to the Vietnamese, the establishment of a popularly based government under Bao Dai, the creation of a national army, and withdrawal from the Chinese frontier. But, as a result of the bitterness of the Generals' Affair, some of these proposals were either forgotten or half-heartedly applied: the Christian Democrats refused to implement a programme put forward by a critic of their policies. Revers, Mast and Xuan had certainly acted indiscreetly, but unfortunately the idea of a compromise solution, for which they and most of the SF10 had stood, was thrown out with the dirty bathwater of the Affair. Although Letourneau denied that the Generals' Affair had any influence on his decision not to withdraw French troops from the Chinese frontier[52] (as recommended by Revers), there seems little doubt that the anti-Revers, anti-Socialist attitude of the MRP, engendered by the Generals' Affair, was one of the prime factors behind the Cao Bang disaster of 1950 and the general hardening of French policy thereafter.

NOTES

1. Interview with Sainteny, 3 April 1967.
2. Interview with Moutet, 20 October 1966.
3. *Journal Officiel* (Assemblée Nationale), 18 September 1946.
4. *Le Populaire,* 3 December 1946.
5. *Le Populaire,* 6 August 1947.
6. See above, pp.30, 37-8.
7. *Journal Officiel* (Assemblée Nationale), 10 March 1949.
8. ibid., 11 March 1949.
9. ibid.
10. ibid.
11. ibid.
12. ibid.
13. *Delahoutre Report,* p.527, (hereafter referred to as Delahoutre). This report was produced by the parliamentary commission appointed to inquire into the Generals' Affair.
14. *Service de Documentation Extérieure et de Contre-Espionnage.*
15. Delahoutre, p.19.
16. ibid., p.19.
17. ibid., p.12.
18. ibid., p.1552.
19. ibid., p.2242.
20. ibid., p.197.
21. ibid., p.39.
22. J. Fauvet, *La IVe République,* p.161.
23. Revers Report in full in Delahoutre Report, appendix I, pp.189-202.
24. ibid., p.192.
25. Interview with Coste-Floret, 20 October 1966.
26. Delahoutre Report, appendix I, pp.194-202.
27. Paul Coste-Floret, 'Rapport sur la situation en Indochine', 13 September 1949.
28. Interview with Coste-Floret, 20 October 1966.
29. Coste-Floret letter of 27 September 1949.
30. J. Fauvet, *La Quatrième République,* p.160.
31. Delahoutre, p.175.
32. Coste-Floret letter of 27 September 1949.
33. ibid.
34. ibid.
35. *Journal Officiel* (Assemblée Nationale), 17 January 1950.
36. *Année Politique,* 1950, p.32.
37. Interview with Michelet, 25 April 1967.
38. *Journal Officiel* (Assemblée Nationale), 5 May 1950.
39. *Journal Officiel* (Assemblée Nationale), 1 December 1950.
40. Delahoutre, p.182.
41. ibid., p.527.

42. ibid., p.541.
43. ibid., p.176.
44. ibid., p.183.
45. ibid., p.531.
46. A. Werth, *France, 1940-1955*, p.460.
47. Interview with Coste-Floret, 20 October 1966.
48. Interview with Pignon, 24 April 1967.
49. Interview with Michelet, 25 April 1967.
50. See J.S. Ambler, *The French Army in Politics, 1945-62*, (Ohio State University Press, 1966), and J. Planchais, *Histoire Politique de l'Armée, 1940-67* (Seuil, 1967).
51. And even after that it was impossible to form a reasonably stable right-centre coalition until after the Gaullist split of March 1952, when 27 conservative Gaullists broke from the RPF to support the investiture of Antoine Pinay as Prime Minister.
52. Interview with Letourneau, 25 November 1966; and see next chapter.

6. INTERNATIONALISATION: LETOURNEAU'S PERIOD OF RESPONSIBILITY FOR INDOCHINA (1949-53)

The eighteen months between Revers' mission (May, 1949) and de Lattre de Tassigny's arrival in Indochina with full military and civil powers after the defeat of Cao Bang marked the end of one phase of the first Indochina War and the beginning of another. Whilst the Generals' Affair was dragging on, the Chinese Communists arrived at the frontier of Vietnam (December 1949); Ho Chi Minh's Government was recognised by China and the Soviet Union (January 1950), and Bao Dai's by the United States and Britain (February); the Korean War began (June), and American and Chinese aid began to arrive in Indochina. The result of these events was that the 'police operations' against the Viet Minh rebels became part of the world struggle against Communism; the forgotten colonial campaign became an 'international' war, with the Chinese, Americans and Russians indirectly involved; and the French Union's struggle to preserve its integrity became a war to make Vietnam independent of foreign influence, so destroying one of France's original motives for fighting in Indochina.

The military and political situation was stabilised during de Lattre's period as High Commissioner and Commander-in-Chief (December 1950-January 1952), and then remained essentially static until the French Government's unilateral decision to devalue the piastre (May 1953) provoked a series of new crises. After checking the Viet Minh invasion of the Tonkinese Delta in early 1951 de Lattre strove to rally the Vietnamese to Bao Dai by referring frequently to Vietnam's 'independence', by creating a national army, and by requesting American aid for it. Bao Dai stopped referring to the Viet Minh as 'the Resistance' and began to urge all-out war against them; the Vietnamese army came into official existence on 8 December 1950, and the full mobilisation of Vietnam was proclaimed by Bao Dai on 15 July 1951. In September 1951 de Lattre went to the United States to request more aid and to persuade the Americans that France was waging an anti-Communist war in Indochina and not a colonial one. In October General Lawton Collins arrived in Saigon with a permanent U.S. aid mission. After de Lattre's death in January 1952 the same policies continued, with the progressive transfer of French administrative services to the Vietnamese, the build-up of Vietnam's armed forces, and, in particular, the replacement of the rather easy-going and corrupt Tran Van Huu by Nguyen Van Tam, a man of considerable energy and decision, as Bao Dai's Prime Minister (June 1952).

The Viet Minh also became more uncompromising, doubtless as part of the bargain for Chinese aid and training facilities.[1] On 19 February 1950 Ho Chi Minh called for total mobilisation against 'the French colonialists and their American allies', and on 3 March the Vietnamese Communist Party, in theory non-existent since November 1945, reappeared as the Lao Dong (Workers' Party), the official party of the new national front, the Lien Viet, into which the Viet Minh was merged.[2] The new intransigence of Ho Chi Minh's Government was shown by the fact that no proposals for peace were put forward between December 1949 and November 1953.

In France itself the supporters of the Bao Dai 'solution' were strengthened by the victory of the Chinese Communists. It could now be argued that the French army was aiding the legitimate Vietnamese sovereign, Bao Dai, against external enemies and their internal puppets. The position of Bao Dai's supporters was further strengthened by the temporary departure of the Socialists from the French Government (February-July 1950) and then by their longer absence (August 1951-January 1956). The four elections between 1951 and 1953 also confirmed the trend towards the Right. The General Election (June 1951) saw the MRP vote cut by half and the Communists and Socialists losing half and three-quarters of a million votes respectively compared with November 1946; the Gaullists, with 20 per cent of votes cast, appeared to be the chief beneficiary, but owing to the system of electoral alliances, the Socialists, MRP, Radicals and Conservatives were all over-represented. The parties opposed to the 'system', Communists and Gaullists, received 46·5 per cent of the votes cast but only 34·8 per cent of the seats in the National Assembly; the other parties, receiving 53·5 per cent of the votes cast, got 65·2 per cent of the seats. The Radicals and Conservatives (Independents and Peasants) did particularly well with a total of 192 deputies compared with 128 in November 1946.[3] The electoral law, designed to preserve the Republic, had achieved its object, but at the cost of over-representation of the conservative parties. The success of the Right was confirmed by the cantonal elections of October 1951, at which gains were registered by all parties except the Communists and Socialists; by the Council of the Republic elections of May 1952, at which the Radicals and Conservatives made substantial gains, mostly at the expense of the Gaullists; and by the municipal elections of April-May 1953, at which the Gaullists and Communists fell back, largely to the profit of the Radicals and Conservatives.

This strengthening of the French Right helped to make possible the rather inflexible colonial policy carried out in North Africa as well as in Indochina between 1950-3.

80

Cao Bang

When the disaster of Cao Bang occurred, Letourneau had been responsible for Indochina for one year. He had shown no signs of initiating a policy. In so far as he had a policy during 1949-50 it was merely one of 'wait and see'. He reflected the indecision of the eighteen months which followed the Revers Report. In much the same way he was later to reflect the revived confidence in a military solution which was one of the consequences of de Lattre's proconsulship.

On 8 October 1950 more than 2,500 out of the 3,500 soldiers who evacuated the frontier fortress of Cao Bang were killed or taken prisoner by the Viet Minh.[4] One of the results of the worst disaster in France's colonial history up to that time was the end of Letourneau's indecision. On 19 October René Pleven, who had been Prime Minister for three months, was faced by a hostile National Assembly. The Opposition, though divided between partisans of military victory and negotiations, were unanimous in blaming the Government for the disaster. Those who believed in war reproached the Government for its indecision, which they attributed, with good reason, to the internal divisions within the Government and the majority. Their point of view was expressed by the Gaullist Edmond Michelet, who claimed that the Government had been composed of such disparate groups for the previous four years that indecision had been inevitable: the disaster of Cao Bang was the logical result of this indecision.[5]

The argument in favour of negotiations was put forward first of all by the Communists. One of their spokesmen recalled that the disaster might have been avoided if the Communist demand for negotiations in July had not been rejected without discussion.[6] A policy of negotiations was also advocated for the first time by Pierre Mendès-France. In a cuttingly logical speech he argued that the Government's policy had been quite incoherent and that France must choose between a military solution and a negotiated settlement. If the former, 'let us get rid of our illusions . . . In order to achieve military victory we will require three times as many troops and three times as much money, and we will need them quickly'; the price of such a policy would be increased taxation and a slower rate of investment, which would be harmful to economic recovery at home; at the same time it would be impossible for France to fulfil her defence commitments in Europe and North Africa or to impose conditions about German rearmament. The alternative was to negotiate 'with those against whom we are fighting; . . . an agreement will entail major concessions, undoubtedly greater than those which would previously have sufficed'.[7] In Mendès-France's view, France had neither the men nor the money to solve the Indochina problem by force, unless of course she was prepared to pay the high price of sending out conscripts and retarding her own economic recovery.

81

Pleven's speeches of 10 and 19 October shed little light on the hesitations, orders and counter-orders which had delayed the evacuation of Cao Bang. Pleven admitted that the Committee of National Defence had approved Revers' recommendation that the frontier posts should be evacuated (at a meeting on 25 July 1949), but 'the decision taken in principle to evacuate Cao Bang was opposed by the High Commissioner and Commander-in-Chief in Indochina for both political and military reasons'.[8] Precisely what happened between July 1949–October 1950 remains uncertain. One thing that is clear, however, is that Letourneau gave no decisive political guidance. It appears that most, but not all, of the soldiers wanted to evacuate the frontier fortresses. The Chiefs of Staff Committee reported in favour of withdrawal on 4 February 1950, but their findings were rejected by the Committee of National Defence ten days later.[9] General Carpentier, the Commander-in-Chief in Indochina, agreed with Revers, but, according to Letourneau, could not make up his mind about the timing of the withdrawal;[10] however, there seems to be some doubt about this opinion, as *L'Observateur* maintained that Carpentier was against withdrawal, because he believed that this course of action would have a bad psychological effect on the Expeditionary Corps.[11] General Alessandri, the Commander in Tonkin, on the other hand, seems to have had no such doubts; he was strongly opposed to withdrawal, and his arguments seem to have impressed Letourneau and Pignon at least as much as those of Revers. Letourneau later maintained that there were arguments both for and against adopting the Revers Report. If, for example, the French withdrew from the fortresses, they would have been conceding a victory to the Viet Minh and at the same time opening the frontier to the Chinese.[12] Pignon, like de Lattre, believed that if Tonkin was even partially surrendered, France would risk losing the whole of Vietnam: 'Tonkin is the key to Indochina, both strategically and because of the character of its people'.[13]

The order to evacuate Cao Bang was eventually given on 16 September 1950, not because the Government had suddenly made up its mind to act decisively, but simply because there was no longer any point in holding on to a fortress which had been by-passed by two new roads built by the Viet Minh. Three days later Alessandri wrote to Pignon, arguing that it was foolish to carry out a withdrawal in Indochina at the very time when the Communists were being routed in Korea. In his reply Pignon agreed that advantage should be taken of Allied successes in Korea; he had pointed this out to Letourneau, 'but it is difficult to bring Paris round to our point of view'.[14] Letourneau himself appears to have been equally indecisive, although he argued in favour of withdrawal at the National Defence Committee of 14 February, but was opposed by Bidault, then Prime Minister.[15]

The debate which began on 19 October 1950 was adjourned till after the return of Letourneau and Juin from Indochina. On 22 November the National Assembly listened to Letourneau's explanation of events. He admitted his responsibility for the Cao Bang disaster, whilst pleading extenuating circumstances, notably that conditions on the ground in Indochina (terrain and weather) made the timing of decisions very difficult.[16] Letourneau doubtless felt quite safe in making this confession, realising that the majority could hardly declare him responsible without admitting its own failure to take any real interest in Indochina over the years. Letourneau went on to say that Lao Kay and Hoa Binh had been evacuated successfully. Tonkin would be saved if 'the true Vietnamese nationalists' stopped their internecine quarrels and rallied to Bao Dai.[17] If they did not, France would consider the possibility of appealing to the United Nations for help — obviously a sop to the Socialists who were beginning to talk of internationalisation. But for the Right wing of the majority he added, 'there can be no question of our abandoning the struggle, and in the meantime recourse to an international body is neither possible nor desirable'.[18] Having appealed, as it were, to all sections of the majority, Letourneau could do no more than outline a vague future policy: in the meantime France would fight on, but she would reserve for herself the right to ask other countries to help in what had become 'a conflict of international character'.[19]

The National Assembly was not particularly satisfied with Letourneau's speech or with the indeterminate policy he proposed. The Communists concentrated on the dangers of internationalising the war: Indochina would become another Korea with Americans fighting Chinese. The extreme Right, led by Frédéric-Dupont and J.-P. Palewski, both Gaullists at this time, also opposed internationalisation: after criticising Letourneau for indecision and for concealing the gravity of the military situation, they argued that the problem should be kept within the French Union, whose own forces, decisively backed by the Métropole, could still defeat the Viet Minh. The Socialists, whose chief spokesman was Pineau, criticised Bao Dai personally, asserting that the promises made to the Vietnamese people by the French Government must be kept, and that some form of internationalisation of the problem might soon be necessary, although, in the meantime, France must continue to fight in order to gain time to work out a political solution, which had become more difficult owing to the fact that part of the Vietnamese nationalist movement had come under Communist control. It appeared that the Socialists wanted an international solution to the war, but in the short term preferred Bao Dai to Ho Chi Minh.

Jean-Jacques Juglas and Paul Coste-Floret were the chief MRP spokesmen. The former attacked Mendès-France for his defeatism and defended Letourneau's proposals. The latter made a long speech in which he discussed the various possibilities — abandoning Indochina, negotiations with Ho Chi Minh, internationalisation — dismissing all; the only honourable course was to persevere with the Bao Dai policy. Mendès-France developed his theme of the previous month, saying it was time to stop 'this vacillating, indecisive, ambiguous policy, which is based neither on popular support nor on irresistible force'. He then outlined his conditions for peace — recognition of the independence of Vietnam, free elections under neutral supervision, evacuation of French troops. Vietnam would then become, he hoped, a neutral State, tied neither to the Soviet Union nor to the United States.

Christian Democrats and Socialists thus contented themselves with some self-criticism and a vague agreement on a future policy of 'internationalisation'. With these two parties united, albeit in uneasy alliance, it was in vain that Mendès-France warned that international-isation would not end the war. Finally Pleven rallied the majority with an emotional appeal to patriotism: 'When French forces are involved, it is not a question of reason, but of the national interest . . . We shall march to the guns behind the tricolour'.[20] The motion, carried by 337-187, gave the Government a mandate 'to reinforce the army as required', but it also insisted that the Government 'should make clear to the free world the international and anti-Communist nature of the war in Vietnam'[21] — in practice a veiled request for American aid, a request which soon met with a favourable response, but which had unforeseen consequences in terms of growing American influence over French policy.[22]

The implication of the motion voted on 22 November 1950 was that the National Assembly had concluded that France was incapable of solving the Indochina problem on her own. But it was unwilling to draw the obvious conclusion. The present Government might be incompetent, but it was preferable to an 'anti-Republican' government dominated by Gaullists or Communists. Thus the Assembly overthrew neither the Government nor the Minister responsible for Indochina. Letourneau had failed to take the political decision necessitated by the arrival of the Chinese Communists at the Vietnamese frontier in December 1949. He had failed despite clear warnings of the dangers created by the new situation. The effect of Chinese aid and Chinese training facilities had been described at length in *Le Monde* on 23 February and 29 July 1950. The Revers Report had painted a gloomy picture as early as June 1949. The debate of October and November 1950 showed that the Government had failed to face up to the alternatives and to come to a decision until it was too late. Frédéric-Dupont told the Assembly on 19 October that on a recent visit to Indochina General Carpentier had complained to him of the Government's inability to make up its mind about Cao Bang.[23] A month later

Frédéric-Dupont criticised Letourneau personally for his inertia and asked why the Minister had not paid a single visit to Indochina during his first year in office; it had required Cao Bang to make him face up to his responsibilities. There can be no doubt that these criticisms were justified and that Letourneau had been indecisive and inefficient; from now on he was to act much more energetically even if no more successfully.

Letourneau's New Policy

Mendès-France had said that France must choose between a massive military effort and negotiations with the enemy. General Juin had contended that the choice was between negotiations with the enemy and internationalisation. After Cao Bang Letourneau chose a policy, but it was not one of those proposed by Mendès-France or Juin. The new policy was worked out in close collaboration with de Lattre, for whom Letourneau had great admiration. Indeed, it is perhaps not unreasonable to say that Letourneau's policy of 1951-3 was as much a reflection of de Lattre's confidence as his policy of 1949-50 had been a reflection of Carpentier's indecision.

The essence of Letourneau's policy was his determination to avoid negotiations with Ho Chi Minh, in itself a negative policy, to which were attached certain positive aspects, the establishment of the pro-French Bao Dai régime, the building up of the Vietnamese national army, and increasing demands for American aid. In his speech of 22 November 1950 Letourneau said the Government was determined to pursue its policy of supporting Bao Dai, granting full self-government to the Associated States and creating a Vietnamese national army,[24] but the most consistently repeated aspect of his policy during the next two-and-a-half years was the negative one — under no circumstances would he consider direct negotiations with the enemy. In his Instructions to de Lattre Letourneau emphasised that it would be necessary to keep in touch with the Viet Minh but only so as to obtain information: 'Such contacts will be able to provide useful information about the situation in the areas controlled by the Viet Minh and about the intentions of the Viet Minh'.[25] In a debate in the National Assembly in April 1952 he maintained that to open negotiations with Ho Chi Minh would break the morale of the expeditionary force and create panic amongst the Vietnamese population.[26] A month later he scotched rumours that the Government was considering a direct approach to Ho Chi Minh: 'When France has set herself a task, she remains loyal to her word and to her traditions. There can be no question of betraying our friends in Indochina . . . If there is to be another policy, it will be pursued by another Government and a different Minister'.[27] And at the end of 1952 he reprimanded Alain Savary, a leading Socialist proponent of direct negotiations with the Viet Minh, for his defeatism.[28] Refusal to negotiate with the enemy was, then, the underlying principle of Letourneau's policy, but, with Ho Chi Minh definitely excluded, it was all the more necessary to make the Bao Dai régime viable. In trying to achieve this Letourneau continued the policy begun by Coste-Floret, introducing new aspects of his own. He tried to accelerate the move towards greater independence; he began the creation of the Vietnamese national army; he strove to obtain the maximum American aid.

Independence

In both public and private statements Letourneau constantly emphasised his desire to 'perfect' the independence of the Associated States of Indochina. After a Cabinet meeting on 18 November 1950 he told the Press that 'we want to increase the independence of the Vietnamese Government'.[29] Four days later he told the National Assembly that France's aim was 'to protect the sovereignty and independence of the Associated States'.[30] And in December 1950 he told General de Lattre that:

> henceforth Vietnam, Cambodia and Laos are fully independent States within the French Union. The only limitations on their sovereignty are those to which they have freely consented. They are the consequences of formal agreements and are justified because of membership of the French Union and the need to fight the Viet Minh.[31]

Two years later Letourneau was saying much the same thing:

> It is essential that we should show these peoples that we are their loyal partners, and that there is no question of our going back on the independence written into our agreements with them.[32]

And in his Instructions to General Salan (July 1952) he wrote:

> It is essential that we should do all we can to assure real independence for the Associated States within the French Union.[33]

There can be little doubt that Letourneau tried hard to grant a significant degree of independence to the Associated States; at the same time, he appears to have been rather slow to recognise the serious limitations of 'independence within the French Union'. One of Bao Dai's former Prime Ministers remarked:

> My impression was that M. Letourneau never really understood

the necessity of granting proper independence to Vietnam . . . It was not simply a question of the war against the Viet Minh; France continued to intervene in all branches of government.[34]

To most nationalist leaders after the Second World War independence meant not only internal self-government, but also independent diplomacy, an independent army, and membership of the United Nations. Independence of this type was possible within the British Commonwealth, but not within the French Union as constituted in 1946. Letourneau was one of those Frenchmen who was willing to stretch the 1946 Constitution to its limit, but he ignored the fact that the degree of independence permitted to even the most advanced territories within the French Union was insufficient to satisfy even moderate nationalist leaders. Within his own terms of reference he did his best to grant independence; within those of the nationalist leaders, or of world opinion, he did not go far enough, even allowing for the fact that a war was being waged in Indochina.

On 19 January 1950 Letourneau told the Assembly of the French Union that the three Associated States had achieved internal sovereignty and that France no longer had any part in the administration of any of the three States.[35] This statement was far from accurate, as the transfer of administrative power only began at the Pau Conference (June-November 1950), and had still not been completed when Letourneau's responsibility for Indochina ended in June 1953. In the course of 1950 the security services were handed over to the Vietnamese (on 10 March in Saigon for Cochinchina, and on 6 June in Hanoi for Tonkin and Annam). After the Cao Bang disaster the French agreed to the establishment of a Vietnamese-officered army (Military Agreement of 8 December 1950), which had hitherto been resisted by the French Army. Otherwise, no visible progress towards independence was made. Nguyen Phan Long, Bao Dai's Prime Minister from January to May 1950, was dismissed because he showed too much 'independence' in making direct approaches to the Americans for aid. His successor, Tran Van Huu, a Cochinchinese landowner and Francophil, was soon disillusioned by Vietnam's lack of independence. He later said that the Conference of Pau opened his eyes to the true position of the Associated States, each of which sent its Prime Minister to the Conference, whilst France, as at Fontainbleau in 1946, sent only civil servants and junior politicians,[36] the leader of the French being the worthy but powerless Albert Sarraut, President of the Assembly of the French Union. In Huu's opinion, the Conference of Pau was a complete failure from the Vietnamese point of view, partly because of Letourneau's attitude, partly because of that of the French delegation. In his opening speech on 29 June Letourneau promised the delegates that administrative independence would be granted as soon as the war situation allowed, but that no degree of independence which might affect 'the cohesion of the French Union' could be considered.[37] Sixteen years later Tran Van Huu said that he was furious not only at the tone of Letourneau's address — 'like that of a Colonial Minister' — but also at Letourneau's failure to appear at the conference after the first day.[38] That Tran Van Huu was disillusioned by the French attitude at Pau is also shown by his remarking to an American journalist in October 1950 that the Elysée and Pau Agreements should be replaced by a new treaty based on the complete equality of France and the Associated States.[39] In the light of criticisms such as these it was in vain that Letourneau protested that France was 'perfecting' the independence of the Associated States with all good faith and speed.

Yet, despite his failure to hasten the movement towards administrative independence, Letourneau's private papers suggest that he *was* trying to achieve this. In his Instructions to de Lattre, for example, he said that the transfer of administrative powers 'ought to be accelerated'. But, if it is true that Letourneau wanted to grant administrative independence, it is also clear that he was determined that French political and economic influence should remain significant. In the concluding part of his Instructions to de Lattre he emphasised the importance of giving political advice (albeit 'as discreetly as possible') to the governments of the Associated States; France must keep her promises about independence, but she had 'the right to ensure that the Associated States are governed effectively'.[40]

Progress towards independence was very slow up to 1951, *Franc-Tireur* commenting that 'even the limited independence granted in 1949 exists only on paper', but under the impulsive de Lattre important advances were made during 1951, and the momentum engendered by de Lattre continued to have an effect in 1952. The development towards complete internal autonomy seemed to be progressing satisfactorily until the whole concept of 'independence within the French Union' was shaken by France's unilateral devaluation of the piastre in May 1953.[41]

On arriving in Vietnam de Lattre had said, 'I have come here to complete your independence, not to limit it'.[42] In terms of paper independence de Lattre fulfilled his promise. During 1951 the Vietnamese gained control of the postal services (January), the customs services (March), the coal mines of Tonkin (April) and the agricultural services (April). On 8 May Bao Dai's first full diplomatic representative, Tran Van Don, arrived in London. A month later the Associated States were admitted to UNESCO, and soon afterwards the Vietnamese were given responsibility for the upkeep of their historical monuments.

The growing diplomatic status of the Associated States was shown when Letourneau persuaded the United States to invite them to the Japanese peace conference at San Francisco (August), and when France applied for U.N. membership for them (December). Progress towards independence was certainly made during 1951 despite de Lattre's exaggeration before the National Press Club in Washington: 'We have no other powers to transfer: everything, except one or two things which the Associated States have themselves asked us to continue to control, has been transfered to the governments of the three independent States'.[43]

De Lattre died suddenly of cancer in January 1952, but the policy he had applied with such energy was continued by Letourneau, who himself took over as High Commissioner whilst remaining a French Cabinet Minister. In May a special 'Commission de réforme française administrative en Indochine' was set up to complete the last stages of the administrative hand-over. Shortly afterwards the Vietnamese were given control of the railways and of the iron and steel industry, and on 17 June Letourneau told the Overseas Writers' Club in Washington that there were only 1,400 French administrators left in Indochina, compared with 7,000 in 1947. Although the Soviet Union refused to let the Associated States join the United Nations, their diplomatic position was enhanced in April 1953 with the reform of the French representation in Indochina. Hitherto there had been one High Commissioner for Indochina with five Commissioners under him, one each for Laos, Cambodia, Tonkin, Annam and Cochinchina. From now on there was a High Commissioner for each of the three Associated States, working under the Minister responsible for relations with the Associated States. The old French High Commission disappeared: the new men were diplomats, not colonial governors.

Letourneau also encouraged Nguyen Van Tam, Bao Dai's new Prime Minister, in his attempts to broaden the popular basis of the Vietnamese State. Nguyen Van Tam succeeded Tran Van Huu as Prime Minister at the beginning of June 1952. Hitherto the only move towards democratic institutions had been the announcement in February 1952 that a provisional Vietnamese National Assembly would meet with forty members nominated by Bao Dai, forty elected, and five representing the minority groups of the highlands. In fact this Assembly never met. Nguyen Van Tam, however, told *Le Monde* in November 1952 that he intended introducing democratic institutions as soon as possible. He said that he wanted to ensure that the Vietnamese, now independent, also had the right to express themselves freely in elections. He hoped to begin by having councils elected to help the governments of the three provinces of Vietnam; eventually there would be a properly elected National Assembly.[44] Nguyen Van Tam did, in fact, set up a provisional

National Council of twenty-one nominated members with consultative rights on the budget (8 August 1952), and he also held municipal elections on 25 January 1953. These were restricted to communes which were not in recognised Viet Minh areas, but 80 per cent of the 89,000 electors appear to have voted despite the efforts of the Viet Minh to discourage them. The government party won the elections although not by outstanding majorities, but at least Nguyen Van Tam had had the courage to hold elections at all. It was also Tam who was responsible for the inauguration of free trade unionism in Vietnam (16 November 1952). Tam was later to be as critical of Bao Dai's attitude to these reforms, as he was appreciative of Letourneau's support. According to Tam, he had the greatest difficulty in persuading Bao Dai to hold the municipal elections, whilst he would not hear of national ones. Tam tried to convince Bao Dai that only by holding elections could his régime acquire any popular legitimacy, but Bao Dai apparently insisted on regarding himself as an Emperor who did not require to have his political position confirmed in any way.[45]

Despite his efforts to strengthen the Bao Dai régime by granting more internal autonomy and by encouraging Nguyen Van Tam's political reforms, Letourneau's policy between 1951-3 continued, as before, to be somewhat contradictory. This, in turn, aroused dissatisfaction within the Associated States. In the 1952 debate on the military budget for Indochina Letourneau said that France was doing all she could to 'perfect' the independence of the Associated States; he also referred to the disinterested character of France's military involvement in Vietnam. But he then went on to emphasise 'France's determination to remain in Indochina'.[46] Such contradictory statements were no doubt necessary to placate the more conservative members of Pinay's parliamentary majority, but they were hardly designed to make the Governments of the Associated States believe that Letourneau's repeated statements about 'independence' were to be taken literally.

Letourneau's Instructions to de Lattre showed the same inconsistency. On the one hand, the maximum independence was to be granted; on the other, 'your powers as High Commissioner allow you to expel from Indochina any suspect persons'.[47] One such summary expulsion occurred in July 1951, when Nguyen Manh Ha, a leading Vietnamese Catholic and former Minister of Ho Chi Minh (but with no sympathy for the Viet Minh by 1951), was arrested and deported to France. According to Nguyen Manh Ha, this expulsion was unjustified, as his only 'crime' had been to criticise Bao Dai and express doubts about the possibility of achieving a military victory over the Viet Minh in an interview with an Indonesian journalist.[48] De Lattre's contention, however, was that Nguyen Manh Ha constituted a serious political threat owing to the left-wing bookshop he ran in Hanoi (the Librairie du Square). Moreover, as Ha was a French citizen - his wife was the daughter of a Communist mayor in France - his 'expulsion' was in fact only 'repatriation'. Whatever the merits of Ha's case, his summary eviction gave the impression that France was still very much a colonial power. There is no reason to doubt that both de Lattre and Letourneau were sincere in their claim that by 1951 the French were fighting in Indochina only to preserve the newly independent Associated States from Communism. But each autocratic decision seemed to contradict this claim. Vietnamese nationalists were understandably more interested in actions than in semantics.

Perhaps the greatest contradiction in Letourneau's policy was his decision to combine the positions of French Cabinet Minister and High Commissioner in Indochina after the death of de Lattre in January 1952. Letourneau later defended his decision on the grounds that it helped him to hasten the movement towards independence and that it increased his authority in negotiations with the Americans.[49] Purely from a functional point of view, however, it was an impractical concentration of powers. As the Gaullist Raymond Dronne remarked in 1952: 'It is not possible for one man, whatever his capacities, to be both a Minister in Paris and a High Commissioner in Indochina'.[50] But perhaps even more important was the unfortunate impression given by this dual office of the weakness of Bao Dai's position and of the extent of French control. Letourneau already had wide powers in Indochina in virtue of his position as Minister in charge of relations with the Associated States; these powers were immeasurably increased when he became High Commissioner as well. François Borella has shown that the decrees of 1950, establishing the powers of the Minister of the Associated States, and of 1952, combining these powers with those of the High Commissioner, resulted in Letourneau wielding huge civil and military powers throughout Indochina.[51]

In view of the above situation it was not surprising that none of the Associated States was satisfied with its degree of independence. Arriving in France for the first meeting of the High Council of the French Union (November 1951), Tran Van Huu told reporters at Orly that he wanted to see the revision of the Franco-Vietnamese Agreements and of the whole structure of the French Union, which ought to be 'a union of free, equal and sovereign peoples. We would like to see a French Union modelled on the British Commonwealth'.[52] A few months later Tran Van Huu complained to Robert Guillain of France's slowness in handing over the administrative services to the Vietnamese.[53] Guillain went on to criticise his own countrymen for using the military situation as an excuse for not granting a larger measure of independence, − a stricture repeated a year later in *L'Express.*[54] Bao Dai himself was dissatisfied with the situation, and apparently asked for greater diplomatic independence at his meeting with President Auriol on 4 September 1952. No official communiqué was issued after this meeting at Muret, but *Le Monde* remarked that it was understood that Bao Dai had asked that Prince Buu Loc should become Ambassador, instead of High Commissioner, to France.[55] Nor was it only the Vietnamese who were dissatisfied. In April 1953 King Norodom Sihanouk of Cambodia told an American audience that if the Cambodians were not granted greater economic and military independence there was a real danger that they would go over to the Viet Minh.[56]

These constant criticisms had some effect. In his Instructions to General Salan in 1952, Letourneau said that it was his intention to hand over all the administrative services to the Associated States before the end of 1953.[57] This was the first time a specific date had been mentioned, but, as with all too many decisions about Indochina, it was a case of 'too little and too late'.

The Vietnamese National Army

One of the chief aspects of Letourneau's policy of 'independence' for Vietnam was the creation of a National Army. His attempt to create this army was no more successful than his scheme for administrative independence. Moreover the need for American aid to build up the new army had unforeseen and contradictory results.

Letourneau's decision to build a Vietnamese National Army was one of the consequences of the Cao Bang disaster. On 22 October 1950 Letourneau, Juin, Bao Dai and Tran Van Huu agreed on the principle of a National Army.[58] The project took shape at Dalat (4-5 November), when Letourneau, Pignon, Bao Dai and Tran Van Huu decided that an army of 115,000, equipped by the Americans, should be established by the end of 1951. At first the majority of officers were to be seconded from French units. This was the genesis of the Vietnamese National Army, on which Letourneau was to pin so much faith. He told the National Assembly in November 1950 that the establishment of a National Army was one of the cornerstones of his policy,[59] and de Lattre was told that 'the creation of national armies in the Associated States has become a matter of urgency. . . . Everything must be done to establish them'.[60] Letourneau continued to lay great emphasis on this aspect of his policy. In April 1952 he told the National Assembly that the newly-created Vietnamese battalions were already proving their worth,[61] and when General Salan became Commander-in-Chief in July 1952, he was told that one of his principal tasks was 'the development and strengthening of the Vietnamese National Army'.[62]

The Vietnamese National Army, however, ran into difficulties from the beginning. The French military authorities in Vietnam were at first sceptical about its value. At the same time Bao Dai wanted the National Army to be independent of the French Union forces. The French were opposed to this; but by the Military Convention of 8 December 1950, which replaced that of 30 December 1949, it was agreed that the National Army would be directly under Bao Dai rather than the French High Command.[63] In return for this concession, Bao Dai promised to have an army of 115,000 in the field by the end of 1951. With de Lattre's support the National Army came into being during 1951, but the figure of 115,000 was not reached until 1953.[64] De Lattre used all his powerful influence to build up the National Army. In March 1951 he persuaded the National Defence Committee to send out 10,000 men as reinforcements on the express condition that the extra troops would be used only as a stop-gap whilst he built up the Vietnamese Army.[65] He strove to recruit Vietnamese youths into the Army, urging them to end their 'attentisme': 'Behave like men. If you are Communists, join the Viet Minh . . . But if you are patriots, fight for your country, because this war is your war. It only concerns France in so far as she has made a number of promises to Vietnam. For France this is the most disinterested war since the Crusades'.[66] Rhetoric of this sort did not have much more effect than Bao Dai's mobilisation order of 15 July 1951. By the end of 1951 the Vietnamese National Army had reached a theoretical total of 38,000, but already it was plagued with two problems, desertion and shortage of officers. Conscripted soldiers preferred to go back to their villages at the first opportunity, whilst the educated classes continued their 'attentisme'.[67]

At Dalat in January 1952 Bao Dai promised Letourneau that he would build up the Vietnamese Army more quickly than hitherto,[68] and in June Bao Dai's new Prime Minister, Nguyen Van Tam, promised the same thing.[69] In the same month Letourneau told the Americans that the Vietnamese Army now had forty battalions (about 40,000 men), and Nguyen Van Tam gave an optimistic report of the Army's progress in an interview with *Le Monde* in November.[70] Early in 1953 General Juin and Letourneau were continuing to talk optimistically about the development and ability of the Vietnamese National Army,[71] but Letourneau later admitted privately that he was very disappointed by the progress of the Vietnamese Army, laying much of the blame on Bao Dai for his failure to put himself at the head of the Army, if not by appearing in the front line, at least by taking every opportunity to inspect troops and visit training camps.[72] Even in 1952-3 Letourneau showed occasional signs of pessimism. Anxiety about the development of the Vietnamese Army was apparent when he told the National Assembly that 'every effort will be required to build up the national armies of the Associated States',[73] and even more when he told

General Salan that it might take 'several years' to bring the national armies up to the necessary standard.[74]

Meanwhile the military situation worsened during 1952. Robert Guillain wrote that although the Vietnamese National Army might have 100,000 men by the end of the year, there could be no question of a reduction of French Union forces, partly because the National Army was still no match for the Viet Minh, and partly because the Viet Minh forces were steadily increasing.[75] In March *Le Monde* criticised the Hoa Binh operation, which had created a salient, denuded the Tonkin Delta of troops, and allowed further Viet Minh infiltration.[76] But at the end of the year Letourneau denied that the military situation had worsened; indeed he even rashly stated that military expenditure for 1952 would be down for the first year since the war began and that two battalions would be brought back and not replaced.[77] In fact, the heavy fighting of November and December put paid to both these projects. The year ended with Bao Dai appealing once again for young men to end their 'attentisme' by joining his army to defend the 'independence' of Vietnam against 'red imperialism', and with Letourneau assuring the National Assembly about the efficacy of Vietnam's military effort.

The Vietnamese National Army, however, was still not functioning properly. Early in February 1953 Letourneau left for Saigon, announcing on his departure the formation of a new force of Vietnamese light infantry battalions.[78] A special military committee met at Dalat on 24 February to draw up plans for the galvanisation of the National Army. Bao Dai presided, and Letourneau, Salan, Nguyen Van Tam, Le Quang Huy (Minister of Defence) and General Hinh (Chief of Staff) were present. Hinh's proposal that 54 new commando battalions should be created was accepted; these troops were to be tried out first in the south, later in the north, and they were to be entirely under Vietnamese command. Letourneau conceded that the reconstituted Vietnamese Army should be independent of the French Union forces rather than integrated into them as before. Letourneau's acceptance of this condition betrayed his now desperate wish that an effective Vietnamese Army should be constituted at almost any cost. The Vietnamese Army had at last achieved its independence, but the Viet Minh had now had an independent army for seven years. Moreover, the new Vietnamese National Army was always faced with the very difficult task of fighting a defensive war.[79]

The Vietnamese National Army scarcely had time to prove itself, as Dien Bien Phu occurred within a year of its birth as an independent entity. But even if Dien Bien Phu had not occurred, there is no reason to believe that the National Army could have defeated the Viet Minh. The Vietnamese National Army would have been unlikely to have been really effective, unless major political reforms had been carried out; otherwise, the soldiers had nothing to fight for. So long as the Bao Dai Government had such a limited popular basis, being supported chiefly by the landowning classes, no effective National Army could have been created. It was by no means clear to the landless peasant why he should fight for a government which refused to carry out agrarian reforms, when Ho Chi Minh offered land redistribution. Nor was it clear to nationalists, except those with strong anti-Communist convictions, why they should fight for a rather dilettante Emperor, supported by French bayonets and American money, when the ascetic Ho Chi Minh had been fighting for national independence in the company only of Vietnamese since 1946.

NOTES

1. Honey, pp.41-2.
2. Strictly speaking the Viet Minh ceased to exist after 3 March 1951, but the term continued in current use (rather than Lien Viet). Viet Minh is therefore used in the text to describe the Communist-led national liberation front even after 1951.
3. For details, see Peter Campbell, *French Electoral Systems and Elections since 1789* (Faber, 1958), pp.110-23.
4. *Année Politique,* 1950, p.211. Bernard Fall, in *Street Without Joy,* gives the total losses as 6,000 troops, 13 heavy guns, 125 mortars, 450 lorries, 950 heavy machine-guns, 1,200 light machine-guns and 8,000 rifles, i.e. enough to equip a new Viet Minh division.
5. *Journal Officiel* (Assemblée Nationale), 19 October 1950.
6. ibid.
7. ibid.
8. ibid.
9. ibid.
10. Interview with Letourneau, 25 November 1966. But Carpentier claimed (interview, 4 December 1967) that the withdrawal would have taken place sooner but for the Committee of National Defence's opposition to it for political reasons.
11. *L'Observateur,* 12 October 1950.
12. Interview with Letourneau, 25 November 1966.
13. Interview with Pignon, 1 December 1966.
14. Pignon letter quoted in C. Paillat, *Dossier Secret de l'Indochine* (Paris, 1964), p.191.
15. Interview with Letourneau, 25 November 1966.
16. *Journal Officiel* (Assemblée Nationale), 22 November 1950.
17. ibid.
18. ibid.
19. ibid.
20. ibid.
21. ibid.
22. See below, pp.98-107.
23. A view with which Carpentier later agreed in private conversation;

interview, 4 December 1967.

24. *Journal Officiel* (Assemblée Nationale), 22 November 1950.
25. Letourneau Papers (Instructions to de Lattre, December 1950).
26. *Journal Officiel* (Assemblée Nationale), 9 April 1952.
27. *Le Monde,* 13 May 1952.
28. *Journal Officiel* (Assemblée Nationale), 19 December 1952.
29. *Le Monde,* 19/20 November 1950.
30. *Journal Officiel* (Assemblée Nationale), 22 November 1950.
31. Letourneau Papers (Instructions to de Lattre).
32. *Journal Officiel* (Assemblée Nationale), 19 February 1952.
33. Letourneau Papers (Instructions to Salan).
34. Interview with Tran Van Huu, 3 December 1966; Bao Dai's *chef de cabinet,* Nguyen De, agreed with this view, interview 1 May 1974.
35. *Journal Officiel* (Assemblée de l'Union française), 19 January 1950.
36. Interview with Tran Van Huu, 3 December 1966.
37. *Le Monde,* 29 June 1950.
38. Interview with Tran Van Huu, 3 December 1966.
39. *New York Times,* 23 October 1950.
40. Letourneau Papers.
41. See below, pp.107-11.
42. Quoted Grosser, p.282.
43. *Année Politique,* 1951, p.235.
44. *Le Monde,* 17 November 1952.
45. Interview with Tam, 23 December 1966.
46. *Journal Officiel* (Assemblée Nationale), 19 December 1952.
47. Letourneau Papers.
48. Interview with Nguyen Manh Ha, 14 January 1967. The interview with the Indonesian journalist was certainly the *occasion* for Ha's expulsion; the Expulsion Order makes this clear. But whether it was the fundamental *cause* remains undertain. P.J. Honey thinks the real reason was that Ha was a fellow-traveller.
49. Interview with Letourneau, 6 February 1967.
50. *Journal Officiel* (Assemblée Nationale), 19 December 1952.
51. François Borella, *L'évolution politique et juridique de l'Union française* (Thesis, Nancy, 1957).
52. *Le Monde,* 25/26 November 1951.
53. *Le Monde,* 7 February 1952.
54. *L'Express,* 23 May 1953.
55. *Le Monde,* 5 September 1952.
56. *Le Monde,* 21 April 1953.
57. Letourneau Papers.
58. *L'Année Politique,* 1950, p.212.
59. *Journal Officiel* (Assemblée Nationale), 22 November 1950.
60. Letourneau Papers.
61. *Journal Officiel* (Assemblée Nationale), 10 April 1952.
62. Letourneau Papers.
63. *L'Année Politique,* 1950, p.267.
64. *Le Monde,* 19 March 1953.
65. *Le Monde,* 22 March 1951.
66. Quoted, Paillat, p.300.
67. *Temps Modernes,* Aug. 1953, p.293 ff.
68. *Le Monde,* 29 January 1952.
69. *L'Année Politique,* 1952, p.231.

70. *Le Monde,* 17 November 1952.
71. e.g. Juin in Saigon in February (*Le Monde,* 18 February 1953), and Letourneau in Hanoi in March (*Le Monde,* 3 March 1952).
72. Interview with Letourneau, 25 November 1966.
73. *Journal Officiel* (Assemblée Nationale), 10 April 1952.
74. Letourneau Papers.
75. *Le Monde,* 7 February 1952.
76. *Le Monde,* 16/17 March 1952.
77. *Journal Officiel* (Assemblée Nationale), 19 December 1952.
78. *Le Monde,* 5 February 1953.
79. The very real difficulties of fighting such a war have been emphasised by Dennis Duncanson in *Conflict Study,* October 1973, pp. 7-8.

7.   AMERICAN INVOLVEMENT IN INDOCHINA, 1949-54.

Letourneau's determination to build a Vietnamese National Army made it essential for him to get American aid. His hope was that the Vietnamese National Army, financed by the United States, would prepare the way for substantial French military and financial reductions in Indochina. At the same time Letourneau still hoped that Indochina would remain firmly within France's sphere of influence, i.e. within the French Union. American aid, however, had unexpected and unwelcome consequences. On the one hand, the Americans insisted that in return for aid the French must further loosen their ties with Indochina — in other words France must give up her attempt to build a close-knit French Union. By acceding to this demand France had to abandon a major motive for her continued fight in Indochina. On the other hand, the Americans expected the French to commit *more*, not fewer, forces to the struggle against the Communists as the price for greater financial and military aid.

The United States had been directly involved in Indochina from 1941-5 through its support of Ho Chi Minh's anti-Japanese resistance organisation, the Viet Minh, but recent studies, including the Pentagon Papers on *United States - Vietnam Relations 1945-67,*[1] clearly show that, although the Office of Strategic Services supported Ho Chi Minh both militarily during the war and politically after his declaration of Vietnamese independence in 1945,[2] the OSS was not implementing United States government policy.[3] Indeed President Roosevelt, supposedly the arch-enemy of European colonialism, had decided by the summer of 1944 that it would be impossible either to make Indochina a United Nations trustee territory after the war or to hand it over to the Chinese Nationalists, and shortly before his death in April 1945 he had sanctioned a policy of non-interference in post-war Indochina, which in practice meant that the United States was agreeing to a restoration of the status quo. France was the ally of the United States, and the United States Government realised that it was important to have France on her side in Europe: conceding to French wishes in South East Asia seemed a small price to pay for cementing the Western Alliance. Moreover, the United States Government was aware of Ho Chi Minh's Communism from an early date. In spite of the fact that in September 1946 Ho succeeded in persuading George Abbot, an American embassy official in Paris, that he was no more than a

98

Vietnamese patriot and nationalist, the State Department was well aware of Ho's connections with Moscow. On 5 December 1946, i.e. before the outbreak of full-scale war between the French and the Viet Minh, Dean Acheson, the Acting Secretary of State, warned that Ho Chi Minh was an 'agent of international Communism . . . with Moscow affiliations . . . receiving the support of the French Communist Party'. Acheson went on to warn that a 'Communist-dominated, Moscow-orientated Indochina' would be directly against the interests of the United States, which consequently would do all it could to support 'the non-Communist elements in Vietnam'.[4] As Geoffrey Warner has pointed out, Acheson's cable illustrates the early emergence of what have been the two related aims of United States' Vietnam policy ever since: 'to deny the country to the Communists; and to find an alternative around which Vietnamese nationalism could coalesce.'[5]

But over the years the Americans found that it was difficult to implement this dual policy. By fighting the Viet Minh the French were helping to achieve the first objective, but by refusing to grant something comparable to 'dominion status' to the Associated States of Indochina they were frustrating the second. 'A series of French-established puppet governments', noted a State Department policy statement of September 1948, 'have tended to enhance the prestige of Ho's government and to call into question, on the part of the Vietnamese, the sincerity of French intentions to accord an independent status to Vietnam'.[6] The United States frankly did not know what to propose at this stage. On the one hand they could not deny 'the unpleasant fact that the Communist Ho Chi Minh is the strongest and perhaps the ablest figure in Indochina', and on the other hand, they felt that they could not press the French Government too hard to concede full independence to the non-Communist Vietnamese nationalists, because 'we have an immediate interest in maintaining in power a friendly French government, to assist in the furtherance of our aims in Europe. This immediate and vital interest has in consequence taken precedence over active steps looking toward the realisation of our objectives in Indochina'.[7] In the late 1940s and early 1950s the Rhine was not surprisingly more important to the Americans than the Mekong.

As for Bao Dai, the State Department was clearly unhappy about him: he was, according to a despatch of May 1949, 'an expedient of uncertain outcome'.[8] However, the State Department emphasised the desirability of the success of the Bao Dai policy, because there appeared to be 'no other alternative to the establishment of a Communist pattern in Vietnam'. The Department believed that 'no effort should be spared by France, other Western powers, and non-Communist Asian nations to assure the experiment its best chance of succeeding'.[9] At the appropriate moment the United States would recognise Bao Dai's Government [it did so in February 1950], and would 'explore the possibility of complying with any request by the [Bao Dai] government for U.S. arms and economic assistance'. However, 'it must first be clear that France will offer all necessary concessions to make the Bao Dai solution attractive to the nationalists', and 'the Bao Dai government must through its own efforts demonstrate its capacity to organise and conduct affairs wisely'.[10]

Although American aid did not begin to arrive in Indochina in appreciable quantities until 1951, it should be emphasised that serious American involvement in Vietnam began *before* the outbreak of the Korean War in June 1950. A draft National Security Council study of December 1949 emphasised the Free World's need to stand firm in South East Asia, (the first example of what was later to be known as the domino theory):

> It is now clear that South East Asia is the target of a coordinated offensive directed by the Kremlin . . . . The extension of Communist authority in China represents a grievous political defeat for us; if South East Asia is swept by Communism we shall have suffered a major political rout, the repercussions of which will be felt throughout the world, especially in the Middle East and in a then critically exposed Australia.[11]

Within ten days of the United States' recognition of the governments of Vietnam, Laos and Cambodia (7 February 1950), the French had appealed to the Americans for direct military aid for Indochina, arguing that their own commitment was 'such a drain on France that a long-term programme of assistance is necessary . . . . Otherwise, it is very likely that France may be forced to reconsider her entire policy with a possible view to cutting her losses and withdrawing from Indochina'.[12] This was, as Geoffrey Warner has remarked, 'a shrewd piece of political blackmail',[13] but the French did not press their point too hard at this stage, nor did the Americans do much about it except to promise action in the near future. The Korean War and the disaster of Cao Bang were the catalysts which resulted in words being transformed into deeds.

Although American aid began to filter into Vietnam before the disaster of Cao Bang, it was not until the parliamentary debate of 22 November 1950 that Letourneau finally made it clear that his policy of destroying the Viet Minh and making the Bao Dai régime viable was to be based on the twin pillars of American aid and the Vietnamese National Army.[14] From now on the *idée fixe* of successive French governments was the building of a Vietnamese National Army equipped by the Americans. The result of this policy was that France became increasingly dependent on the United States, and in consequence the prospect of negotiating directly with Ho Chi Minh, advocated by Pierre Mendès-France at the end of 1950 and by many Socialists (as well as Communists) during the next three-and-a-half years, became increasingly remote. For the Americans had already laid down their terms for aid. On 11 April 1950 Dean Acheson told Schuman and Letourneau that the United States Government was opposed to France negotiating with the Vietnamese Communists or recognising Mao Tse-tung.[15] On 6 May Bidault, Schuman and Acheson had talks in Paris on the subject of American aid. Acheson promised an immediate stepping-up of the aid programme on condition that the French granted a larger measure of independence to the Associated States. He also wanted 'the majority of the aid' to go directly to the Associated States.[16] General Carpentier, the French Commander-in-Chief, however, told the Americans that he would 'never agree to this equipment being given directly to the Vietnamese'.[17] At the same time Letourneau denied that there was any question of exchanging 'independence' for American aid: in his view the Associated States already had 'full independence within the French Union'.[18] In the same interview Letourneau complained of allied slowness in recognising what France was doing in Indochina:

> France does not intend to let her sons be killed in Indochina like mercenaries without any recognition of the task she is accomplishing. France has the right to speak out clearly in the knowledge of the justice of her cause. If this is not understood, France will have no alternative but to leave to others the defence of positions which are of vital importance to the whole free world.[19]

This was a complaint which was to be voiced frequently over the next four years, and from a French point of view it seemed quite justifiable. Many Americans, however, remained unconvinced about French motives in Indochina, Walter Lippmann expressing their doubts in a scathing attack on French colonialism in the *New York Herald Tribune* on 17 May 1950.

The outbreak of the Korean War (25 June 1950), it is true, led to a reduction of Franco-American differences over Indochina. On 26 June Truman announced that 'the despatch of military aid to the forces of France and of the Associated States in Indochina will be accelerated, and a military mission will be sent to Indochina to work closely with these forces'.[20] In July Donald Heath arrived as American Ambassador to the Associated States. He was accompanied by the new military mission, but American aid remained meagre throughout 1950, partly owing to continued misunderstandings about French policy, partly because Korea had first priority. Tran Van Huu, who had many conversations with Heath in late 1950, contended, justifiably it would seem, that the main reason for the slow arrival of American aid was the divergence of Franco-American views on the degree of independence which should be given to the Associated States.[21] According to *L'Année Politique* the sum total of American aid during 1950 was seven Dakotas, forty Hellcat fighters and three shiploads of light arms, the last being mostly reserved for the Associated States. The Cao Bang disaster, however, had the effect of producing a written aid agreement, even if it did not remove American reservations about French policy. By now it was clear that Vietnam might become a Communist state if Bao Dai and the French were not given military aid in large quantities. At the end of December, Letourneau, de Lattre, Tran Van Huu and Heath signed an aid agreement in Saigon. Letourneau paid homage to the United States, and went on to say:

> I am sure that the day will soon come when the national armies of the Associated States of Indochina, effectively supported by the other forces of the French Union, will not only constitute an effective military force, which is the attribute of all sovereign States, but will also make a valuable contribution to the defence of free people throughout the world.[22]

In his reply Heath said that American aid implied no military, economic or political control, in contrast to Communist claims. The years which followed, however, showed that this claim was not entirely accurate.

Despite its inauspicious beginnings Letourneau continued to attach great importance to the American aid programme. At a press conference in January 1951 he said that France's allies should give more aid in view of the nature of the war in Indochina.[23] After their talks of 29-30 January Truman and Pleven issued a communiqué announcing Franco-American agreement on Far Eastern problems. The Indochina war was recognised as part of the world struggle against Communist aggression; more aid was to be given to France and the Associated States; the United States would not intervene in Indochina unless the Chinese did so.[24] In February forty American fighter-bombers and six heavy bombers arrived in Indochina. On a visit to the United States in April Auriol was given the same assurances as Pleven in January, but the French remained dissatisfied with the volume of American aid. Letourneau, therefore, decided to send General de Lattre de Tassigny, the Commander-in-Chief in Indochina, to appeal for more help.

During his American visit (13-24 September 1951) de Lattre appeared on television and held press conferences as well as putting his case to the United States Government. He told the National Press Club in Washington that 'this war is in no sense a colonial war, because

Indochina is no longer a colony'.[25] He went on to emphasise the strategic importance of Tonkin: 'Once Tonkin has been lost, there is no barrier to Communism before Suez . . . . Hanoi is the Berlin of South East Asia.' He claimed that France was doing all she possibly could to win the war against the Communists: 'We have given our shirts (*notre chemise*); now we are giving our blood. What more do you expect of us?' France's aim was to build up the Vietnamese National Army, and he had come unashamedly to ask for more American money and arms to do this. Two days after this speech the American State Department issued a communiqué emphasising the identity of views of the United States and France on Indochina (as in January) and promising more rapid delivery of American aid. The result of this promise was the arrival in Saigon of General Lawton Collins with a permanent aid mission. Meanwhile, the *New York Times* advocated enough aid to equip eight Vietnamese divisions.[26] But, although American aid was greater in 1951 than it had been in 1950, it still remained insufficient to satisfy the French.[27] And, despite their promises, the Americans remained uneasy about French policy. Certainly, the replacement of the Pignon-Carpentier team by de Lattre and Letourneau helped to allay their fears about colonialism,[28] but they continued to be critical of the limited degree of independence granted to the Associated States, whilst their own involvement in Korea seemed to justify the slow delivery of equipment to Indochina.

In 1952 Letourneau continued where de Lattre had left off. He went to the United States for a fortnight in June, announcing on his departure that the prime object of his visit was to ask the United States for the means to build up the Vietnamese National Army and so prepare for the relief of the Expeditionary Corps.[29] Letourneau tried, like de Lattre, to reassure the Americans about French policy. He told the Overseas Writers' Club that the Associated States were now virtually independent. Moreover, he had not come to ask for American troops, only for aid, with which France and the Associated States could defeat the Viet Minh. Asked about relations between France and the Associated States after the war was over, he said he saw no reason why they should not be similar to those between the United States and the Philippines. The official talks with Truman and Acheson (16-17 June) led to yet another communiqué recognising Asian-European interdependence and the efforts of France and the Associated States in the struggle against Communist aggression. The Americans promised increased aid, although the exact amount was to be fixed later by Congress.[30] On his return to Paris, Letourneau said the talks had been very satisfactory: 'We have received firm assurances about the more rapid delivery of aid and equipment'.[31] And three months later Letourneau announced that American aid, hitherto disappointing, was arriving in Indochina in steadily increasing quantities. As the volume of Chinese aid appeared to be static, he estimated that Indochina would become less of a burden for France after 1952.[32]

Although it is true that by early 1953 the United States was paying for over half the cost of the war in Indochina, Letourneau's hopes were partially disappointed. For in October 1952 Congress decided to make cuts in all overseas aid. As a result the $650 million promised for Indochina was reduced to $525 million. France therefore had to find an extra 43 milliard francs to pay for the war.[33] French reaction to this American decision was voiced by President Auriol, who complained that France was paying a disproportionate amount, both in men and money, for the defence of the free world. France had now spent Fr.1,600 milliard on the Indochina War, whereas total American aid to France - including Marshall Aid, which could not be used for Indochina - amounted to 800 milliards.[34]

The Viet Minh capture of Nghia Lo, followed by attacks in the Thai country during October and November 1952, ended any possibility of a reduction in the size of the Expeditionary Corps for 1953, but Letourneau optimistically continued to claim that American aid would soon lead to an improvement in the war situation. In the debate on the 1953 military budget (19 December 1952) he even said that he hoped to reduce the Expeditionary Corps by 20,000 men in 1953, saving Fr.14 milliard, but he admitted that this reduction would depend as much on the progress of the Vietnamese army as on the volume of American aid.[35] In March 1953 Letourneau went to the United States again, accompanied by René Mayer, the Prime Minister, and Georges Bidault, the Minister for Foreign Affairs. After three days of talks with Eisenhower, Dulles and Wilson (the Secretary of Defence), a communiqué was issued, which emphasised again the interdependence of Korea and Indochina. In return for increased American military and financial aid, the French Government undertook to strengthen the forces of the French Union and the Associated States. At the same time China was warned again not to intervene in Indochina.[36] A month later, however, the French Government received the Memorandum of 26 April, in which the United States promised more aid, but insisted on greater control over its use, in particular demanding that it should go mainly to the forces of the Associated States. At the same time the Memorandum stated that an increase in direct aid to France would be 'dependent upon the French Government drawing up a plan - satisfactory in all respects - for ensuring military success in Indochina'.[37] The United States had at last made it absolutely clear that American aid entailed more, not less, military commitment by France in Indochina. Letourneau's hope that American aid would somehow relieve France of the military and financial burdens of the Indochina War had thus been as badly disappointed as his hope that the Vietnamese National Army would become a substitute for the French Expeditionary Corps.

Despite the warning signs the French Government had shown little foresight about the effect of American aid. *L'Observateur* had pointed out the price of American aid in late 1950 and early 1951.[38] In February 1952 Robert Guillain of *Le Monde,* reporting from Indochina, had said that the effect of American and Chinese aid was simply to nourish the war. Neither the United States nor China had any wish to get involved directly in Vietnam, but both were content to see their enemies suffering there – hence, 'we (the French) will remain alone in this war of attrition'.[39] A week later Guillain warned that 'the United States help those who are prepared to help themselves: if we give up, we will be given up. They tell us to hold fast – "You're not at war in Europe; in Asia you are; keep up the fight, and we'll take care of Europe".'[40] He criticised France for having no constructive policy: her only aim seemed to be to hold on in the hope that American aid and the Vietnamese National Army would somehow turn the scales, a hope best summarised by de Lattre when he had optimistically claimed that, 'If we are given the means, we shall see the end of the tunnel in eighteen months'. Guillain suggested that the metaphor of the bottomless pit might be more appropriate than that of the tunnel. And when Jean Letourneau and René Mayer were in Washington in March 1953, Jacques Fauvet of *Le Monde* again emphasised France's dilemma when he pointed out that the United States would never give France whole-hearted support in Indochina so long as France gave the impression that she only wanted aid to balance her budget. He quoted extracts from *U.S.News* and *Newsweek* suggesting that France was not making sufficient effort in Indochina to deserve more American aid; in particular the Americans wanted to know why France refused to send national servicemen to Indochina and why most of the casualties there were not metropolitan Frenchmen. This article by Fauvet indicated the extent to which Letourneau had miscalculated in his hope that American aid could be a substitute for French effort.[41]

Even before the Memorandum of April 1953 the Americans had spoken bluntly of the price of their aid. In December 1952 the *New York Herald Tribune* described the Eisenhower-Dulles plan to win the war as follows:

> The French will be urged to make an unequivocal offer of independence to Indochina within a specific time limit. They will be asked to send two more divisions to Indochina. In return, the United States will recognise France's rôle there and increase aid substantially. . . . The aim will be to destroy the Viet Minh regular forces within two years, and thereafter to deal with any remaining

pockets of resistance.[42]

The *New York Herald Tribune* commented that this was a bold plan; it remained to be seen whether the Administration could persuade Congress to support it and the French to carry it out. Three months later a leading article in *L'Aurore* contended that 'If the United States takes over the cost of the war in Indochina, France will be able to devote herself entirely to Europe and Africa'.[43] This was precisely the delusion under which Letourneau had been labouring for the past three years, for it showed a complete misunderstanding of the nature of American aid. As Jean-Jacques Servan-Schreiber pointed out in *Le Monde* in January 1953, American aid made it *more* difficult for France to get out of the Indochina impasse, because the Americans were opposed to any compromise solution involving negotiations with Ho Chi Minh. Admiral Radford, for example, had stated that the Viet Minh must be 'completely destroyed'. Hence the illusion of those, like Letourneau, who imagined that increased American aid would miraculously reduce France's burden in Indochina. On the contrary,

> American aid is given in direct proportion to the anti-Communist effort made by each country. The Americans do not intend to replace France's sacrifices in Indochina, but to make them more effective by increasing them. If we [the French] increase our military budget, the Americans will increase their aid; if we reduce our budget, they will reduce their aid. That is the mechanism.

More aid would also mean greater American direction of the war: 'In the case of Indochina, the situation is already clear: the plans are being made in Washington; . . . with the arrival of every American bomber in Indochina, France's control of the war is reduced and her sacrifices in it are increased.'[44]

Servan-Schreiber was doubtless exaggerating the degree of France's subservience to the United States at the beginning of 1953, but by the end of that year — with the United States paying for two-thirds of the cost of the war and the American-inspired Navarre Plan in full swing[45] — it would have been difficult to dispute the accuracy of his remarks. Pierre-Henri Teitgen, Laniel's Deputy Prime Minister from June 1953 - June 1954, described American pressure as 'very constricting'[46] (*très gênante*) during the last year of the war, whilst Letourneau agreed that 'one must recognise that American pressure increased steadily in the later stages of the war'.[47] However, in defence of the Americans, Letourneau emphasised that they never tried to influence the details of French policy, only its broad outlines. The Americans apparently talked a great deal about 'the evolution of the agreements

106

made with the Associated States', but never explained precisely what they wanted. As an illustration of American strategic pressure, however, Letourneau mentioned the secret agreement signed in Paris on 17 December 1952, by which the British and French agreed to rid Malaya and Indochina respectively of Communist infiltration, whilst the Americans were to defend Korea at the 38th parallel and prevent any Communist advances into Formosa and the offshore islands. This agreement was signed by Acheson, Eden and Schuman after an Atlantic Council meeting, and it was essentially the result of American diplomatic pressure.[48]

In his Instructions to de Lattre in December 1950 Letourneau had emphasised that France must not be controlled by her allies: 'If it is true that our policy in Indochina is closely linked with that of the Anglo-Saxons in Asia, it is no less true that it must remain above all French. France must not yield to the views of Washington. Alliance does not signify subservience'.[49] And yet, after two years of supplicating for American aid, the French Government was no longer in a position to resist American pressure. This pressure did not reach its maximum until after Letourneau's departure from the Government (June 1953), but his American aid policy had prepared the way for the American-inspired Navarre Plan (which in turn led to Dien Bien Phu) and for the French Government's refusal — or inability — to reply to Ho Chi Minh's offer of negotiations in December 1953, five months before the climacteric of Dien Bien Phu.

The Devaluation of the Indochinese Piastre, and the Collapse of Letourneau's Policy

Before discussing the final phase of the first Indochina War, it is necessary to comment briefly on the French Government's unilateral decision to devalue the Indochinese piastre (May 1953). The decision to devalue was economically justifiable but politically inept, exposing, as it did, the artificiality of the independence of the Associated States. It destroyed Bao Dai's limited confidence in France and marked the end of the French Government's awkward political balancing act, i.e. its attempt to hand over an increasing number of powers to the Associated States whilst at the same time maintaining a considerable degree of French influence in Indochina. It destroyed the political career of Jean Letourneau, who had identified himself wholly with the delicate intricacies of the Bao Dai policy. It also provoked widespread criticism amongst the ruling élites in all three Associated States, but especially in Vietnam. It led directly to the French Governmental Declaration of 3 July, promising an extension of independence, and to the far-reaching concessions made to Laos, Cambodia and Vietnam between August and November 1953 - concessions which in effect amounted to the death of the French Union, at least as conceived in the Constitution of 1946. Finally, it led to important changes in the French administrative and command structure in Indochina. These developments accorded to a large extent with American wishes, as did the most important military decision of 1953, the adoption of the ambitious Navarre Plan in response to the Viet Minh invasion of Laos in April.[50] By this stage the Americans had come to the conclusion that the Bao Dai experiment had little chance of succeeding unless the Vietnamese nationalists were seen (a) to have a degree of independence incompatible with membership of the French Union; and (b) to have moved on to the offensive against the Communists.

At 8.00 p.m. on Saturday 8 May 1953 Jean Letourneau, who was still both Minister of the Associated States and High Commissioner in Indochina, received a cable in Saigon announcing the devaluation of the piastre as from Monday 10 May. He summoned Bao Dai's Prime Minister, Nguyen Van Tam, in the middle of the night to give him the news, apologising profusely for his government's failure to consult the Vietnamese Government.[51] Letourneau had been told nothing about the devaluation in advance by the French Prime Minister, Bourgès-Maunoury, or the Finance Minister, René Mayer, who later made the standard claim for such shock devaluations, namely that speed and secrecy were vital.[52] A year after the devaluation Letourneau told the Mondon Commission, which had been set up to inquire into the whole business of trafficking in piastres: 'When I received René Mayer's telegram announcing the devaluation of the piastre, I had two choices: either to pass myself off as an imbecile or as a false witness. I preferred the former.'[53]

The devaluation of the piastre put an end to a scandal, the origin of which was a decree of December 1945 fixing the value of the piastre at 17 francs.[54] The real value of a piastre was never more than about 7 francs. Thus in effect the French taxpayer was subsidising the Indochinese economy. This was reasonable in itself, as it was a form of aid, but the trouble was that speculators soon became wise to the profits which could be made out of trading piastres for francs.[55] Up to 1949 the chief beneficiaries were the Viet Minh and French administrators (and a few soldiers). Thereafter the chief beneficiaries were Vietnamese government officials, but France had agreed at the Conference of Pau in 1950 to interfere as little as possible in the affairs of the Associated States. Consequently she could put an end to the traffic only at the price of appearing as the manipulator of a puppet government: hence Letourneau's refusal to touch this political dynamite. It was a strange irony that the well-meaning and conscientious Letourneau could implement his policy of minimum interference in the internal affairs of the Associated States only by refusing to tackle the thoroughly dishonest piastres traffic.

The Mondon Commission (established 3 July 1953; final report published 17 June 1954) was given the task of (a) inquiring into the mechanisms of the piastres traffic, and (b) discovering who was responsible for it. The section on the mechanisms produced little that had not already been revealed by Jacques Despuech,[56] and the second section failed to attribute responsibility with any precision. After the collapse of Dien Bien Phu most French politicians simply wanted to wash their hands of *la sale guerre,* and the National Assembly never even debated the Mondon Report.

But in the context of French policy in Indochina, the Report contained some interesting comments. It condemned the French Government for taking so long to devalue the piastre, whilst conceding that it was difficult for it to do so after the (nominal) granting of independence to the Associated States in 1949-50. It concluded that there was no evidence that French Ministers had been involved in the traffic, but Letourneau was reprimanded for his failure to try to halt it during his 'forty-five months of responsibility for Indochina'.[57] The Report also suggested that Letourneau had been negligent in the performance of his duties, notably with regard to the fact that, although he admitted to the commission of inquiry that he knew that Bao Dai had himself transferred 176 million francs to Paris and that other transfers had leapt from Fr.40 milliard in 1951 to 230 milliard in 1952, he had done nothing to check the traffic.[58] Letourneau also agreed that in his dual capacity as Minister of the Associated States and High Commissioner he had 'all the necessary military and civil powers' to deal with the traffic. Yet, with all this authority, Letourneau did nothing to check the activities of the Exchange Office or of the speculators.[59] Why? The most charitable verdict is that Letourneau wanted to implement the Elysée and Pau Agreements with the maximum of good faith, i.e. to intervene in the internal affairs of the Associated States as little as possible.[60] Only by doing this could he help to build up the reputation of Bao Dai's nationalist government and attract support away from the Viet Minh. Letourneau's basic argument throughout the hearings of the Mondon Commission was that a mistake had been made when the piastre was overvalued in 1945, but that once this initial mistake had been made *and* independence had been granted to the Associated States, it was impossible to rectify the situation: 'we could not unilaterally devalue the piastre without destroying Vietnamese confidence in the word of France.' Indeed, 'the decision to devalue went completely against the tide of all our policy in Indochina, which was based on respect for the independence of the Associated States.'[61]

In defence of Letourneau it cannot be denied that the political situation in Indochina deteriorated rapidly after the devaluation, with all three Associated States demanding greater independence and virtually rejecting the French Union as then constituted. Under Indochinese and American pressure the French issued the Declaration of 3 July 1953, promising 'to perfect the independence and sovereignty of the Associated States, and to ensure, with the agreement of the three governments concerned, the transfer to the Associated States of those powers retained by France only because of the perilous circumstances arising from the war.'[62] The July Declaration was partially successful. It satisfied the Americans who had asked for more independence for the Associated States in their Memorandum of 26 April. It also led to better relations with Cambodia, as it was agreed that French troops should evacuate the right bank of the Mekong, handing over all responsibility for security to the Khmer Government, and with Laos, whom France promised to help in the event of external aggression, whilst otherwise leaving all internal administration to the royal Government. The conversations with Vietnam, however, soon ran into difficulties. Bao Dai told Paul Reynaud, the French Deputy Prime Minister, that he did not want total independence, as he feared he would fall under the influence of the extreme nationalists. And the French Government was itself rather divided, with Reynaud and Pleven adopting a relatively flexible attitude, and Bidault demanding that, in return for their new independence, the Associated States should declare their solemn allegiance to the French Union, with all the restrictions implied by the 1946 Constitution.[63] In October, however, a congress of Vietnamese nationalists called for 'the withdrawal of Vietnam from the French Union', and it was only under pressure from the Bao Dai Government that the words 'in its present form' were added to the above phrase.[64]

Another consequence of the collapse of Letourneau's policy was that the Ministry responsible for relations with the Associated States was abolished, as was the dual position held by Letourneau as Cabinet Minister and High Commissioner. As from July 1953 there was a Minister of State for Indochina (the first was the Gaullist Marc Jacquet), whilst in Indochina itself the new High Commissioner, renamed Commissioner General, was a civil servant, Maurice Dejean. The whole nature of the High Commission was changed, so that Dejean was little more than a special ambassador. Although the object of these changes was to remove the impression that France was interfering in the internal affairs of the Associated States, they were not entirely successful. On the one hand, they destroyed an essential link in the chain of command between Paris and the Commander-in-Chief of the Expeditionary Corps. (General Navarre later complained that neither Jacquet nor Dejean ever told him whether or not he was responsible for the defence of Laos.[65] On the other hand, the changes did little to satisfy the more extreme Vietnamese nationalists.

Letourneau's failure to tackle the piastres' traffic, followed by the French Government's unilateral devaluation of the piastre, therefore, had profound repercussions on France's relations with the Associated States. Letourneau could hardly have been unaware of the fact that one of the chief beneficiaries of the traffic was the Viet Minh.[66] And yet he failed to check the traffic, ostensibly on the grounds that any attempt to do so would have been regarded as unwarranted interference by the French Government in the affairs of the Associated States. However, it is difficult to understand why Letourneau could not have devalued the piastre after consultation with the Governments of the Associated States; France could still have given economic aid to the Associated States, but without subsidising the Viet Minh, and conditions could have been laid down to ensure that a proportion of the aid was earmarked for social and agrarian reforms. Alternatively he could have controlled the Exchange Office properly (he certainly had the power to do so). Instead, there was so little control over the transfer of piastres that Léon Pignon could say that 'under the regulations then in force there was in effect no penalty for transferring piastres'.[67] Letourneau neither stopped nor controlled the traffic in piastres. He preferred instead to support Bao Dai's régime, even although this entailed turning a blind eye to the piastres scandal. In the meantime he hoped that the Vietnamese National Army, aided by the Americans, would somehow transform the situation. Letourneau staked his career and reputation on supporting Bao Dai. The gamble did not come off, and from mid-1953 until the end of the first Indochina War France carried on what was in effect little more than a holding operation in Vietnam. Bao Dai's non-Communist Government could no more survive without outside help than could Ho Chi Minh's Communist 'Government', but France had almost lost the will to support a government which seemed all too ready to slap her in the face at the slightest 'provocation'. Meanwhile, the Americans were still not prepared to cross their Rubicon, i.e. to commit themselves unreservedly (including, if need be, militarily) to the Vietnamese National Government.

NOTES

1. *United States - Vietnam Relations, 1945-67* (Washington: U.S. Government Printing Office, 1971) (Henceforth, cited as *U.S. - Vietnam Rels.*)
2. For OSS involvement, see Dennis Duncanson, *Conflict Studies,* October 1973, p.3.
3. For the view that the OSS was not acting with official backing, see

Edward R. Drachman, *United States Policy Toward Vietnam,* 1940-45 (Cranbury, N.J., 1970), and Geoffrey Warner, 'The United States and Vietnam', *International Affairs,* July 1972, pp.381-2.

4.   *U.S.-Vietnam Rels.,* vol.8, p.85.

5.   Geoffrey Warner, 'The United States and Vietnam', *International Affairs,* July 1972, p.382. (For much of the information in this paragraph, and the two which follow, I am indebted to Warner's excellent article).

6.   *U.S.-Vietnam Rels.,* vol.8, p.145.

7.   ibid., pp.148-9.

8   ibid., p.153.

9.   ibid., pp.190-91.

10.   ibid., pp.190-91.

11.   ibid., p.267.

12.   ibid,, vol.I, p.22.

13.   *International Affairs,* July 1972, p.384.

14.   *Journal Officiel* (Assemblée Nationale), 22 October 1950.

15.   *Le Monde,* 13 April 1950.

16.   *Le Monde,* 8 May 1950.

17.   *Année Politique,* 1950, p.59.

18.   *Le Monde,* 17 April 1950.

19.   ibid.

20.   *Le Monde,* 28 June 1950.

21.   Interview with Tran Van Huu, 3 December 1966.

22.   *Le Monde,* 24 December 1950.

23.   *Le Monde,* 25 January 1951.

24.   *Le Monde,* 1 February 1951.

25.   *New York Times,* 21 September 1951.

26.   *New York Times,* 24 September 1951.

27.   *Année Politique,* 1952, p.177.

28.   Grosser, p.282.

29.   *Le Monde,* 11 June 1952.

30.   *Le Monde,* 20 June 1952.

31.   ibid., 24 June 1952.

32.   ibid., 2 October 1952.

33.   ibid., 15 October 1952.

34.   ibid., 26 October 1952.

35.   *Journal Officiel* (Assemblée Nationale), 19 December 1952.

36.   *Le Monde,* 31 March 1953.

37.   26 April 1953 U.S. Memorandum on Indochina, published in full in *Le Monde,* 26 July 1953.

38.   e.g. on 8 February 1951.

39.   *Le Monde,* 2 February 1952.

40.   ibid., 9 February 1952.

41.   *Le Monde,* 18 March 1953.

42.   *New York Herald Tribune,* 23 December 1952.

43.   *L'Aurore,* 16 March 1953.

44.   *Le Monde,* 31 January 1953.

45.   For the Navarre Plan, see below, pp.

46.   Interview with Teitgen, 24 April 1967.

47.   Interview with Letourneau, 6 February 1967.

48.   ibid.

49.   Letourneau Papers.

50.   For Navarre Plan, see below p.114.

51.   Interview with Nguyen Van Tam, 23 December 1966.

52. Interview with Letourneau, 6 February 1967.
53. *Rapport de la Commission Mondon,* p.2247 (Henceforth referred to as Mondon).
54. J. Despuech, *Le Trafic de Piastres* (Paris, 1953), p.47.
55. The mechanism was as follows: American dollars were bought in Paris and taken to Indochina where they were sold for piastres, which were then exchanged for francs at the bargain rate. American dollars were always in demand, because the Viet Minh needed them to buy arms on the Hong Kong black market. This method of trafficking gave a profit of 100-120 per cent. It was also possible to make handsome profits simply by sending piastres direct to France. Such transfers were particularly popular with Bao Dai and his entourage. It was necessary to obtain permission from the Exchange Office in Saigon, but this was easily obtainable, especially for the influential. There were also other less lucrative methods of trafficking. For details see Despuech, pp.66-82.
56. In *Le Trafic de Piastres* (Paris, 1953).
57. Mondon, p.1169.
58. ibid., p.2244.
59. ibid., p.2240.
60. Not surprisingly this was Letourneau's contention; interview, 6 February 1967.
61. Mondon, p.60.
62. Mercier, p.298.
63. Lacouture and Devillers, p.39.
64. Mercier, p.405.
65. H. Navarre, *Agonie de l'Indochine,* p.68.
66. In his evidence to the Mondon Commission Letourneau denied that the Viet Minh benefited from the traffic; he maintained that they financed themselves by forced loans and the sale of opium (pp.43-4). But both in his book and in his evidence before the Commission, Despuech provided clear evidence that the Viet Minh took full advantage of the over-valuation of the piastre. The method employed was as follows: within Viet Minh controlled territory the 'Ho Chi Minh piastre' (issued from Dec. 1946 onwards) was used for all normal exchange. Meanwhile, all genuine piastres, i.e. those issued by the Indochinese Bank, were confiscated by the Viet Minh both in their own territory and outside on threat of reprisals. They were then transferred into francs on the Saigon black market, and the francs were exchanged for dollars or gold to buy arms in Hong Kong or Manila. Even after 1950 the Viet Minh still needed gold or dollars to buy arms from the Chinese, who insisted on payment for their 'aid'. It was thus that the Viet Minh benefited from the 'generosity' of the French taxpayer.
67. Interview with Pignon, 24 April 1967.

8. THE LAST PHASE: THE NAVARRE PLAN, DIEN BIEN PHU AND THE GENEVA AGREEMENT

During the last year of the first Indochina War the French Government acted without much conviction. France wanted peace, but, understandably, not at any price. She could hardly abandon Bao Dai in favour of the Communist Ho Chi Minh. Yet by 1953 it was all too apparent that Bao Dai was having only limited success in rallying the Vietnamese nationalists. At the same time it was clear that the Viet Minh were growing in strength, with their troops being trained by the Chinese and armed by the Russians. When the Viet Minh attacked the Tai country in the autumn of 1952 and moved into Laos in the spring of 1953, they showed that they could move at will (at least by night) throughout most of Vietnam and Laos. This was a depressing situation for the French Government, which had tacitly given up all hope of building a close-knit French Union, but failed in the process to boost the popularity of Bao Dai's nationalist government. Indeed the unilateral devaluation of the piastre looked like an act of political despair, and the National Assembly debates of June and October 1953 showed that the parties were seriously divided over Indochina. There was neither a majority for pulling out, nor one favouring an all-out fight against the Viet Minh.

Georges Bidault, the Foreign Minister in Laniel's Government (June 1953 - June 1954) and the man chiefly responsible for Indochina policy in this period, was personally in favour of forcing the Communists to negotiate from a position of weakness. But he was under no illusions about the possibility of an outright victory. However, he agreed with the Americans that the Communists must be shown that they could never win. Hence, he supported the Navarre Plan, which aimed at consolidation south of the eighteenth parallel by 1953-4, followed by offensive action in the north in the 1954-5 campaign season. In the course of the northern offensive it was hoped that the Viet Minh would be drawn into a series of large-scale battles against powerfully armed mobile groups, whose victories would lead to 'oil stain pacification' of ever larger areas of territory.[1] But, although Bidault personally favoured a decisive anti-Communist policy, he was severely constrained in his attempts to implement one. Not only were there over a hundred Communists in the National Assembly (one-sixth of its membership) calling for direct negotiation with Ho Chi Minh, but there were also influential Radicals and Socialists, led by Pierre Mendès-

France and Alain Savary, who were demanding negotiations with Ho Chi Minh as the sole way out of the impasse. The Christian Democrats too were becoming increasingly restive over Indochina policy. Although five-sixths of their eighty-five deputies supported Bidault to the end, there was a significant minority who voted against him or abstained in the debates of late 1953 - early 1954. On the other hand, Bidault was in a reasonably strong position in the French Cabinet. The Prime Minister, Joseph Laniel, a wealthy Norman who had played a prominent part in the Resistance, was not particularly interested in Indochina, but he supported Bidault throughout his premiership. Bidault could also rely on the whole-hearted support of Pierre de Chevigné, the MRP Minister of War, and René Pleven, the UDSR Minister of National Defence.[2] Bidault's position in the Cabinet was further strengthened when François Mitterrand of the UDSR resigned as Minister of Overseas France in protest at the Government's illiberal policy in Morocco.[3] Mitterrand was known to hold views similar to those of Mendès-France, i.e. he was prepared to consider the possibility of negotiating with Ho Chi Minh. On the debit side from Bidault's point of view was the fact that Paul Reynaud, a Deputy Prime Minister in Laniel's Government, had come to the conclusion that France ought to loosen her ties with the other countries of the French Union and pull out of Indochina as soon as this could be done with some degree of honour. Thus, Georges Bidault found himself in a rather difficult position. He realised that French public opinion was rapidly losing interest in Indochina (Communist propaganda against *la sale guerre* was at last beginning to bite), but he was determined that France should not renegue on her commitments to the Governments of the Associated States. This entailed following an 'American-style' programme of aggressive resistance to the Communists, whilst at the same time trying to avoid the appearance of being an American puppet. Moreover, unlike politicians in Britain or the United States, Bidault had to keep a constant eye on the fluctuating parliamentary majority in the National Assembly.

The thirty-six day political crisis between the fall of René Mayer (21 May 1953) and the investiture of Joseph Laniel as Prime Minister (27 June) showed the indecision reigning in the National Assembly. Paul Reynaud proposed negotiations with China, 'without whose aid the Viet Minh could not wage war in Indochina'.[4] Pierre Mendès-France, who had been urging direct negotiations with the Viet Minh since 1950, made a rather *nuancé* speech in which he suggested that such negotiations would be necessary in due course; but prior to their taking place he wanted to discuss the whole Indochina problem with the United States and Britain.[5] Georges Bidault made it clear that he was not *a priori* against a negotiated solution. He said his aim was to

115

hasten 'the conclusion of the war by every means'. This, of course, could equally well have been taken to mean negotiations with the enemy or the use of American air power. Bidault clarified his position by going on to say:

> The only end [to the war], which we could not possibly accept, would be a straightforward withdrawal, which would be incompatible with the respect we owe to those who have died in the fighting; incompatible with the promises of support we have given to our friends; incompatible with the nature of the work we have accomplished in the past in Indochina, and which we are still accomplishing in all countries where there is a French presence.[6]

The Assembly obviously took it that Bidault intended to pursue the war to victory. He was thus supported by Gaullists like Raymond Dronne and Conservatives like General Aumeran, whilst being condemned by the Communists and some Radicals and Socialists. Bidault failed to get invested as Prime Minister by only one vote. *Le Monde* suggested that the crucial factor was the refusal of several UDSR deputies to vote for him, because Max André had described François Mitterrand as 'a defeatist, who wanted to see France 'leaving Indochina, i.e. abandoning those who have placed their confidence in France'.[7] Thus, by a strange irony, one of Bidault's closest supporters, Max André, may have been responsible for his failure to become Prime Minister in 1953.

In the end Joseph Laniel, a little known Conservative who was a compromise candidate, was elected Prime Minister in order to end the ministerial crisis. Laniel stated in his investiture speech that France would not abandon her friends in Indochina, but at the same time she would explore all avenues for achieving a just peace.[8] In the October debate on Indochina, however, he made it clear that France would negotiate with the Viet Minh only from a position of strength. He contended that the Vietnamese National Army was growing stronger daily, as American arms and equipment arrived in increasing quantities, whilst at the same time Viet Minh strength had passed its peak. Laniel went on to say that the Viet Minh were beginning to look less and less like a national liberation movement and more like a satellite of Moscow, a development which was helping to consolidate Bao Dai's position as a national leader. It was not the aim of the French Government or of the Associated States' Governments to pursue a war of extermination against the declining Viet Minh; if and when Ho Chi Minh and his friends realised the hopelessness of their position and wanted negotiations, France and the Associated States would also be ready to negotiate.[9]

However, the hollowness of Laniel's public statements was exposed shortly afterwards when the French Government did not reply to Ho Chi Minh's offer of negotiations made through the Swedish weekly, *Expressen.* A Swedish journalist, Svante Löfgren, had been present at the Indochina debate at the end of October, and, having listened to Laniel's hints about the possibility of negotiations, sent a series of questions to Ho Chi Minh by way of the Swedish ambassador in Pekin.[10] In his reply, Ho Chi Minh predictably blamed the whole war on the French, but added, 'If the French Government, having drawn the lessons of these years of war, wishes to conclude an armistice and resolve the question of Vietnam by negotiations, the Government of the Democratic Republic of Vietnam is ready to examine France's propositions.'[11] Ho Chi Minh went on to say that he would welcome the mediation of a neutral country, but the substantive negotiations must be between France and the Democratic Republic of Vietnam. Bidault immediately condemned the *Expressen* offer as 'a propaganda manoeuvre'.[12] Chevigné, the Minister responsible for the Army, described it in similar terms.[13] The Conservative Motais de Narbonne advised the Government to ignore Ho Chi Minh's offer on the ground that France had supported Bao Dai for four years and could not now abandon him.[14] A Christian Democrat, André-François Mercier, wrote that the *Expressen* offer was merely a propaganda ruse inspired by Moscow and Pekin.[15]

But if the conservative wing of the National Assembly (and of the Senate) was undivided in its views about the *Expressen* offer, the Government was not. Reynaud believed that the Government should at least test the genuineness of Ho Chi Minh's offer of negotiations by making preliminary approaches to China and the Viet Minh. Pleven and Laniel wanted to send Alain Savary to make an initial contact with the Viet Minh, but Bidault was opposed to this. He told Savary: 'Ho Chi Minh is on the point of capitulating: we are going to beat him. Do not strengthen his position by a contact of this sort', to which Savary replied, 'You are taking a terrible responsibility upon yourself by making this decision'.[16] On 14 December Ho Chi Minh again offered an armistice and negotiations (over the radio), but, as before, the French Government made no reply. General Navarre had already dropped his paratroopers into the valley of Dien Bien Phu, where he hoped he could draw the Viet Minh into battle and inflict a serious defeat on them.

Chevigné later maintained that he and Bidault were against replying to the *Expressen* offer for both political and military reasons. If France had negotiated directly with the Viet Minh, even with the approval of Bao Dai, the only result would have been the partition of Vietnam; at this stage Bidault was firmly opposed to partition because this would have been a major concession to the Communists. Secondly, the military situation appeared to be improving; Operation Mouette, a clearing operation in the Delta, had gone well, and the soldiers were promising greater successes in 1954. Chevigné, who had been seconded to the U.S. Marines during the Second World War, later stated that he was very apprehensive when he visited Dien Bien Phu in February 1954 (the valley was overlooked by hills in all directions), and he agreed that the politicians made a serious mistake in putting too much reliance on Navarre's optimism in late 1953. Chevigné maintained that the main reason for France's rejection of the *Expresson* offer was the (supposed) improvement in the military situation at this time. He denied that American pressure had anything to do with it.[17] However, although there is no evidence that the Americans attempted to tell the French Government what to do, they had already made it clear that they wanted the Navarre Plan implemented and were opposed to direct negotiations with the Viet Minh. It was doubtless no accident that Bidault told Dulles at the Bermuda Conference in December 1953: 'We do not want to miss any chance to end the war, but at the same time we do not intend to end it at any cost . . . In particular, we have no intention of negotiating directly with Ho Chi Minh.'[18]

The Conferences of Berlin and Geneva

In December 1953 the Heads of Government of the United States, France and Britain, accompanied by their Foreign Ministers, met in Bermuda to discuss Russia's proposal for a summit meeting and to work out a common policy. The Western Powers accepted Molotov's invitation, and it was agreed that there would be a four-power conference at Berlin, starting in January 1954, to discuss problems of world peace with special reference to the problems of Germany and Austria. Far Eastern problems were not on the agenda, although preliminary talks on Korea and Indochina were not excluded. The final communiqué from Bermuda was vague on Indochina. It paid homage to the military efforts of France and the Associated States, but said nothing specific about how to conclude the war: 'We will continue to act together in order to restore peace and stability in this region'.[19] At Berlin no decision was reached about the German or Austrian questions, but at the meetings on the Far East, which came after the main conference, it was decided that a further conference should be held to discuss Korea and Indochina. The final communiqué from Berlin (18 February) announced that a conference on Korea would open at Geneva on 26 April, and 'the Ministers have also agreed that the problem of restoring peace in Indochina will be discussed at the conference'.[20] France, Great Britain, the United States, the Soviet Union, China and 'other interested States' were to be invited to send representatives.

Bidault's conduct at the Conferences of Berlin and Geneva was to be criticised by his political opponents but was consistent with his previous pronouncements on Indochina. Bidault was not opposed to a negotiated solution, but he wanted to negotiate only from a position of strength, i.e. after an improvement in the military situation, and in any case not directly with the Viet Minh; he was opposed, in principle, to any solution involving the partition of Vietnam on the grounds that sooner or later the whole country would be liable to go Communist. He was supported in these views by the Americans, who, however, were more interested in a military victory than a conference table one. With Mendès-France, the Communists, many Socialists, a few Christian Democrats and a large number of French newspapers demanding a negotiated solution, Bidault had to be careful not to appear to be too intransigent at Berlin. When the Soviet Union proposed a five-power conference on Asian problems, Bidault and Dulles opposed the suggestion, arguing that China should not be invited to a conference on Indochina until she stopped sending arms to the Viet Minh. However, the French Government, no doubt worried at the likely reaction of public opinion if no conference on Indochina ensued, told Bidault to do all he could to get a Far Eastern conference convened. Reynaud was apparently the man chiefly responsible for this decision, although Pleven was also coming round to the view that a negotiated solution was the only way out of the impasse.[21] Bidault, therefore, organised preparatory meetings of the Western Powers in early February to try to work out an agreed position on Far Eastern problems. Dulles was at first adamantly against the idea of 'recognising' China through inviting her to the conference, but on 8 February agreed to the principle of China being allowed to discuss Asian problems, provided this did not imply American diplomatic recognition of China. Dulles and Bidault proposed again that China should show signs of her desire for peace by stopping (or decreasing) her aid to the Viet Minh. Molotov argued that China had nothing to do with events in Indochina, which began long before 1949. Nor could she be expected to attend a conference on the assumption that she was already guilty. The Soviet Union, however, remained in favour of a Conference of Five limited to Korea and Indochina. Eden got round the problem by proposing that all who were 'interested' (i.e. there was to be no order of precedence) should be invited to the conference at Geneva, with Korea as the main subject on the agenda and Indochina as the second one.

At the same time as the Four Powers were conferring at Berlin René Pleven, the French Minister of National Defence, was making a tour of inspection in Indochina. Returning to France a week after the decision to hold the Geneva Conference (26 February) Pleven gave a gloomy report of the military situation. Chinese aid was increasing; the French

119

Union forces were holding their own, but only with heavy losses; the Vietnamese National Army was becoming an effective fighting unit very slowly. The best that France could do was to try to maintain the present military situation and negotiate peace at Geneva.[22] All depended on Dien Bien Phu, the entrenched camp in North-West Vietnam, which Navarre had occupied with 10,000 men in November and December 1953, partly to protect Laos, partly to tempt the Viet Minh to fight an open battle, in which he was sure that the French would triumph on account of their superior equipment. A similar entrenched camp at Na San in 1952-3 had been relatively successful, all Viet Minh attacks having being repulsed, although in some cases only with difficulty. But, whereas Na San was seventy miles from the Hanoi airfields, Dien Bien Phu was over two hundred, and all depended on the aerial bridge, assuming, of course, that the ground troops held their positions as at Na San.

Bidault had told Alain Savary that he would not hear of direct negotiations with the Viet Minh, as France's military position was getting better and Ho Chi Minh was on the verge of collapse.[23] After the Conference of Berlin he told J.-R. Tournoux that he was hopeful about Geneva. He based his hopes on the fact that since Stalin's death (March 1953) the Russians had shown greater interest in negotiated solutions; moreover, he would be negotiating from a position of strength, at the heart of which would be Dien Bien Phu.[24] The French Government's determination not to show any weakness at this stage was emphasised by their rejection of Nehru's proposal that there should be a ceasefire before the Conference of Geneva began. But on 13 March France's position of strength was suddenly and severely eroded, when on the first night of the Viet Minh attack on Dien Bien Phu two of the three strongpoints protecting the landing-strip were captured. General Ely, the French Chief of Staff, went to Washington to ask the Americans for increased aid and to tell them about the critical situation at Dien Bien Phu. The American Government agreed to back France as much as possible, and Admiral Radford offered to bomb the area around Dien Bien Phu by Operation Vautour. A special French war Cabinet comprising the Prime Minister, Foreign Minister, Defence Minister and military Ministers of State, after consulting Navarre, asked the American Government to carry out Operation Vautour, but on 5 April Dulles changed his mind, suggesting that an alliance of the United States, Britain, France, New Zealand and Australia should jointly offer to guarantee Vietnam against Communist aggression. Both Bidault and Eden opposed this, believing that such a threat to China might prejudice the Geneva conference. Thus Dulles, worried about the reactions of Congress to direct American intervention in Vietnam, turned down Bidault's request to implement Operation Vautour, whilst Bidault, anxious about the threat to Geneva implied by allied guarantees to Vietnam, opposed Dulles's suggested South-East Asia alliance. Bidault remained determined to negotiate from a position of strength, but he knew that the Laniel Government could not survive the postponement or cancellation of the Geneva Conference. Nevertheless, in a final bid to save Dien Bien Phu, Laniel and Bidault tried again on 23 and 24 April to persuade the Americans to carry out Operation Vautour, i.e. to reverse the decision of 5 April. The American Government was willing to comply with the French request (although by late April it was doubtful whether even massive bomber raids could have saved the garrison at Dien Bien Phu), provided the British gave token support. Churchill and Eden, however, thought that any attempt to save Dien Bien Phu would both fail in its objectives and remove any chance of a negotiated solution.[25] In these circumstances the Americans refused to intervene, and Dien Bien Phu fell on 7 May, a week after the opening of the Geneva Conference.

Bidault was, therefore, not in a strong position at Geneva. He told Eden that he had very poor cards, only 'the two of clubs and the three of diamonds'.[26] At home he was subjected to constant criticism. *Témoignage Chrétien* wondered whether Bidault was the right man to lead the French delegation. His two main aims appeared to be not to cause any split in the Western Alliance and not consider a compromise solution. He had also refused Nehru's cease-fire offer. Could a man with such a negative attitude be expected to negotiate peace at Geneva?[27] On 9 March Mendès-France contended that 'certain members' of Laniel's Government did not really want peace. Mendès-France, who was soon to make a cutting personal attack on Bidault for his conduct of the Geneva negotiations, was clearly thinking of Bidault when he told the deputies that 'France is carrying out a subtle diplomacy in order to disguise a policy whose objective is to continue the war. For that is exactly what some people want: to continue the war after having given the impression that they have tried to find a peaceful solution to it'.[28] In fact, Bidault was in an extremely difficult position after the fall of Dien Bien Phu; he genuinely wanted a peaceful solution, but not one forced upon him in the wake of the worst defeat in France's colonial history. However, he had one considerable advantage in that he was a skilful and experienced diplomatist, who had spent almost six years in charge of the Quai d'Orsay since the Second World War. Besides his own mental agility, Bidault had, or hoped to have, other cards at his disposal. The chief of these was the threat of American intervention if the Conference failed. Allied to this was the Soviet Union's fear that if the United States became openly involved in South-East Asia, China might invoke the Sino-Soviet pact, and the Soviet Union had no wish to get involved in a world war over Indochina, especially at a time when she had only atomic weapons to pit against America's hydrogen bombs.[29]

Bidault's aim at Geneva was to negotiate a ceasefire, but an immediate political solution was not expected. Bidault did not at first favour partition, partly because of promises given to Bao Dai by the French Government, partly because he feared this would lead sooner or later to a Communist Vietnam; instead, his objective was 'leopard-skin' regroupment with each side controlling specific geographical areas; his other chief aim was to ensure that the Viet Minh evacuated Laos and Cambodia. In Jean Lacouture's opinion[30] there is no reason to doubt that Bidault genuinely wanted to get a ceasefire at Geneva despite the views expressed, for example, by Mendès-France in the National Assembly, or by *Esprit,* which maintained that Bidault was negotiating only to improve his position to continue the war: 'total victory against the Viet Minh, the aim of the Navarre Plan, remains the prime objective both in Paris and in Washington.'[31] But Bidault's aims and methods contrasted noticeably with those of his successor Mendès-France. Whilst Bidault was opposed to partition, Mendès-France strove to achieve it. Whilst Bidault avoided direct negotiations with the enemy,[32] Mendès-France went out of his way to contact Pham Van Dong and Chou En-lai. Whilst Bidault tried to use the threat of American intervention, Mendès-France said he would send national servicemen to Indochina if peace was not made.

For almost a month — in Eden's opinion for longer[33]— very little progress was made at Geneva. Within the first week Dulles left, certain that no solution could be expected, although he left behind a representative, Bedell Smith. Up to 24 May the French, Chinese and Viet Minh limited themselves to diatribes against each other. There were signs that Eden in particular was anxious to find a solution, but it was not at all obvious how he was going to achieve one. In the early stages of the Conference Bidault indicated that he wanted a ceasefire and a regroupment of forces; he did not envisage partition as a military or political solution. Thus, on 6 May he assured Bao Dai that the French Government would not consider any solution unacceptable to the Vietnamese Government, and on 3 May Maurice Dejean, the High Commissioner in Indochina, made a press declaration to the same effect: 'The French Government has no intention of accepting a solution based on the partition of Vietnam . . . this would be contrary to our promises to the Vietnamese Government'.[34] Bidault believed that a ceasefire without partition was possible if the Americans backed him with the threat of intervention. He wanted to apply constant pressure on the Communists, so that a ceasefire with definite guarantees would result. He disagreed with Reynaud's proposal that a ceasefire should be arranged as quickly as possible. Maurice Schumann supported

Bidault, and it was decided that a controlled and guaranteed armistice should be the French Government's objective. Bidault explained his aims in more detail in his first major speech at the Conference (8 May). After paying homage to the men of Dien Bien Phu, describing France's work of civilisation in Indochina, and blaming the Viet Minh for starting the war, he explained France's proposals for ending the hostilities: 'We propose in the first place that the Conference agrees to the principle of a general ceasefire in Indochina, based on guarantees for the troops and civilians on both sides.' In Laos and Cambodia, he claimed, it was a simple matter of invasion by the Viet Minh terrorists: 'The solution, therefore, is for the invaders to withdraw and restore the territorial integrity of Laos and Cambodia.' In Vietnam, on the other hand, there was a civil war. France wanted to see a 'Vietnamese State, whose unity, territorial integrity and independence are guaranteed', but first it was essential to end the fighting; hence he foresaw 'a transitional armistice phase, in the course of which the political problems can be solved one by one'. In the execution of this ceasefire plan two steps were necessary: 'Firstly, whilst the irregular forces are being disarmed, the regular forces of the two sides should be concentrated into clearly defined regroupment areas. Secondly, the implementation of the ceasefire agreement should be placed under the control of an international commission.'[35] Bidault's proposals were, therefore, essentially military. He intended leaving the political solution to the Government of Vietnam, by which of course he meant Bao Dai's Government and not that of the Viet Minh, whose presence at the conference he recognised only because of the need to get a military solution first.

On 10 May the Viet Minh leader, Pham Van Dong, read out a thirty-seven page 'history' of France's occupation of Indochina. Without making any reference to Bidault's proposals, he put forward an eight-point plan of his own. France should recognise the independence of Vietnam, Cambodia and Laos; all French troops should depart from Vietnam with appropriate guarantees; free elections, organised by 'all the democratic organisations' within the three countries, should follow; the three countries should examine the conditions for entering the French Union; agreements should be worked out about France's economic and cultural facilities within the three states; there should be no persecution of those who had supported the other side in the war; prisoners of war should be exchanged; fighting should cease on the basis of a general and simultaneous ceasefire, controlled by mixed commissions, consisting of representatives of all the belligerent parties in the three states.[36]

Bidault himself made no immediate comment on Pham Van Dong's proposals, but his press secretary, Jacques Baeyens, condemned them out of hand.[37] The Viet Minh proposals were certainly very different from the French, demanding that a political solution precede a military solution and, in practice, the capitulation of France, but Bidault and his colleagues probably made an error in condemning the proposals without taking the trouble to consider at least some of them as a basis for discussion. Bidault's inflexibility certainly did not help the Government, who on 12 May managed to carry a vote of confidence by only two votes.

On 12 May Chou En-lai supported the Viet Minh proposals and condemned Bidault's which, he said, betrayed 'a colonialist mentality'. So far there seemed to be no common ground between the two sides, a factor which was further emphasised by Bidault's refusal to speak to the Viet Minh representatives. Bidault later explained his attitude to Lacouture and Devillers: 'It would have been a waste of time . . . what would have been the point of seeing Pham Van Dong. I knew that he had only one aim: to kick us out of the door.'[38] Bidault's inflexibility at this time is explicable partly in terms of his consistently held view that the Viet Minh were Communist rebels and that Ho Chi Minh's 'Government' was not really a government at all, and partly because of the Franco-American diplomatic discussions then going on. Bidault still hoped that the Americans would openly declare their support for France, threatening intervention if the French proposals were not accepted. He knew that since Dien Bien Phu his only strong card was the threat of American intervention. Without this he could not hope to see his proposals of 8 May being accepted, even in a modified form. On 12 May Maurice Schumann was instructed to ask the Department of State what its attitude would be if the Geneva Conference failed. This was not a demand for intervention. The French Government simply wanted the United States to *threaten* intervention in order to strengthen Bidault's negotiating position. The Americans were, however, very divided. Admiral Radford, Vice-President Nixon and the 'China lobby' were against making any concessions to the Communists; others like Charles Wilson, the Defence Secretary, and certain military chiefs, notably Ridgway and Twining, were in favour of letting France negotiate a peace if at all reasonable terms were available. Between the two sides was Dulles, anxious to help the French, but aware that American public opinion was not yet prepared to accept direct intervention in Vietnam. He aimed to win over Congress by proposing a collective security system for South-East Asia, which would entail, if necessary, American intervention with allied support. On 15 May the United States' Government replied to Schumann that seven conditions must be fulfilled before the Americans would intervene after the failure of the conference. France and the Associated States must ask for American assistance; this request must be supported by

Thailand, the Philippines, Australia, New Zealand and Britain; the United Nations must approve the intervention; the French Government must declare again the total independence of the Associated States, giving them the right to secede from the French Union if they wished; American intervention would be naval and aerial, with French troops continuing to fight on the ground; arrangements would be made between the United States and France about a command structure; the French National Assembly must approve the Government's request for intervention. These proposals did not close the door to American intervention, but they showed the indecisive attitude of the United States; the Americans did not want a Communist Vietnam, but they had no wish to intervene militarily if this could be avoided. But, as Lacouture and Devillers have pointed out, it was largely owing to Bidault that America's indecision was publicly proclaimed.[39] Thus unwittingly Bidault strengthened the negotiating position of the Viet Minh.

Meanwhile, Britain was opposed to all threats of intervention until Geneva had failed, and Eden was annoyed with the French and Americans for engaging in what he saw as underhand talks.[40] It seems quite probable that the Conference of Geneva would have broken down eventually if it had not been for Britain and Russia. Eden believed that a compromise peace was possible; rightly or wrongly, he steadily pushed the idea of partition, and he was eventually supported by Molotov, who in turn seems to have persuaded Pham Van Dong to accept the idea of partition, at least as a preliminary step towards a solution. In his speech on 12 May Eden suggested that there was no point in the two sides engaging in diatribes against each other or in arguing about who was responsible for the war. He went on to say that the French and Viet Minh proposals seemed to have some points in common — both, for example, talked of a ceasefire and of regroupment in specific areas. He proposed that the questions of Laos and Cambodia be separated from that of Vietnam, and that there should be some form of international control of the ceasefire. Two days later Molotov supported the idea of an international Control Commission, agreeing that a military, rather than a political, solution should be the first priority. Bidault also made his first concession by announcing that France was willing to withdraw her troops from Cambodia and Laos if the Viet Minh would agree to do the same. On 20 May Eden and Molotov dined privately to discuss the situation, and Eden emphasised that time was working against the Communists, especially in view of the Franco-American talks going on. This meeting may have been partially responsible for Molotov's five point plan of 21 May: ceasefire; regroupment by zones; measures to prevent any reinforcement of the belligerents after the ceasefire; international control of the ceasefire;

international guarantee of the agreements. These proposals were followed by two important Viet Minh statements. On 24 May Hoang Van Hoan, the Viet Minh Foreign Minister, told *Le Monde*: 'Our first requirement is a ceasefire. We are not going to lay down any political conditions at this stage.'[41] Thus the Viet Minh conceded, as Molotov had done ten days before, that a military solution could precede a political one. And on 25 May Pham Van Dong suggested that the Viet Minh would be prepared to consider partition; he used phrases like 'demarcation lines' and 'areas reserved to one side', which seemed to be very different from the 'leopard-skin' type of partition envisaged by Bidault. Nevertheless, the French negotiators were probably secretly delighted with this proposal, which they themselves could never have made owing to their promises to Bao Dai.

Thus, by 25 May it was clear that Britain and the Soviet Union were determined to find a compromise solution. Molotov had persuaded the Viet Minh to aim at a ceasefire with partition as an essential aspect of any final solution, whilst Eden had been given a verbal promise by Bidault that there would be no further requests for American intervention unless the Conference failed. Although there were further rumours of American intervention on 29 May, these were finally scotched on 8 June when Dulles declared that 'the United States do not envisage unilateral action in Indochina unless China intervenes openly.'[42] The United States thus came out against the French Government's request for an open American declaration of intention to intervene if the Conference failed. Bidault was therefore condemned to negotiate *nolens volens*. But his continued determination to be relatively inflexible with the Communists was shown by his decision to appoint the outspokenly anti-Communist Frédéric-Dupont as Minister of State with special responsibility for Indochina (20 May).

The Conference went into temporary suspension from 29 May to 8 June, whilst the Foreign Ministers reported to their Governments. On 8 June Molotov made a violent attack on Bidault, probably not because he feared Bidault would persuade the Americans to intervene in Indochina — it was already clear that they had no wish to do so — but because the Soviet Union wanted to remove a partisan (albeit a reluctant one) of the European Defence Community (EDC) from the Quai d'Orsay. Perhaps Molotov also wanted merely to make a mockery of a man who now had few assets and could no longer threaten strong action. The *Journal de Genève* may have been close to the mark, when it commented that 'Molotov wishes to show the French Parliament that Bidault is not the man with whom Moscow and her partners want to negotiate.'[43] A few days previously François Mitterrand had justifiably written that the fate of the French Government appeared to be dependent on the smiles of Molotov.[44] On 9 June Bidault had to defend himself in the National Assembly. He maintained that he was the victim of Russian propaganda, and that he had been single-minded in his determination to achieve an honourable peace at Geneva:

> Some people have said that a double game has been going on at Geneva, and that the negotiations have been undertaken only on the assumption that they will fail ... If anyone can produce a single piece of evidence to show that I have been against peace or in favour of war, let him stand up and speak ... It has been said that the Government will fall if I do not achieve peace. If you know of another negotiator, who has a better chance of succeeding, I am quite ready to hand over my responsibilities to him.[45]

Mendès-France was unable to produce definite evidence that Bidault had been 'against peace or in favour of war', but he made a strong attack on him on the grounds that he had failed to negotiate directly with France's chief opponents, the Viet Minh and Chinese, and that he had been playing 'some devilish game of poker' by trying to get the Americans to intervene.[46]

Meanwhile at Geneva Frédéric-Dupont had organised the first of a series of unofficial contacts between the French and the Viet Minh, at which the Communists again made it clear that they were willing to envisage partition as a military solution.[47] However, it was by now too late for Bidault and Frédéric-Dupont to succeed, as Laniel's Government was overthrown on its Indochina policy on 12 June by 306-293.[48] On 17 June Mendès-France was invested as Prime Minister. He promised to obtain peace within a month or resign. This promise probably weakened his bargaining position at Geneva, although arguably it was tactically shrewd, indicating to Molotov that he would have to deliver peace quickly or face the possibility of once more dealing with a man like Bidault. In the meantime Bidault remained in charge of the French delegation until 18 June, and in his last few days encouraged more unofficial meetings with the Viet Minh as well as congratulating Eden on the important break-through of 16 June, when Chou En-lai said that the Communists would withdraw all their forces from Cambodia and Laos if the French would do likewise.

By the time Mendès-France took over the negotiations the problems of Cambodia and Laos had been largely solved, whilst the Communists were ready to discuss the partition of Vietnam. At secret negotiations they had already suggested the seventeenth parallel as a possible line of partition.[49] Indeed, it is now clear that the major break-through at Geneva came *before* Mendès-France replaced Bidault, and that Bidault deserves much greater credit for what he did than was allowed by Mendès-France and his supporters at that time. It would, of course, be easy for a cynic to argue that Bidault became less intransigent during the last ten days at Geneva only because he realised that his fall was imminent; after his speech of 9 June in the Assembly he had to try to put the record straight and give the impression that he had done all he could to achieve peace. But, as Lacouture and Devillers point out, an experienced diplomatist is unlikely to change his mind on the spur of the moment.[50] It is much more likely that Bidault's basic attitude did not change much at Geneva. He arrived at the Conference as a tough pessimist, expecting the negotiations to fail and the Americans to have to intervene, or to threaten to intervene. Bidault put forward his proposals and assumed that the Communists would make no concessions. He then strove to get the Americans to support him by threatening to use force. But as it became apparent that Molotov was genuinely interested in peace, and that he was capable of influencing the Viet Minh, Bidault's views about the possibility of a negotiated solution began to change, even if his basic cynicism about a peace based on partition did not. When the Viet Minh – no doubt largely on Molotov's prompting – agreed to give first priority to a ceasefire (24 May) and then to suggest partition (25 May), and later to withdraw their forces from Cambodia and Laos (16 June), Bidault realised that a negotiated peace, which did not entail a humiliating surrender, was possible. Other factors were no doubt also important. The National Assembly made it clear on 4 May, 12 May and 9 June, that it expected Bidault to do all he could to achieve peace. Eden and Molotov also wanted the Conference to succeed. Bidault's only ally, Dulles, could not risk the wrath of Congress. Bidault was, therefore, condemned to negotiate. But, right to the end, he remained unhappy about partition, unless the French Union forces retained control of at least part of Tonkin as well.[51] After Mendès-France had achieved the ceasefire Bidault told the National Assembly that he was glad the war had ended, but he was critical of the terms of the armistice.[52] He quoted Mendès-France's own words of 4 June 1953; 'France will never abandon her friends . . . Those Vietnamese who have put their confidence in us, and whom we have protected, will never be abandoned.'[53] Bidault maintained that Mendès-France had now gone back on this promise. Moreover, there was no guarantee that the agreements would be kept; he quoted Eisenhower as saying on 22 July: 'The United States have not been party to the decisions taken at the Conference and are not bound by them.' He recalled Article 62 of the Constitution, to which they all subscribed, and asked what right the Government had to abandon parts of the French Union. To Bidault Geneva was a new Munich with Mendès-France playing the role of Chamberlain. To the end of his political career Bidault refused to accept with equanimity the loss of any part of the old French Empire.

Twenty years later it is clear that Bidault's scepticism about the Geneva Peace Agreement was justified. Vietnam north of the seventeenth parallel was, as Bidault had forecast, lost to the Communists, although a considerable proportion of the population had no wish to be ruled by Ho Chi Minh's dictatorial government (almost a million people left the North to settle in the South before the deadline date of 20 July 1955; only 80,000 moved from the South to the North).[54] The United States Government and Bao Dai's Government specifically dissociated themselves from the final agreement, which, amongst other things, laid down that no new troops were to be introduced into either zone after withdrawal by the two sides, and that elections were to be held in July 1956 to decide on the reunification of Vietnam. The first of these conditions was soon broken by the North, which by 1959 was infiltrating large numbers of troops into the South. Meanwhile, the South refused to hold an election on reunification on the perfectly understandable grounds that the population of the North was greater than that of the South and that the election would not be 'free' (as laid down in paragraph 7 of the final Agreement) in the Communist part of the country. Publicly the United States Government cautiously accepted the Geneva Agreement (without, however, signing it),[55] but privately it regarded it as 'a major defeat for Western diplomacy and a potential disaster for U.S. security interests in the Far East'.[56] The Communists had gained an important salient from which to extend their influence in South East Asia. Arguably the Americans have exaggerated the importance of the 'domino theory' in South East Asia. It is possible that the Communists would be satisfied with control of a united Vietnam. It is equally possible that they would not; after all Ho Chi Minh founded the *Indochinese* Communist Party in 1930, not the *Vietnamese* Communist Party. And Communist activity in Laos and Cambodia since 1954 certainly gives the impression that control of all of Indochina is part of the Communist strategy. Only the future will show whether the Communists will be able to fulfil their strategic aims, and whether, having achieved them, they will attempt to extend their influence further.

In the circumstances of the late 1950s and early 1960s, however, it was almost inevitable that the United States would do all it could to support nationalist governments in Indochina and throughout South East Asia. At first the United States attempted to do this by means of aid programmes and through the South East Asia Treaty Organisation, but as Communist infiltration and guerrilla activity increased in the late 1950s and early 1960s, the United States decided to commit 'advisers' and then ground troops to South Vietnam.[57] And so the second Indochina War began in earnest. In February 1965 there were only two battalions of marines in South Vietnam; within a year there were almost half a million American troops in Indochina, and the North was being heavily bombarded. After eight inconclusive years of war the United States finally withdrew after making as unsatisfactory a peace as that which ended the first Indochina War.

It is not the purpose of this book to discuss the second Indochina (Vietnam) War, i.e. that of 1965-73. But it is legitimate to point out that the unsatisfactory 'peace' agreement of 1954 led almost inevitably to further conflict in Indochina. It is perhaps not unreasonable to compare the Geneva Agreement of 1954 with the Versailles Treaty of 1919, in the sense that neither did much to clear the atmosphere of bitterness and resentment. But whereas the Second World War was to bring peace — albeit uneasy at times — to Europe, the second Indochina War appears to have done little to resolve the power struggle in South East Asia.[58]

NOTES

1. See Henri Navarre, *Agonie de l'Indochine* (Paris, 1958), esp. p.68 ff.
2. In public Pleven stood four-square behind Bidault, but in private he was beginning to doubt whether the Communists could be forced into negotiations by military defeats; interview with Pleven's *chef de cabinet*, Alain Dutheillet de Lamothe, 24 April 1967. (UDSR = Union Démocratique et Socialiste de la Résistance, a small left-of-centre party).
3. The Sultan was deposed with Bidault's connivance in September 1953. Mitterrand resigned immediately afterwards.
4. *Journal Officiel* (Assemblée Nationale), 27 May 1953. Reynaud obtained 276 votes; he required 314, an absolute majority of the National Assembly's membership.
5. ibid., 3 June 1953. Mendès-France got 301 votes, failing by 13 to get invested as Prime Minister.
6. *Journal Officiel,* 10 June 1953.
7. *Le Monde,* 12 June 1953.
8. *Journal Officiel* (Assemblée Nationale), 27 June 1953.
9. *Journal Officiel* (Assemblée Nationale), 27 October 1953.
10. It is possible that the original initiative came from Pekin, not from Löfgren. This is the view of Dennis Duncanson (letter of 12 March 1974).
11. *Le Monde,* 1 December 1953.
12. ibid.
13. ibid., 12 January 1954.
14. *Journal Officiel* (Conseil de la République), 4 December 1953.
15. Mercier, p.43.
16. Quoted, Lacouture and Devillers, *La fin d'une guerre,* p.47, n.2.
17. Interview with Chevigné, 24 November 1966.
18. Quoted, J.-R. Tournoux, p.29.
19. *Le Monde,* 10 December 1953.
20. ibid., 19 February 1954.
21. Interview with Dutheillet de Lamothe, 26 April 1967. (Lamothe was Pleven's *chef de cabinet*).

22. See Lacouture and Devillers, pp.63-5.
23. Above p.117.
24. Tournoux, p.34.
25. Eden, p.101.
26. ibid.
27. *Témoignage Chrétien*, 5 March 1954.
28. *Journal Officiel* (Assemblée Nationale), 9 March 1954.
29. Eden, pp.117 and 124.
30. Interview with Lacouture, 7 February 1967.
31. *Esprit,* May, 1953, p.758.
32. Pierre-Henri Teitgen, who was Deputy Prime Minister in Laniel's Government, emphasised that Bidault was 'always opposed to bilateral negotiations with the Viet Minh'; interview, 24 April 1967.
33. Eden regarded 16 June, the day on which Chou En-lai agreed to recognise the problems of Laos and Cambodia separately from that of Vietnam, as the first major breakthrough; Eden, p.129.
34. Quoted, Lacouture and Devillers, p.123, n.3.
35. *Le Monde,* 11 May 1954.
36. *Le Monde,* 12 May 1954.
37. ibid.
38. Lacouture and Devillers, p.154, n.17.
39. Lacouture and Devillers, p.180.
40. Eden, p.119. On 17 May Eden received a promise from Bidault that France would not ask the Americans to intervene in Vietnam *before* the Conference failed.
41. *Le Monde,* 26 May 1953.
42. *Le Monde,* 10 June 1954.
43. *Journal de Genève,* 10 June 1954.
44. *Courrier de la Nièvre,* 30 May 1954.
45. *Journal Officiel* (Assemblée Nationale), 9 June 1954.
46. ibid.
47. Frédéric-Dupont, p.156.
48. 101 Communists, 106 Socialists, 33 Radicals, 44 Gaullists and 22 others (mainly UDSR) voted against Laniel's Government in a motion of no confidence.
49. The secret negotiations of 6-16 June were carried out by two soldiers (Col. Brétisson of France and Col. Lau of the Viet Minh) and two diplomats (Chauvel of France and Buu of the Viet Minh); Frédéric-Dupont, p.162.
50. Lacouture and Devillers, p.228.
51. Frédéric-Dupont, p.156.
52. For details of the Geneva Agreement, see below p.129.
53. *Journal Officiel* (Assemblée Nationale), 23 July 1953.
54. Nearly all of the 80,000 were Viet Minh soldiers, who were transported north in Polish ships. For the ruthless establishment of the Communist dictatorship in the north between 1954-6, see P.J. Honey, *Communism in North Vietnam* (London, 1963).
55. Strictly speaking no country signed the Geneva Agreement, although the French and Viet Minh high commands signed the military clauses. See Robert F. Randle, *Geneva 1954: the Settlement of the Indochina War* (Princeton University Press, 1969).
56. *U.S. - Vietnam Rels:* vol 1, section 3, p.14. Cited Geoffrey Warner, 'The United States and Vietnam'. *International Affairs,* July 1972, p.394.

57. Professor Geoffrey Warner of the University of Hull (formerly of the Australian National University) is at present working on a detailed study of United States policy in Indochina in this period. In the meantime, he has written two articles on 'The United States and Vietnam' in *International Affairs*, July and October 1972. See also Dennis Duncanson, *Government and Revolution in Vietnam*, and the same author's articles in *Conflict Study*, October 1973, *International Affairs*, October 1973, and *The World Today*, March 1974.

58. See, for example, *International Affairs*, October 1973, special number on 'Asia after Vietnam'; and Dennis Duncanson, 'The ceasefire in Vietnam', *The World Today*, March 1973, and 'One year of peace in Indochina', *The World Today*, March 1974.

9.   MOTIVES FOR INDOCHINA POLICY

The preceding chapters have shown that French governments were rarely in full control of their Indochina policy. On several occasions up to 1949 French administrators and soldiers took preemptive action without the authorisation of Paris (e.g. the setting up of the Cochinchinese Republic in June 1946 and the bombardment of Haiphong in November 1946), whilst from 1950 onwards American influence on the decision-making process became steadily greater as the United States got more involved, albeit still indirectly, in Indochina. Nevertheless, the French political parties, and notably the one which was the lynch-pin of all the centre coalitions from 1946-54, the Christian Democratic MRP, continued to play an important, and often a determinant, role in the formulation of Indochina policy. It is, therefore, appropriate to analyse the motives which lay behind the policies pursued by the Christian Democrats and their coalition partners during the first Indochina War.

Anti-Communism

Anti-Communism does not seem to have been an important motive for the Christian Democrats in the early stages of the Indochina conflict. It was only after 1949 that it became a major motive for continuing the war. Many Christian Democrats claim that anti-Communism was always *the* major reason for the policies they pursued. But there is little evidence to support their claim.

Max André, Maurice Schumann and Paul Coste-Floret, for example, all asserted that for them anti-Communism was the essential motive for the position they adopted over Indochina from the beginning.[1] André emphasised that the Fontainebleau Conference broke down owing to the intransigence of the Communists, who refused to 'negotiate' in the normal sense of the word. They wanted simply to convert Vietnam into a Communist state, and André, the leader of the French delegation, was quite unwilling to be party to the spread of Communism. Maurice Schumann was equally adamant about the importance of anti-Communism as early as 1946. He emphasised the monolithic nature of world Communism at the time when Stalin controlled the movement with an iron hand and Mao Tse-tung was still an unknown leader. The effect of this was that non-Communists in France felt that it was as important to resist Ho Chi Minh in Indochina as General Markos in Greece. Both Schumann and

Coste-Floret pointed out that France could never have agreed to a Communist government within the French Union — Ho Chi Minh would simply have conveyed all the defence secrets of the Union to Moscow.

Despite the assertions of André, Schumann and Coste-Floret, there seems to be no evidence that anti-Communism was an important motive for the Christian Democrats in 1946 or even in 1947. André made no reference to the Communism of the Viet Minh in his despatch to *L'Aube* at the time of the first Dalat Conference.[2] Nor did he refer to it during his speech on Indochina at the MRP Congress in March 1947, although this took place three months after the Viet Minh *coup* of December 1946. Schumann was equally silent about Ho Chi Minh's Communism, both in the National Assembly and in his many leading articles in *L'Aube* during 1946 and 1947.[3] Indeed, he is not found openly condemning the Viet Minh as a Communist organisation until August 1948.[4] It could be argued that André and Schumann were exercising tactical restraint so long as the French Communists were still in the Government, but this would not apply after May 1947. If anti-Communism was really as important to Schumann in the immediate post-war period as he later claimed, it is surprising that he did not refer to Ho Chi Minh's allegiance to Moscow until late 1948. Indeed, it was only after Ho Chi Minh's Government was recognised by China and the Soviet Union in January 1950 that *L'Aube* began to refer to anti-Communism as *the* motive for the war in Indochina.

That anti-Communism was a relatively minor MRP motive in the early stages of the Indochina conflict was in fact confirmed by Jean Letourneau and Pierre de Chevigné (neither of whom had any sympathy for Communism). Both men considered that the most important reason for the breakdown of the Fontainebleau Conference and the rupture with Ho Chi Minh was that France was not ready to accept the dismemberment of her Empire,[5] i.e. *initially* the prime reason for the clash with Ho Chi Minh was that France was determined to reassert herself after the humiliations of the Second World War, and she was totally against losing control of any territory which had been hers in 1939. And this attitude affected the parties of the Left as much as to those of the Right or Centre. As Chevigné put it:

> Everyone knew that Ho Chi Minh was a Communist, but we (the MRP) were partners of the Communists in government, and the Communists, whilst in power, showed no more desire to grant Ho Chi Minh's requests than we did.[6]

It was thus that in May 1946 Maurice Thorez, the Communist leader, told General Xuan that he had 'no intention of being remembered as

134

the liquidator of French power in Indochina'.[7] Even Georges Bidault, the MRP Prime Minister at the time of the Fontainebleau Conference, and later an outspoken anti-Communist, did not attack Ho Chi Minh as a Communist in 1946. Paul Vignaux, who knew Bidault well before and during the war (Bidault was Head of the National Resistance Council from 1943-4), pointed out that Bidault was not particularly anti-Communist immediately after the war. His great driving force, like General de Gaulle's, was his concept of French greatness, and he had no objection to co-operating with Communists, provided they did not try to frustrate his objective.[8] This view of Bidault was supported by Léon Pignon, High Commissioner in Indochina from 1948-50, and even more emphatically by Robert Buron, who emphasised that Bidault was personally very friendly with Maurice Thorez and seemed even to prefer the Communists to the Socialists as partners in the tripartite governments of 1944-7 — perhaps because the Communist record in the Resistance had been so much more impressive than that of the Socialists.[9] In Buron's view the decisive break between Bidault and the Communists did not occur until June 1947, when Stalin publicly insulted Bidault over the Saar problem.

Although most of the evidence suggests that anti-Communism was not the prime reason for the failure of the Fontainebleau Conference, nor even for the abortive peace initiatives of Bollaert in 1947, it would be wrong to infer that anti-Communism was not an important influence in the MRP's decision to support the Bao Dai policy. Georges Le Brun-Kéris, an MRP liberal, considered that anti-Communism became a major motive for the MRP's inflexibility towards Ho Chi Minh after the end of tripartism, i.e. after May 1947,[10] and it was certainly during the summer of 1947 that Bidault began to orientate French foreign policy decisively in favour of the West and against the Soviet Union. The major French strikes of the autumn of 1947 and the Marshall Plan also had the effect of hardening France against international Communism. The MRP began to appear as the great anti-Communist party, a role emphasised by the investiture of Robert Schuman as Prime Minister in November 1947 to deal with the Communist-fomented economic and social crisis. Robert Schuman, who was a devout Catholic, was considered to be more anti-Communist than Bidault in the immediate post-war period. He was also a firm protagonist of the Bao Dai policy, the essence of which was the promotion of a non-Communist alternative to Ho Chi Minh. It seems, then, that anti-Communism became a major factor in the formulation of the MRP's Indochina policy only during the Schuman Ministry (November 1947 - July 1948) — the Prime Minister (Schuman), Foreign Minister (Bidault), and Minister for Overseas France (Coste-Floret), all taking a firm stand against further contacts with

Ho Chi Minh.[11]

One of the effects of Mao Tse-tung's victory in China in 1949 was that the war in Indochina was transformed into a major ideological struggle. China and the Soviet Union recognised and armed the Viet Minh; the United States did the same for Bao Dai. In March 1951 Ho Chi Minh recreated the Indochinese Communist Party (its predecessor having been officially dissolved in 1945), and announced that the Viet Minh was a Communist movement.[12] This was doubtless part of the price which had to be paid for Chinese assistance. At the same time the French, partly in order to persuade the Americans to increase their supplies of military aid, began to emphasise that they were fighting for the free world against the Communists. Letourneau stated that the lesson to be drawn from the disaster of Cao Bang was that Indochina and Korea were part of the same struggle between the free world and the Communists.[13] In December 1950 the Christian Democratic Senator Jacques de Menditte said that the war in Indochina was not between Ho Chi Minh and Bao Dai, but between Communism and Democracy.[14] Just over a year later Letourneau wrote that 'the problem of Indochina has become part of the world struggle for freedom'.[15] And during the last two years of the war the Christian Democrats continued to lay great stress on the ideological nature of the struggle. Kenneth Vignes told the party congress in 1953 that France was fighting to prevent the spread of world Communism.[16] A.-F. Mercier wrote that anti-Communism was the chief reason for France's continued presence in Indochina,[17] and the MRP National Committee called for 'a positive anti-Communism throughout the French Union'.[18]

The MRP had changed its views a great deal since the time when Bidault and Thorez were in agreement that Ho Chi Minh's most dangerous characteristic was not his Communism, but his nationalism. The party's persistent emphasis on anti-Communism no doubt had much to do with the fact that by 1953 the United States was paying for two-thirds of the cost of the war in Indochina. But it did little to solve Vietnam's basic problems. As Danielle Hunebelle commented in *Le Monde:*

> When we say: 'Ho Chi Minh is a Communist', the Vietnamese replies: 'Ho Chi Minh is my father in the rice-paddy, my brother in the maquis. Do you wish me to take up arms against my father and my brother?' When we say: 'But your father and your brother are fighting for Communism. We are fighting to save you from Communism', the Vietnamese replies: 'I am fighting for my independence. My father and my brother are fighting for their independence. As for your Communism, I have no idea what you

are talking about.'

Catholicism

If a rather nationalistic determination to preserve the integrity of the French Union was the main reason for France's reluctance to decolonise, religion was a factor which cannot be ignored, particularly in the case of Indochina, where about one-tenth of the population was Catholic. The possibility that Catholic MRP Ministers were influenced by the Church in their Vietnam policy was originally suggested by Philip Williams and Philippe Devillers.[19] All the evidence confirms the validity of their hypothesis.

In estimating the influence of Catholicism on the French Christian Democrats, one is faced with much the same problem as William Bosworth in his attempt to analyse the political influence of Catholicism within France as a whole.[20] It is not too difficult to discuss the political opinions expressed in the Catholic press and by Catholic Action groups, but it is harder to be precise about the effect of such influences on politicians. One can note that the Vietnamese Catholics, at first indecisive towards the Viet Minh, who in fact made some effort to woo them up to 1947, later became intransigent opponents of Ho Chi Minh, accepting the advice of the Vatican and of the influential *Missions Etrangères,* who played an important role in running the Vietnamese Church and training the clergy. The similarities between the policies advocated by the *Bulletin des Missions Etrangères* and those advocated by the MRP can be noted. A sociological study of MRP shows that, *malgré soi,* the MRP was essentially a Catholic party, and that most of its leaders had risen through the hierarchy of Catholic Action groups. But although the *precise* political effect of Catholicism on the MRP cannot be measured, there is sufficient documentary and oral evidence to confirm the view that it was important.[21]

The only Catholic Minister in Ho Chi Minh's provisional government of September 1945 - December 1946, Nguyen Manh Ha, once remarked: 'If you wish to understand the Indochina policy of the MRP, you should begin by studying the history of Catholicism in Vietnam'.[22] The early history of Catholicism in Indochina has already been briefly sketched.[23] The immediate post-war period produced circumstances in which Catholics and Communists, at least in the North, at first co-operated to achieve Vietnamese unity and independence. Ho Chi Minh tried to win over the Catholics, doubtless partly for the tactical reason that there were a large number of Catholics in Tonkin, the only part of Vietnam where the Viet Minh had any real strength. Independence was declared on 2 September 1945, significantly a Sunday and the day of remembrance for the Annamite

137

Catholic martyrs. Nguyen Manh Ha recalls that all the members of Ho Chi Minh's Government attended Church on Christmas Day 1945. If Ho Chi Minh wanted the support of the Catholics, it seems equally clear that they were not unwilling supporters of the Communist-led Viet Minh. As Nguyen Manh Ha pointed out, the vast majority of Catholics being poor, their social and economic objectives were similar to those of the Communists, whilst on a political level both wanted national unity and independence. What mattered most to the native Catholics was the practical side of Christianity. They would support a government which protected their churches, carried out land reforms, and encouraged education. On 20 September 1945 Ho Chi Minh ordered the cessation of attacks on churches, pagodas and other places of worship,[24] and in return the Vietnamese bishops proclaimed their support for Ho Chi Minh's Government on 20 October 1945. An uneasy entente between Catholics and Communists continued throughout the winter of 1945-6, although attacks were still being made by the latter on the former, particularly in the northern dioceses of Phat Diem and Bui Chu.

However, the Communist-Catholic 'marriage' gradually broke down during 1946. The Vietnamese Catholics had shown comparatively little interest in the ideological differences between Communism and Catholicism, but to the Paris-trained priests who returned to Indochina in increasing numbers during 1946 Communism was anathema. It was not long before they convinced the Vietnamese clergy that co-operation with the Viet Minh was contrary to their faith, but the slowness with which some Vietnamese clergy accepted this point of view indicated their reluctance to agree with this 'European' interpretation of Catholicism. The diocese of Phat Diem, for example, under Monseigneur Le Huu Tu, continued to maintain a neutral position between the French and the Viet Minh until 1949. Gradually, however, the French and Vatican point of view prevailed, partly owing to the important influence of the *Missions Etrangères* within the Vietnamese Church, and partly owing to the strongly anti-Communist attitude of Pope Pius XII in the late 1940s, culminating in the formal condemnation of Communism by the Holy Office on 15 July 1949. In June 1948 the Vietnamese bishops issued an official proclamation condemning the Viet Minh as a Communist organisation, and in 1949 they declared their support for Bao Dai against Ho Chi Minh. Even the recalcitrant Le Huu Tu, Bishop of Phat Diem, rallied to Bao Dai after the Elysée Agreement of March 1949. But not all Catholics followed his example, and in the early 1950s a few were still to be found serving in the ranks of the Viet Minh.[25] Between 1946-9, however, the vast majority of Vietnamese Catholics broke with the Viet Minh and became supporters of Bao Dai.

The suggestion that the Indochina policy of France's Christian Democratic Ministers was influenced by the Vatican and, more specifically, by the Catholics of Vietnam seems to be both true and false. It is true in so far as the MRP, which was to all intents and purposes a confessional party, paid close attention to the views of the Vatican in all fields; the outspoken anti-Communism of the Vatican in the late 1940s was no exception.[26] It is false in so far as it assumes that the Vietnamese Catholics were united as a body against the Viet Minh. As has been shown, at least up to 1949 they were not; Catholics like Nguyen Manh Ha and Bishop Le Huu Tu would have preferred to have come to a compromise with the Viet Minh if this had been possible. The *Missions Etrangères*, on the other hand, showed themselves from the first to be against the Viet Minh, and they were fully supported by Vietnamese bishops like Nguyen Ba Tong, Ho Ngoc Can and Ngo Dinh Tuc.[27] These men condemned the Viet Minh from early 1947 and supported the restoration of Bao Dai as Head of State in 1949.

Although the majority of the Vietnamese clergy and the MRP favoured an intransigent policy towards the Viet Minh, it does not necessarily follow that the one influenced the other or vice versa. There is, however, sufficient circumstantial evidence to make it clear that a connection between the two did exist. In May 1954, for example, Bidault told his Minister of State at the Foreign Ministry, Frédéric-Dupont, that his desire to protect the Catholics of Tonkin was the main reason for his refusal to negotiate with Ho Chi Minh.[28] Marius Moutet and Nguyen Manh Ha both considered that one of the reasons for the MRP's support for Bao Dai was that the ex-Emperor's wife and most of his entourage were Catholics, and when Paul Rivet, a Socialist deputy, made this assertion in the National Assembly in 1949, no MRP spokesman refuted it.[29] At the end of 1947 the Vietnamese bishops appealed to Robert Schuman, the MRP Prime Minister, to make no further contacts with the Viet Minh, and from this time until 1954 there were no negotiations between the French and the Communists. Robert Buron, an MRP liberal who was later to play an important role in the negotiations with the Algerian nationalists, emphasised that the general influence of Catholicism was also against independence for the colonies: 'Why should France agree to granting independence to her colonies when the Papacy did not favour 'independent' national entities within the Catholic church as a whole?'[30] The fact that so many members of the MRP came from a Catholic Action background ensured that they were interested in the world-wide role of the Catholic Church. At the height of the Cold War they could hardly abandon the Catholics of Vietnam to the Communists, a point which was emphasised by Le Brun-Kéris at the

1954 MRP Congress,[31] by Letourneau in the National Assembly in July 1954,[32] and by Teitgen in private conversation thirteen years later.[33]

Circumstantial evidence does not prove a case, but when it all points in the same direction, it is probable that it is leading to something significant. This is all the more likely when the known facts point in the same direction. In this case the known facts are that there was a distinct similarity between the political policies advocated by the Vietnamese Catholics and those pursued by the French Christian Democrats, and that the Catholics of Vietnam and France were inevitably on the same psychological wavelength, for both were bound to follow the anti-Communist instructions of the Vatican. In these circumstances there can be no doubt that Catholic pressure was a vital factor in discouraging the MRP from considering a policy of negotiations with the Viet Minh between 1946-54.

Gaullism

Many members of the MRP denied that General de Gaulle had any influence on the party's policies after his resignation from the government in January 1946: 'Perhaps some members of the party were subject to the General's influence, . . . but not the vast majority; certainly not the party workers or the militants.'[34] This opinion of Pierre-Henri Teitgen's was echoed by Max André, Pierre de Chevigné, Paul Coste-Floret and Jean-Jacques Juglas, who all maintained that de Gaulle's influence on the MRP was negligible after January 1946.[35] There is strong evidence, however, that de Gaulle's influence on the MRP's colonial policy was considerable, not only in the months immediately after his leaving the government, but also throughout the Fourth Republic, particularly during the years 1947-52 when the Gaullist *Rassemblement du Peuple Français* (RPF) was a powerful political force, although none of its members held ministerial office. The fundamental reason for this influence was that the Christian Democrats and Gaullists appealed to the same Catholic, largely conservative electorate. They also had a similar wartime heritage — de Gaulle had been the leader of the Free French in England and later in North Africa, while the Christian Democrats had played a key role in the home Resistance. De Gaulle never forgave *le parti de la fidélité*, as the MRP was labelled at the time of the Liberation, for not following him into opposition in January 1946. When he founded his RPF in April 1947, a handful of Christian Democratic deputies joined him, notably Edmond Michelet and Louis Terrenoire, but the vast majority remained in the MRP. Christian Democratic voters, however, went over in droves to the RPF at the municipal elections of October 1947, and thereafter the MRP was always under Gaullist electoral

140

pressure. This was confirmed at the 1951 General Election when approximately half of the MRP's 1946 electors voted for the RPF. In these circumstances it was not surprising that the Christian Democrats often deferred to Gaullist views.

Referring to the immediate post-war period, the Gaullist Edmond Michelet said: 'At that time the General was totally against the dismemberment of the French Empire'.[36] Michelet, who was MRP Minister for the Armed Forces at the time of the Fontainebleau Conference in 1946, went on to say that General de Gaulle brought pressure to bear on the MRP to adopt an intransigent attitude towards Ho Chi Minh at the Conference. He appealed directly to Bidault to make no concessions to Ho Chi Minh,[37] and on 3 August 1946 Admiral d'Argenlieu, a Gaullist *inconditionnel* since 1940, told Devillers that he too had appealed to the MRP to reject Ho Chi Minh's demands.[38] Robert Delavignette, later Letourneau's *chef de cabinet*, commented: 'Admiral d'Argenlieu was the puppet of General de Gaulle, and the Admiral's influence was considerable in 1946. It is certain that he brought pressure to bear on the MRP and that he won over Bidault'.[39]

De Gaulle kept up his pressure in the autumn of 1946 when the final draft of the Constitution of the Fourth Republic was being drawn up. At a press conference on 28 August 1946 he rejected the Socialist proposals for a French Union with a confederal structure: 'The Constitution must emphasise the close ties between France and the overseas territories, . . . In particular it must emphasise France's preeminent responsibility for the foreign and defence policy of the whole French Union'.[40] And at Epinal in September he said: 'It is essential that the French Union be French, i.e. that France maintains its control over the Union's foreign policy, defence policy, communications and economic affairs'.[41] It is probable that Bidault himself did not require any Gaullist encouragement to insist on the need for a tightly-knit French Union, closely controlled from Paris, but there seems no reason to doubt the claim of Alain Dutheillet de Lamothe, René Pleven's *chef de cabinet*, that Gaullist pressure was a major factor in uniting the MRP as a whole behind Bidault,[42] for earlier in the summer several Christian Democrats had advocated a loosely structured French Union. By the autumn they were silent. As a result a French Union with a rigid, centralised structure came into being, and this ensured that France found it all the more difficult to work out new relationships with her former colonial territories in the years to come.

After the Constitution had been ratified (October 1946) and the Indochina War had begun (December 1946), the Gaullists continued to oppose any concessions to nationalists in the French Union. They did this in spite of the fact that their leader probably realised by 1950 that negotiation was the only solution in Indochina, and that generosity alone could save North Africa. Edmond Michelet, a close confidant of the General's and always a liberal Gaullist, was not alone in claiming that de Gaulle continued to be against decolonisation when out of office whilst privately realising its necessity,[43] and Jean-Paul Palewski once told Devillers that the Gaullist party strove to prevent liberal colonial policies, not because they were opposed to them, but because they did not want the despised centre governments of the Fourth Republic to get any credit for such policies.[44] In the summer of 1947 de Gaulle threatened that anyone responsible for the loss of any French territory would be impeached when he (the General) returned to power.[45] Pressure of this type was almost certainly the main reason for Coste-Floret's failure to implement Vietnamese independence after declaring it in June 1948, so ruining any chance of establishing a successful non-Communist government under Bao Dai at a time when this might have been a possibility.

The Gaullist barrage of criticisms continued in the late 1940s and early 1950s, ending only with the disintegration of the RPF in 1952-3 after twenty-seven Gaullist deputies deserted the General's banner to support the conservative government of Antoine Pinay in 1952. The Gaullist newspaper, *Carrefour,* criticised the Socialists and Mendès-France for suggesting negotiations with Ho Chi Minh.[46] In the National Assembly Palewski castigated Mendès-France as a defeatist.[47] In July 1953 the Gaullist General Billotte called for the total mobilisation of the Vietnamese people against the Viet Minh, and in October 1953 Raymond Dronne rejected the suggestion that France should consider withdrawing from Indochina: 'Have you forgotten that Munich was the first step to the disaster of 1940? An Asiatic Munich would sound the death-knell of France as a world power.'[48]

Statements such as these by Gaullists, some of whom were former members of the MRP, were bound to affect the MRP's attitude towards the French Union, because, as already emphasised, the Christian Democrats and Gaullists vied with each other for the same electorate. Various members of the MRP, notably Robert Buron, Henri Bouret and Pierre Corval, all agreed that Gaullist pressure of this type, aimed indirectly at the MRP-Gaullist electorate, was an important reason for the intransigent colonial policy of a party whose colonial aims were theoretically liberal and generous.[49] The MRP could hardly preside over the 'disintegration' of the French Union so long as General de Gaulle and his followers continued to describe every concession to colonial nationalists as 'treason'. Indeed the Gaullists must bear a heavy responsibility for the fact that concessions in Indochina were usually too little and always too late.

Economic Motives

There is no evidence that the MRP Ministers who were largely responsible for Indochina policy from 1945-54 were strongly motivated by economic considerations, certainly not in terms of direct benefits. However, economic motives were not as unimportant as Ministers later claimed,[50] largely because hopes of reviving the pre-war 'profitability' of Indochina took a long time to die.

Before the Second World War 70 per cent of French imperial trade had been with Indochina.[51] Indochinese rice, rubber and anthracite were exported; French manufactured goods were imported. In 1939 five-sixths of the rice-fields of Cochinchina were owned by Frenchmen; the rubber plantations were entirely French-owned; the minerals of Tonkin, notably anthracite, were mined by French companies; the *grandes sociétés* – Terres Rouges, Ciment Portland, Distillerie d'Indochine, La Banque d'Indochine – played a dominant role in the economy of Indochina. In 1946 the French hoped to revive the profitable business of pre-war days, their early optimism being shown by the foundation of new companies such as La Société des Phosphates de l'Extrême-Orient (founded in July 1946). In 1947 Emile Bollaert, the High Commissioner, spoke optimistically of the economic future of Indochina. But the war against the Viet Minh ruined these hopes. Exports in 1950 amounted to only one-tenth of the volume of those of 1939. Indochina's trade deficit increased sixfold between 1947-51. The war cost an estimated Fr.3,000 milliard between 1946-54.[52] Most of the big companies realised early on that there could be no profitable future in Indochina – by 1951 the Bank of Indochina had transferred seven-eighths of its capital to France or North Africa. Only the piastres traffic left much hope for gain, and it was a very speculative business.[53]

Despite the above factors, Letourneau's *chef de cabinet*, Robert Delavignette, considered that economic motives were important for the MRP, as for the other political parties except the Communists, not in the traditional sense of making quick profits, but because it seemed that France could only recover from the devastation of the War by exploiting to the full the economic resources of the French Union.[54] Although the directors of the large companies soon realised that profits could not be made in war-torn Indochina, the politicians continued to profess optimism about the federation's economic future. In this way the economic myth about the potential profitability of Indochina was allowed to persist for longer than the facts of the situation justified. The politicians allowed themselves to be deceived, or perhaps merely tried to deceive their followers, into believing in economic pie in the sky. Thus in 1949 the MRP leader Robert Lecourt claimed that if more money were invested in Indochina, both Indochina and France would benefit enormously.[55] And in 1950 Letourneau told de Lattre on his appointment as Commander-in-Chief that:

> It is essential that France's economic interests in Indochina are safeguarded. The economies of France and Indochina are complementary, France receiving natural resources and agricultural produce from Indochina, and Indochina receiving manufactured goods from France.[56]

In fact by 1950 the trade with Indochina had been greatly reduced (to one-tenth of its 1940 level). But the optimism of the politicians died hard. By the early 1950s the French taxpayer found himself subsidising the piastres traffic, paying for a considerable part of the war, and defraying the cost of the budgetary deficits of the Associated States. It was not surprising that the politicians responsible for Indochina policy stopped talking about the economic advantages of remaining in Indochina after 1950.

National Prestige

In the immediate post-war period there was a strong feeling that France must hold on to her colonies to compensate for the defeat of 1940.[57] Many Frenchmen who had followed de Gaulle or fought in the home Resistance saw the building of the French Union, one hundred million strong, as the sole means by which France could recover her national greatness. At the same time they were determined that Paris should control the Union, for without unity of purpose it would have no strength. In 1946 the Communist Thorez, the Radical Herriot, the Christian Democrat Bidault and General de Gaulle were equally nationalistic and intransigent, because the French were a humiliated people who had no wish to be humiliated again. For the MRP, with their Resistance background, the motive of national prestige was probably more important than any other single factor in their Indochina policy.

At the 1945 MRP Congress Juglas said that 'France will only be a great power so long as our flag continues to fly in all the overseas territories',[58] a statement which was to be repeated in many forms over the years by members of the MRP. A few examples will suffice. In September 1947 Maurice Schumann wrote that the French Union must be built in order to create 'une plus grande France'.[59] At the

1952 party congress Teitgen said that 'There can be no choice between Indochina and the Metropole: the security and greatness of France and of the French Union are indivisible'.[60] And in 1953 Mercier wrote that 'Without the French Union France would no longer be France. It is through the French Union that France can play her role in the world'.[61]

If France were to play this major role in world affairs, it was important for her not only to build and protect the French Union but to control it. Bidault emphasised this to Max André on the eve of the Fontainebleau Conference in 1946,[62] and two months later Maurice Schumann wrote that the French Union must have 'one head, one diplomacy and one army'.[63] A major reason for the determination of Paris to control the Union was the fear that if a large measure of self-government were given to any one overseas territory a chain reaction would set in, culminating in the disintegration of the whole French Union. Bidault and Teitgen were opposed to Bollaert pronouncing the word 'independence' at Hadong in September 1947 for fear of the repercussions in North Africa,[64] and René Plantade, editor of *Forces Nouvelles*, claimed that 'The MRP always looked at Indochina with its eyes on North Africa'.[65] In an article on the motives behind Letourneau's Indochina policy, Robert Guillain wrote:

> The last and most emotive argument is the following: the integrity of the French Union requires us to remain in Indochina; if we do not remain there, a chain reaction could set in, beginning perhaps in North Africa.[66]

France, then, was determined to build a strong and united French Union in order to recover her prestige in the world, but the war in Indochina proved to be her Achilles heel. In the first major debate on Indochina (March 1947) Maurice Schumann had emphasised that the war was purely an internal problem of the French Union, and at Bordeaux in 1952 Coste-Floret rejected the idea of internationalising the war, i.e. bringing in U.N. forces, for the same reason. But, as the war grew in scale, France's policy of guarding the French Union from all external influences gradually disintegrated. France was unable to fight the Viet Minh, aided after 1949 by the Chinese, without herself getting American aid. At first she hoped to get American aid without strings: the United States would provide the necessary arms, but Indochina would remain French. It has already been shown how American aid led to American demands for control over its use, culminating in the Memorandum of 26 April 1953, by which the United States promised more aid only in exchange for increased direction of the war and the promise of total independence for the

Associated States, i.e. the end of the French Union as conceived in the Constitution of 1946.

In concluding this chapter on the motives for French policy during the first Indochina War, it seems clear that the MRP, as a Resistance party, opposed colonial concessions above all for patriotic or nationalistic reasons. The MRP Ministers, who formulated so much of France's Indochina policy between 1945-54, were encouraged by the Vatican and the clergy in Vietnam to stand by their fellow Catholics, and they were pressurised by the Gaullists, who could threaten their electorate, into making no concessions to the nationalists, whether Communist or non-Communist, until it was too late. On the other hand, there is no real evidence that economic interests or pressures had any real influence on the MRP. But in the last analysis it was nationalism which was the driving force behind French policy. In some ways this was understandable. The Resistance leaders, who became France's political leaders after the Second World War, wanted to build a new and stronger France. One means seemed to be the construction of a powerful French Union. But they found themselves running against the tide of history in Indochina, and later in North Africa. At least it can be said of the Christian Democrats that they learnt their lesson in Indochina, for in the second phase of decolonisation — in Morocco, Tunisia and Algeria — the Christian Democrats were generally to be found on the side of those who favoured making concessions to the nationalist leaders before it was too late.

NOTES

1. Interviews with André, 3 October 1966; Schumann, 21 October 1966; and Coste-Floret, 20 October 1966.
2. *L'Aube,* 11 May 1946.
3. e.g. no reference was made to Communism in his major speech on Indochina, 13 March 1947.
4. See *L'Aube,* 8 August 1948.
5. Interviews with Letourneau, 25 November 1966; and Chevigné, 24 November 1966.
6. Interview with Chevigné, 24 November 1966.
7. J. Lacouture, *Ho Chi Minh,* p.125.
8. Interview with Vignaux, 23 December 1966.
9. Interview with Buron, 23 December 1966.
10. Interview with Le Brun-Kéris, 14 October 1966.
11. For details, see above, Chapter 4, pp.54-63.
12. *Année Politique,* 1951, p.113.
13. *Le Monde,* 19 October 1950.
14. *Journal Officiel* (Conseil de la République), 7 December 1950.
15. *Forces Nouvelles,* 22 March 1952.

16.   MRP National Congress, Paris, 1953.

17.   Mercier, p.91.

18.   *Le Monde,* 7 July 1953.

19.   P.M. Williams, *Crisis and Compromise: Politics in the Fourth Republic,* p.112; and Philippe Devillers, interview 12 January 1967.

20.   W. Bosworth, *Catholicism and Crisis in Modern France.*

21.   For a detailed discussion of this problem, see R.E.M. Irving, 'The MRP and the impact of Catholicism on French Indochina policy', *France-Asie,* summer 1969, pp. 257-71.

22.   Interview with Nguyen Manh Ha (who now lives in Paris), 14 January 1967.

23.   See above, Chapter I, p.9.

24.   He was not always obeyed. A French priest, Père Fournier, was murdered a few days later by a Viet Minh band in Hanoi, *Bulletin des Missions Etrangères,* 1947, p.56.

25.   *Etudes,* December 1950, p.338; and Mercier, p.42.

26.   For the extent to which the MRP was a confessional party, see R.E.M. Irving, *Christian Democracy in France,* pp.11-14, 78-91.

27.   *Etudes,* December 1950.

28.   Frédéric-Dupont, *Mission de la France en Asie,* p.157.

29.   *Journal Officiel* (Assemblée Nationale), 10 March 1949.

30.   Interview with Buron, 23 December 1966.

31.   MRP National Congress Report, 1954.

32.   *Journal Officiel* (Assemblée Nationale), 23 July 1954.

33.   Interview with Teitgen, 24 April 1967.

34.   Interview with Teitgen, 24 April 1967.

35.   Interviews with André. 3 October 1966; Chevigné, 24 November 1966; Coste-Floret, 29 October 1966; Juglas, 2 December 1966.

36.   Interview with Michelet, 25 April 1967.

37.   ibid.

38.   Interview with Devillers, 22 December 1966.

39.   Interview with Delavignette, 13 January 1967.

40.   *Le Monde,* 29 August 1946.

41.   *Le Monde,* 1 October 1946.

42.   Interview with Dutheillet de Lamothe, 26 April 1967.

43.   Interview with Michelet, 25 April 1967; see also J. Lacouture, *Cinq Hommes et la France.*

44.   Interview with Devillers, 21 December 1966. (Judging by de Gaulle's Algerian policy after he came to power in 1958, Palewski's statement undoubtedly has the ring of truth about it.)

45.   Lacouture, *Ho Chi Minh,* p.151; *Le Monde,* 11 January 1967.

46.   e.g. on 30 March 1949.

47.   On 22 November 1950.

48.   *Journal Officiel* (Assemblée Nationale), 23 October 1953.

49.   Interviews with Buron, 23 December 1966; Bouret, 7 June 1967; Corval, 7 February 1967.

50.   e.g. interviews with Coste-Floret, 29 October 1966, and with Letourneau, 5 May 1967.

51.   Unless otherwise stated, the statistics which follow can be found in *L'Annuaire Statistique du Vietnam,* 1949-53.

52.   *Le Monde,* 21 July 1954.

53.   See above, Chap. 7, p.113.

54.   Interview with Delavignette, 13 January 1967.

55.   *L'Aube,* 1 January 1949.
56.   Letourneau Papers (Instructions to de Lattre, 22 December 1950).
57.   Interviews with Fontaine, 27 April 1966, and Lacouture, 7 February 1967.
58.   *L'Aube,* 16 December 1945.
59.   *L'Aube,* 12 September 1947.
60.   MRP National Congress Report, 1952.
61.   Mercier, p.16.
62.   Interview with André, 3 October 1966.
63.   *L'Aube,* 10 September 1946.
64.   Interview with Bollaert, 29 October 1966.
65.   Interview with Plantade, 24 April 1967.
66.   *Le Monde,* 9 February 1952.

The decolonisation of French Indochina during the decade after the end of the Second World War appears to have been a classic case of 'too little and too late'. But there is not much point in discussing what might have happened if the history of those times had been different. It is conceivable that Ho Chi Minh *might* have become the Tito of South-East Asia if the French had been more accommodating in 1946. It is possible that Bao Dai might have rallied all the Vietnamese non-Communists (including the large number in the Viet Minh), if the French had granted unity and independence in 1947-8, i.e. before Mao Tse-tung came to power in China. But these events did not take place, and the duty of the historian or of the political scientist is not to speculate about what might have happened, but to try to discover exactly what did happen, why it happened, and what effect it had then and subsequently.

The story of the decolonisation of Indochina has been told by propagandists, hagiographers, journalists and scholars.[1] All in their different ways have added either a few or many pieces to a complicated jigsaw puzzle. The final story will not be written until all the official documents have been released by all the countries involved directly or indirectly in the process of decolonising Indochina, notably France, the United States, the Republic of China, the Soviet Union, both parts of Vietnam, Laos and Cambodia. And even then the facts will be interpreted in different ways. The primary purpose of this book has been to put a few more pieces of the jigsaw into place by focusing on the role of the political parties in France, and above all on that of the Christian Democratic MRP which held the key portfolios throughout the period from 1946-54. The second purpose, which is of course a corollary of the first, has been to study the motives not only of the French political parties but also of the Vietnamese (Communists and non-Communists) and of the Americans. The third purpose has been to assess the effect of the process of decolonisation on the principals involved in the dispute.

Before attempting to draw up some tentative conclusions it is important to emphasise again the complexity of the problem. Indochina was 12,000 miles from France. It was the jewel of France's Empire. France had only a Provisional Government when she found herself faced with Ho Chi Minh's demands for the unity and independence of Vietnam. But who was Ho Chi Minh? To what extent was he motivated by nationalism and/or Communism? How far was he representative of Vietnamese opinion as a whole? After all his government had not been elected, and its writ ran only in the northern part of Vietnam, and even there only in certain areas. Conflicting advice was conveyed to the French Government by its own servants. Jean Sainteny, who had been sent to negotiate with Ho Chi Minh, saw the Vietnamese leader primarily as a nationalist and advocated coming to terms with him. Admiral d'Argenlieu, the High Commissioner in Indochina, saw Ho Chi Minh as a Communist rebel who must be eliminated before any attempt could be made to achieve a political solution. General Leclerc, the Commander-in-Chief, hovered between the views of Sainteny and d'Argenlieu, but in the last analysis deferred to those of his wartime commander, General de Gaulle, who was at that time totally opposed to the loss of any part of the old French Empire.

In 1946 most French politicians were genuinely interested in working out new relationships with the former colonial territories. They accepted the Brazzaville Declaration of 1944, in which General de Gaulle had promised new social and economic opportunities for all citizens of the French Union (as the Empire was renamed in 1946). But, like the General, the politicians were opposed to anything comparable to independence or dominion status. And it must be emphasised that *all* parties, including the Communists, were against granting independence in the immediate post-war period. After all, France had in effect lost the war, although she had emerged on the winning side. Gaullists, Christian Democrats, Socialists and Communists were equally determined to build up a French Union of a hundred million people as the sole apparent means by which France could compete on equal terms with the United States, the Soviet Union and Great Britain.

Britain, in contrast, had played a key role in winning the war. She had never been defeated or occupied. She, therefore, found it less difficult to be generous when the Americans and Russians pressed for decolonisation. Moreover, Britain's whole colonial tradition was quite different from France's. Ever since the Durham Report of 1840 Britain had claimed that the final objective for her colonies was self-government within the British Empire. Progress towards this goal had been very limited except in the case of the English-speaking white dominions, but at least *psychologically* Britain was prepared for the era of decolonisation — France was not. Her objective had always been *assimilation.* This was not necessarily an ignoble objective, for in theory it meant that all citizens of the French Empire could aspire in due course to complete equality with their compatriots in France. But self-government, even in the far-distant future, was ruled out. After the Second World War, however, self-government - or independence - was precisely what nationalists in all colonies wanted, because it was *the* passport to the United Nations. Moreover, the United Nations Charter had laid down that all nations should have the right to self-determination.

In these circumstances it was almost inevitable that France should come into conflict with the nationalists of Vietnam, who had not only set up a provisional government in September 1945, but could also lay claim to a national and cultural heritage stretching back two thousand years. Moreover, nationalism had been recently stimulated by the Japanese and encouraged by the Americans. But it was by no means inevitable that the clash should have been violent. It became violent only because extremists on both sides believed that this was the best way to achieve their ends. Thus, against the orders of his Commander-in-Chief, General Valluy bombarded Haiphong in November 1946 as a reprisal for Viet Minh crimes of violence, whilst Vo Nguyen Giap and Pham Van Dong encouraged Ho Chi Minh to attempt the pre-emptive Hanoi *coup* of December 1946. Even then all chance of achieving a peaceful solution had not been lost. But French policy in the crucial years, 1947-9, was tortuous and contradictory. On the one hand, contacts were made with Ho Chi Minh, but, as has been shown, Bollaert's conditions were so tough, owing to party political pressure in France, that they were almost inevitably rejected by the Viet Minh leader. On the other hand, the Bao Dai policy was implemented so slowly and with such obvious ill-grace — again owing largely to party political differences in France — that Bao Dai had almost no chance of rallying the Vietnamese people to his side. Like Ho Chi Minh, Bao Dai insisted on achieving a significant degree of independence, together with the unity of Vietnam, as minimum conditions. But in the end it was only under indirect pressure from the Chinese Communists that the French conceded these demands, for by 1949 it was apparent that Mao Tse-tung was on the verge of defeating the Nationalists in China, and it was clear that he would look favourably upon his fellow-Communist, Ho Chi Minh. If Bao Dai was going to succeed in rallying the Vietnamese nationalists, the French would have to accept his demands — and quickly. Hence, the Elysée Agreement of 1949.

After Mao Tse-tung came to power the situation in Indochina became even more complex. Chinese aid and training facilities for the Viet Minh inevitably fuelled the war. Consequently the French got drawn into a growing financial and military commitment in Indochina, until they eventually needed increasing quantities of American aid in order to fulfil that commitment. But in accepting American aid they had also to accept, even if reluctantly, conditions which made impossible the achievement of the objectives for which they had at first accepted the commitment. It was indeed a vicious circle.

Meanwhile, the Americans, after their experience in Korea, were reluctant to get involved on the ground in Vietnam. They were already committed to the defence of Japan, South Korea and the offshore islands. Moreover, they had no wish to get tainted with French 'colonialism'; yet they could hardly stand by whilst the Communists tightened their grip on Indochina. So, *nolens volens,* the United States got increasingly involved in Indochina in the early 1950s.

The French were faced with yet another dilemma. As members of the Western Alliance, dependent upon United States protection in Europe, they could not be seen to yield to Communist aggression. They were therefore condemned to fight on in Indochina, no longer in order to preserve the French Union, but as part of the world clash of ideologies – until finally the death of Stalin made it possible for the superpowers to take the first steps towards *détente.* From the time of the de Lattre-Letourneau partnership (1950-2) until the end of the war in 1954 there can be no doubt that the French made a serious effort to grant independence. However, they ran into enormous difficulties in transferring the administration to the inexperienced Vietnamese in the midst of a civil war. Thus, once again, the French fell between two stools. They were criticised by their Vietnamese and American allies for granting independence too slowly, yet each move towards full independence put one more nail in the coffin of the French Union as conceived in 1946.

These, then, were the very difficult circumstances in which the French tried to work out a new relationship with the peoples of Indochina. The difficulties were further compounded by the situation at home. France was trying to recover a measure of self-confidence after the humiliation of the Second World War. She was going through a period of economic reconstruction. She was governed by a succession of well-meaning but weak coalitions of the Centre. After the Communists had been evicted from the government in May 1947, they began to condemn *la sale guerre* and to advocate what would have amounted to surrender to Ho Chi Minh. The Communists put pressure on the Socialists, who remained in government, to demand negotiations with Ho Chi Minh, but the Socialists, who believed as strongly in political democracy as in economic and social democracy, had grave doubts about negotiating with a Communist. Meanwhile, the other major party of government, the MRP, came under increasing pressure from the Gaullists to make no concessions to Ho Chi Minh. The latter once remarked that 'the key to the problem of Indochina is to be found in the domestic political situation in France'.[2] This study has shown that there is much truth in this remark. In particular it has been shown that in the crucial years 1947-9 French governments, under Gaullist and Conservative pressure, took away with their left hand what they had granted with their right. Bao Dai might have succeeded if he had received determined backing from French governments in this period. Instead he was treated as a puppet, and felt that he had been duped.[3] As a result he had no chance of rallying the Vietnamese people and the prime — although not the only — reason for his failure is to be found in the French party political situation.

After 1950 the French political parties played a less important role in Indochina policy. The Indochina problem had become 'internationalised'. The forgotten colonial war had become part of the world struggle against Communism. But even then the role of the parties in France was not insignificant. The very fact that the French Communists criticised their government with increasing vehemence resulted in greater cohesion in French policy. Growing American influence in the Indochina theatre further increased the desire to find a solution which excluded negotiations with Ho Chi Minh. But again there was a contradiction in French policy, for, as has been shown, Jean Letourneau wielded enormous powers in Indochina through his combined post as a senior Cabinet Minister in France and High Commissioner in Indochina at the very time when he was trying hard to make independence a reality. The final contradiction occurred when France devalued the piastre unilaterally in May 1953 in direct contravention of the Elysée Agreement of 1949. Thereafter, only two courses of action remained open, either *la guerre à outrance* or negotiations with Ho Chi Minh. The former would have required direct intervention by the United States, but events at the time of Dien Bien Phu showed that the United States Government was not yet ready to commit itself in this way. The latter required the application of diplomatic pressure by the Soviet Union and China on Ho Chi Minh's Government, and this is what finally led to the Geneva Agreement of 1954.

It is now time to comment briefly on the effects of the first Indochina War on those involved in the dispute. The effects of the war on the Soviet Union and China will not be discussed, not because they were unimportant, but because the prime objective of this book has been to concentrate on France and Vietnam, and to a lesser extent on the United States.

As far as the United States was concerned, the first Indochina War brought America to the verge of direct intervention in Vietnam. Secretary of State Dulles was convinced of the need to halt Communism in South-East Asia (he was one of the first apostles of the domino theory). Indeed, he opposed direct intervention at the time of Dien Bien Phu only because he did not believe Dien Bien Phu had any *strategic* value. To have bombed the Viet Minh around the perimeter of Dien Bien Phu would have been no more than a short-term operation, and it would have associated the United States with 'colonialist' France. Dulles seems to have believed sincerely, if naïvely, that if the United States dissociated itself from the colonialism of Britain and France, grateful ex-colonies such as Vietnam would support the Americans in their struggle against Communism.[4] It was for this reason that the United States deliberately encouraged the elimination of French influence in Vietnam in the year after the Geneva Agreement and committed itself to Ngo Dinh Diem, who was both strongly anti-Communist and anti-French. Unfortunately for the Americans he also turned out to be anti-Buddhist (and there were approximately one million Buddhists in South Vietnam) and obsessively suspicious of all opponents and rivals. When Diem was ousted from power, with American connivance, in 1963, the United States was finally faced with the alternative of intervening directly or standing by whilst South Vietnam was taken over by the Communists. But the crucial decisions which led to full-scale American military involvement in Vietnam from 1964-73 had been taken in the wake of the first Indochina War; and it was *during* the first war that the major *volte face* in American policy occurred, because by 1953 the United States had become the most implacable opponent of the man whom it had supported in the years 1941-6, Ho Chi Minh.

As far as Vietnam was concerned, the first Indochina War — like its successor — brought neither unity nor independence, the twin aims of both Ho Chi Minh and Bao Dai. North Vietnam, it is true, became Communist: Ho Chi Minh achieved one half of one of his two main objectives. But ironically, both halves of Vietnam were at least as far from independence in 1954 as in 1946, in the sense that both were dependent on outside powers.[5] Under the terms of the Geneva Agreement people were allowed to move from one zone to the other for up to a year. Over a million (mainly Catholics) moved from the North to the South, and many more would have come South if they had not been prevented from doing so by the Communist authorities who were worried at the scale of the emigration. In contrast, only a handful moved from the South to the North. The Agreement also provided for an election on the issue of reunification, but, as the population of the North was greater than that of the South, and the Communists would never have allowed free elections in the North, Ngo Dinh Diem, with American backing, refused to hold such an election. Thus Vietnam remained divided, and like those other victims of the Cold War, Germany and Korea, seemed likely to remain so unless either half is abandoned by its respective sponsor (or sponsors).

As far as France was concerned, the first Indochina War had a disastrous effect on the Fourth Republic. Indeed it is not an exaggeration to say that the cancer that finally destroyed the brave new Republic, which had been established with such high hopes after the Liberation, began to grow during the war in Indochina. For the war discredited the Republic by showing that its politicians were incapable of pursuing a coherent policy, by demonstrating that they were not prepared to take unpopular decisions, and by hinting that the régime itself was corrupt. The failure of successive governments to deal with the problems of decolonisation — in North Africa as well as in Indochina — undermined the nation's confidence in the Republic, so that when the Army finally challenged the Republic in May 1958, there was no decisive republican response to that challenge. Moreover, the various scandals of the Indochina War, notably those concerned with the leaking of information to the Viet Minh, destroyed the Army's confidence in the Republic, not so much because the scandals hinted at the corruption of the politicians — professional soldiers took this for granted — but because they suggested that the politicians were prepared to betray the army for their own ends. After *l'affaire des fuites* of 1954 an Indochina soldier was heard to remark: 'Now we know that wherever the French Army fights, it will always be stabbed in the back'.[6] By tradition the French Army avoided political involvement, but de Gaulle had himself broken that tradition (*la grande muette*) with his appeal of 18 June 1940. The first Indochina War prepared the way for the tradition to be broken for the second time (in 1958). Various studies of the French Army have indicated the direct connection between the 'betrayal' of 1954 and the *coup* of 1958.[7] The professional soldiers, who were brought back from Indochina to Algeria, were determined not to be 'stabbed in the back' again. When this looked like happening in 1958, it was two Indochina veterans, Generals Salan and Massu, who defied Pierre Pflimlin's 'government of abandon' by setting up a Committee of Public Safety in Algiers.

Finally, Indochina, the first and longest colonial war, helped to discredit the Christian Democratic MRP, which had played the key role in the formulation of Indochina policy. This discrediting of MRP was important, because the party was one of the new elements of the Fourth Republic which had given grounds for the hope that the Fourth Republic would be an improvement on its despised predecessor, the Third. The MRP was the biggest and by far the most important new party of the Fourth Republic. It was to the Fourth Republic what the Radicals had been to the Third, the key party in almost every coalition government. It stood for reconciliation between Church and State, and for economic and social progress. It played an important role in the first steps towards European integration. It was in favour of decolonisation, provided it was carried out in an orderly manner and

155

without undue haste. In practice, however, the idealism and hopes of the MRP disappeared in the swamps of Indochina. The great new party which had emerged out of the Resistance became disillusioned and discredited. At the same time Frenchmen began to lose confidence in the Fourth Republic, and so the way was prepared for *le treize mai* 1958, the day on which the Fourth Republic was not so much killed as declared to be dead.

NOTES

1. See Bibliography, pp.157-63.
2. Devillers, p.371, n.18.
3. Interview with Nguyen De, Bao Dai's *chef de cabinet,* 1950-54, 1 May 1974.
4. See, for example, V. Bator, *Vietnam: a Diplomatic Tragedy* (Oceana, 1965).
5. The same situation pertains after the second Indochina War, because neither North nor South Vietnam has the industrial capacity to wage a modern war, and so long as the war continues — as it does in 1974 after a year of nominal peace — both countries will remain virtual satellites in spite of their nominal independence.
6. H. Navarre, *Agonie de l'Indochine, 1953-4* (Paris, 1958), p.114.
7. See, for example, J.S. Ambler, *The French Army in Politics, 1945-62,* (Ohio State University Press, 1962), and J. Planchais, *Une Histoire Politique de l'Armée, 1940-67* (Paris: Seuil, 1967).

BIBLIOGRAPHY

I have divided this bibliography into three parts. The first is a general bibliographical essay on books which are particularly useful for an understanding of the main themes covered by this book. The second consists of a list of the primary sources which have been consulted, and the third of secondary sources.

Part I.

The most useful historical accounts of pre-war Indochina are contained in P. Devillers, *Histoire du Vietnam de 1940 à 1952* (Paris: Seuil, 1952); P. J. Honey, *Genesis of a Tragedy: the Historical Background to the Vietnam War* (London: Benn, 1968); D. Lancaster, *The Emancipation of French Indochina* (London: Oxford University Press/Royal Institute of International Affairs, 1961); Le Thanh Khoi, *Le Vietnam: Histoire et Civilisation* (Paris: Seuil, 1965); A. Masson, *Histoire du Vietnam* (Paris: Presses Universitaires de France, 1967); G. Pasquier, *L'Annam d'Autrefois* (Paris: 1929); C. Robequain, *The Economic Development of French Indochina* (London: Oxford University Press, 1944); and A. Viollis, *Indochine S.O.S.* (Paris: 1949). The books cited above also all contain accounts of the first Indochina War except for those by Pasquier, Robequain and Viollis. Of those already cited, the most scholarly accounts of the war and of its political repercussions are by Devillers and Lancaster, but perhaps the outstanding work on post-war Indochina is Dennis J. Duncanson's *Government and Revolution in Vietnam* (London: Oxford University Press/Royal Institute of International Affairs, 1968). Some studies by American scholars of the 1950s have worn rather badly, but the following are still useful: J. Buttinger, *The Smaller Dragon: a Political History of Vietnam* (New York: Praeger, 1958) and Ellen J. Hammer, *The Struggle for Indochina* (Stanford: Stanford University Press, 1954). Graphic accounts of the fighting are to be found in Bernard Fall, *Street without Joy: Indochina at War, 1946-54* (Harrisburg: Stackpole, 1961); Edgar O'Ballance, *The Indochina War, 1945-54: a Study in Guerrilla Warfare* (London: Faber and Faber, 1964); and J. Roy, *The Battle of Dien Bien Phu* (New York: Harper and Row, 1965).

For the breakdown of negotiations with Ho Chi Minh in 1946-7, see in particular H. Azeau, *Ho Chi Minh: Dernière Chance?* (Paris: Flammarion, 1968), J. Sainteny, *Histoire d'Une Paix Manquée:*

Indochine, 1945-7 (Paris: Amiot-Dumont, 1953) and D. Schoenbrun, *As France Goes* (London: Gollancz, 1957). For an excellent account of relations between China and Vietnam from earliest times until the end of the first Indochina War, see King Chen, *Vietnam and China, 1938-54* (Princeton: Princeton University Press, 1969). There are two well-documented accounts of United States' policy in Indochina during the period in question: V. Bator, *Vietnam: a Diplomatic Tragedy* (New York: Oceana, 1965), and Arthur M. Schlesinger, Jr., *The Bitter Heritage: Vietnam and American Democracy* (London: Macmillan, 1967). For the last phase of the war, see in particular R. Guillain, *La Fin des Illusions* (Paris: Centre d'Etudes de Politique Etrangère, 1954), an outstanding discussion of the options open to France in 1953-4 by a distinguished *Le Monde* journalist. J. Lacouture and P. Devillers *La Fin d'une Guerre: Indochine, 1954* (Paris: Seuil, 1960), and Robert F. Randle, *Geneva 1954* (Princeton: Princeton University Press, 1969), are both long and thorough accounts of the Geneva negotiations.

Ho Chi Minh was a controversial figure both during the first Indochina War and until his death in 1969. No definitive biography has yet been written, but the most objective (although written by an admirer) is J. Lacouture, *Ho Chi Minh* (Paris: Seuil, 1967). For a more critical view, see P. J. Honey, *Communism in North Vietnam* (Cambridge: M.I.T. Press, 1962), which also shows clearly how the Lao Dong (Workers' Party) runs North Vietnam. And for a positively hostile view of both Ho Chi Minh and the North Vietnamese system of government, see Hoang Van Chi, *From Colonialism to Communism: a Case History of North Vietnam,* (London, 1964). Apart from Honey, the most balanced accounts of the North Vietnamese system of government and of its predecessor, the Viet Minh, are to be found in Bernard Fall, *The Viet Minh Régime* (New York: Institute of Pacific Relations, 1954) and *The Two Vietnams: a Political and Military Analysis* (New York: Praeger, 1964). For a sociological approach, which contributes to our understanding of the social climate in which the Viet Minh flourished, see J. Chesneaux, *Contribution à l'Histoire de la Nation Vietnamienne* (Paris: Editions Sociales, 1955), and in particular the outstanding study by P. Mus, *Vietnam: Sociologie d'une Guerre* (Paris: Seuil, 1952). For the constitutional status of the Associated States of Indochina within the French Union, see F. Borella, *L'Evolution Politique et Juridique de l'Union Française depuis 1946* (Paris: Librairie Générale de Droit et de Jurisprudence); and for the Indochina problem in the context of French foreign policy as a whole, see A. Grosser, *La Quatrième République et sa Politique Extérieure* (Paris: Colin, 1961).

Amongst the various memoirs concerned with the first Indochina War and the Geneva negotiations, the following are useful, although none is an outstanding work of scholarship: Pierre Célerier [pseudonym of a colonial administrator], *Menaces sur le Vietnam* (Saigon, 1950); General Georges Catroux, *Deux Actes du Drâme Indochinois* (Paris: Plon, 1959); General Paul Ely, *L'Indochine dans la Tourmente* (Paris: Plon, 1964); Anthony Eden, *Full Circle*: Vol. III, Memoirs (London: Cassell, 1960); Dwight D. Eisenhower, *Mandate for Change: The White House Years, 1953-6* (New York: Doubleday, 1963); Joseph Laniel, *Le Drâme Indochinois: de Dien Bien Phu au Pari de Genève* (Paris: Plon, 1957); and General Henri Navarre, *Agonie de l'Indochine, 1953-4* (Paris: Plon, 1956). On the Army's involvement in politics, see J. S. Ambler, *The French Army in Politics, 1945-62* (Ohio State University Press, 1962) and J. Planchais, *Une Histoire Politique de l'Armée* (Paris: Seuil, 1967). On the scandals concerned with the Indochina War, see J. Despuech, *Le Trafic des Piastres* (Paris: Deux Rives, 1953) and J.-M. Théolleyre, *Le Procès des Fuites* (Paris: Calmann-Lévy, 1956).

There are no detailed studies of the attitude of French political parties to Indochina, or of their influence over Indochina policy, but the following contain some incidental information. For the attitude of the Gaullists, see A. W. DePorte, *De Gaulle's Foreign Policy, 1944-6* (Cambridge, Mass.: Harvard University Press, 1968); no study has been made of Gaullist attitudes in the important period 1947-54, although there is some scattered information in C. Purtschet, *Le Rassemblement du Peuple Francais, 1947-53* (Paris: Cujas, 1965). The same applies to the Socialists and Radicals, although it is worth consulting B. D. Graham, *The French Socialists and Tripartisme, 1944-7* (London: Weidenfeld and Nicolson, 1965) for the immediate post-war period, and F. De Tarr, *The French Radical Party from Herriot to Mendès-France* (London: Oxford University Press, 1961) for the whole period of the first Indochina War. (De Tarr's excellent book, however, is really only concerned with foreign and colonial policy in so far as it affected the internal balance of forces within the Radical Party). The attitude of the MRP is discussed briefly in R.E.M. Irving, *Christian Democracy in France* (London: Allen and Unwin, 1973).

Incidental information about French policy in Indochina is also to be found in: V. Auriol, *Mon Septennat, 1947-54* (Paris: Gallimard, 1970); R. Aron, *France, Steadfast and Changing* (Cambridge, Mass.: Harvard University Press, 1960); J. Dumaine, *Le Quai d'Orsay, 1945-51* (Paris: Julliard, 1955); G. Elgey, *La République des Illusions, 1945-51* and *La République des Contradictions, 1951-4* (Paris: Fayard, 1965 and 1968); J. Fauvet, *La Quatrième République*; and P. M. Williams, *Crisis and Compromise: Politics in the Fourth Republic* (London: Longmans, 1964).

There are a number of books, which are journalistic in style, but nevertheless useful for the insight they provide into both French politics and the Indochina War. See in particular: L. Bodard, *La Guerre d'Indochine*: I. *L'Enlisement* (1963); II. *L'Humiliation* (1965); III. *L'Aventure* (1967) (Paris: Gallimard); G. Chaffard, *Les Carnets Secrets de la Décolonisation* (Paris: Calmann-Levy, 1965); C. Paillat, *Dossier Secret de l'Indochine* (Paris: Presses de la Cité, 1964); and J.-R. Tournoux, *Secrets d'Etat* (Paris: Plon, 1960).

Finally, the first Indochina War, like its successor, produced a large amount of polemical, hagiographical, or other heavily biased, literature, some of which is nevertheless useful, as it helps to explain the strongly held points of view of the various participants. For a right-wing, strongly anti-Communist interpretation see Frédéric Dupont, *Mission de la France en Asie* (Paris: Editions France-Empire, 1956), and André-François Mercier, *Faut-il Abandonner l'Indochine?* (Paris: Editions France-Empire, 1954). Amongst the important Viet Minh apologia are the works of Ho Chi Minh, notably *Selected Works,* 4 vols. (Hanoi: Foreign Languages Publishing House, 1961-2). See also Wilfrid Burchett, *Au Nord du 17e Parallèle* (Hanoi, 1965); Pham Van Dong and the Committee for the Study of the History of the Vietnamese Workers' Party, *President Ho Chi Minh* (Hanoi: Foreign Languages Publishing House, 1960); Jean Rous, *Chronique de la Décolonisation* [Collection of articles from *Les Temps Modernes* and *L'Observateur*] (Paris, 1956); Truong Chinh, *The Resistance Will Win* (Hanoi: Foreign Language Publishing House, 1960); and Vo Nguyen Giap, *People's War, People's Army* (New York: Praeger, 1962).

Part II: Primary Sources

(a) Documents

The most useful collection of documents in English on the first Indochina War is contained in Allan B. Cole (ed.), *Conflict in Indochina and International Repercussions: a Documentary History, 1945-55* (Ithaca: Cornell University Press, 1956). See also P. V. Curl (ed.), *Documents on American Foreign Relations, 1950-54* (New York: Harper, 1955); *Documents on International Affairs, 1955* (London: Oxford University Press/Royal Institute of International Affairs, 1956); *American Foreign Policy, 1950-55: Basic Documents,* 2 vols. (Washington: Department of State, 1957): *Vietnam: Report by Walter H. Judd* (Washington: U.S. House of Representatives, 1955); *Report of Senator Mike Mansfield on a Study Mission to the Associated States of Indochina: Vietnam, Cambodia and Laos* (Washington: U.S. Senate, 1954); *Pentagon Papers on United States-Vietnam Relations, 1945-67,* 12 vols. (Washington: U.S. Government Printing Office, 1971); *Documents Relating to the Discussion of Korea and Indochina at the Geneva Conference, April 27 - June 15, 1954* (London: Foreign Office,

Cmd. 9186, 1954); *Further Documents Relating to the Discussion of Indochina at the Geneva Conference, June 16 - July 21, 1954* (London: Foreign Office, Cmd. 9239, 1954).

The most important French documents are: *Les Accords Franco-Vietnamiens du 8 mars 1949* [Elysée Agreements] (Paris: Notes et Études Documentaires, 1949); *Conventions Inter-Etats Conclues en Application de l'Accord Franco-Vietnamien du 8 mars 1949* (Paris: Notes et Études Documentaires, 1950); *Premier Rapport de la Sous-Commission de Modernisation de l'Indochine* (Paris: Présidence du Conseil, 1948); *Annuaire Statistique du Vietnam, 1949-52*, 3 vols. (Saigon: Institut de la Statistique et des Études Economiques, 1951-53); *Documents de la Conférence de Berlin* (Paris: La Documentation Française, 1954); *Les Accords de Genève* (Paris: La Documentation Française, 1954); *Rapport de la Commission Delahoutre* [Generals' Affair] (Paris: Assemblée Nationale, 1954); and *Rapport de la Commission Mondon* [Piastres traffic] (Paris: Assemblée Nationale, 1954). For French Parliamentary Debates on Indochina, see *Journal Officiel de l'Assemblée Nationale, Journal Officiel de la Conseil de la République* and *Journal Officiel de l'Assemblée de l'Union Française* [of these the most important is the first, i.e. the debates of the National Assembly]. For party attitudes, see *Rapports des Congrès des Partis Politiques* [Microfilm reports of party congresses, Fondation Nationale des Sciences Politiques, Paris] ; and for party publications, see J. Charlot (ed.), *Répertoire des Publications des Partis Politiques Français, 1944-67* (Paris: Colin, 1967).

(b)   Interviews and Correspondence

The following were kind enough to discuss the problems of Indochina with me on one or more occasions between 1966-74. Unless otherwise stated personal interviews took place.

Scholars and journalists: Philippe Devillers, historian of Indochina; Dennis Duncanson, Reader in South-East Asian Studies, University of Kent, Canterbury [correspondence] ; Patrick Honey, Reader in Vietnamese Studies, School of Oriental and African Studies, University of London [correspondence] ; André Fontaine, chief foreign correspondent of *Le Monde*; Jean Lacouture, scholar of Indochina, biographer of Ho Chi Minh; René Plantade, editor of *Forces Nouvelles*.

French politicians: Max André, conservative Christian Democrat, leader of French delegation at Fontainebleau Conference, 1946; Henri Bouret, liberal Christian Democrat; Robert Buron, liberal Christian Democrat, Minister of Overseas France, 1954-5; Pierre de Chevigné, MRP Minister of State for War, 1951-4; André Colin, Secretary-General of MRP, 1945-55; Robert Delavignette, *chef de cabinet* of Marius Moutet, 1936-8, Director of Political Affairs, Ministry of Overseas

161

France, 1947-51; Paul Coste-Floret, MRP Minister of Overseas France, 1947-9; Pierre Corval, liberal Christian Democrat; Alain Dutheillet de Lamothe, *chef de cabinet* of René Pleven (UDSR); Léo Hamon, Christian Democrat, later Gaullist, politician; Jean-Jacques Juglas, Christian Democrat, President of Overseas Committee of National Assembly, 1946-55; Louis Jacquinot, Conservative (Independent) politician, Minister of Overseas France, 1951-2 and 1953-4; Georges Le Brun-Kéris, Assistant Secretary-General of MRP, 1951-8; Francine Lefebvre, liberal Christian Democrat; Jean Letourneau, MRP Minister of Overseas France, 1949-50, Minister with Special Responsibility for Indochina, 1950-3; André-François Mercier, conservative Christian Democrat; Pierre Mendès-France, Radical, Prime Minister of France, 1954-5 [correspondence]; Edmond Michelet, Gaullist, Minister of Armed Forces, 1946-7; Marius Moutet, Socialist, Minister of Overseas France, 1946-7; Alain Poher, *chef de cabinet* of Robert Schuman (Minister of Foreign Affairs, 1948-52); Maurice Schumann, President of MRP 1945-9, Minister of State at Foreign Ministry, 1951-4; Pierre-Henri Teitgen, MRP Minister of Armed Forces, 1947-8, deputy Prime Minister, 1948 and 1953-4, Minister of Overseas France 1955-6; Paul Vignaux, trade union leader.

Vietnamese politicians: Nguyen De, chief adviser (*chef de cabinet*) to Bao Dai, Head of State, Associated State of Vietnam, 1949-54; Nguyen Manh Ha, Minister in Ho Chi Minh's provisional government, 1945-6; Nguyen Van Tam, Bao Dai's Prime Minister, 1952-3; Tran Van Huu, Bao Dai's Prime Minister, 1950-2.

Colonial civil servants and soldiers: Emile Bollaert, High Commissioner in Indochina, 1947-8; Léon Pignon, High Commissioner in Indochina, 1948-50; Jean Sainteny, Representative of French Government sent to negotiate with Ho Chi Minh, 1945-6; General Marcel Carpentier, Commander-in-Chief, Indochina, 1949-50.

Part III: Secondary Sources

For a full list of articles on Indochina, including those on French and American policy in the period under discussion, the *fichier* at the Centre de Documentation, Foundation Nationale des Sciences Politiques, Paris, should be consulted; for press cuttings, the Press Archives at the Royal Institute of International Affairs, London, should be consulted. The following newspapers and journals were found to be particularly useful. Where appropriate a brief comment on their approximate political position is included:

L'Année Politique (Independent; annual publication including documents, analysis of important political developments, etc; published by Presses Universitaires de France).

L'Aube (Christian Democrat daily newspaper; ceased publication in 1951).
Carrefour (Gaullist weekly).
Ecrits de Paris (extreme Right monthly).
Esprit (progressive Catholic monthly).
Etudes (Jesuit monthly).
L'Express (progressive Socialist/Radical weekly).
Le Figaro (independent/conservative daily).
Forces Nouvelles (Christian Democrat weekly).
France-Asie (quarterly academic journal).
L'Humanité (Communist daily).
International Affairs (quarterly academic journal).
Le Monde (independent daily).
New York Herald Tribune (independent daily).
New York Times (independent daily).
Le Populaire (Socialist daily).
Revue de Défense Nationale (monthly academic journal).
Revue des Deux Mondes (Conservative quarterly).
Revue Française de Science Politique (quarterly academic journal).
Témoignage Chrétien (progressive Catholic weekly).
The Times (independent daily).
The World Today (monthly academic journal).

INDEX

Abbas, Ferhat, 65
Acheson, Dean, 99, 101, 103, 107
affaire des fuites, see Leakages' Affair
affaire des généraux, see Generals'
    Affair
Alessandri, General, 82
Algeria, 1, 75, 155
American policy in Indochina: initially
    favourable to Ho Chi Minh, 10,
    98; changing attitude to Ho Chi
    Minh, 99-100; policy aims,
    99-100; effect of Korean War,
    101; aid programme, 79, 100-7,
    145-6; differences with French,
    101-2, 105-7; favourable view of
    de Lattre, 79; attitude to Bao
    Dai, 99-100; pressure on French,
    105-7, 153; April 1953 Memo-
    randum, 104-5, 110; military
    defeat of Viet Minh as prime
    objective, 104, 106, 115, 119;
    against direct American military
    involvement in Indochina, 124-6;
    paying for two-thirds of cost of
    war by 1953-54, 136; role at
    Geneva Conference, 118-22,
    124-5; refusal to sign Geneva
    Agreement, 128-9; effect of First
    Indochina War on American
    policy in South East Asia, 153-4
André, Max, 14, 21, 22, 26, 37, 116,
    133
Annam, 4, 7, 8, 66, 69
Argenlieu, Admiral Thierry d', High
    Commissioner in Indochina,
    1945-47: appointed High Com-
    missioner by de Gaulle, 13;
    character, 13, 14, 15, 17; acts
    without government instructions,
    4; policy, 14, 38, 54; encourages
    Cochinese 'autonomy', 20;
    supports Bao Dai 'solution', 54
Associated States (of Indochina); 7,
    12n, 58, 88, 90, 92, 99, 101-2,
    103-4, 107, 109-11, 115-6, 144-6;
    see also Cambodia, Laos,

Vietnam, Indochina
Atlantic Charter, 3, 32
Aube, L', 30, 38, 39, 50, 134
Aurore, L', 106
Auriol, President Vincent, 48-49,
    102, 104

Bao Dai, Emperor of Annam
    (1925-45); Head of State, Vietnam
    (1949-55); character, 54, 65 6;
    declares independence of Vietnam,
    4; dilemmas facing, 54, 56; Bao Dai
    'solution', 55-8, 80, 85-95; agrees to
    form provisional government, 57;
    signs Elysée Agreement (1949), 58;
    as French protegé, 59; Socialist
    criticisms of, 65-6; relations with
    General Xuan, 62; builds Vietnamese
    National Army, 92-5; role at Geneva
    Conference, 122-3; rejects Geneva
    Agreement, 129
Berlin, Conference of, 118-9
Bermuda, Conference of, 118
Bidault, Georges, Prime Minister of
    France (1946; 1949-50); Foreign
    Minister (1944-48; 1953-54);
    character, 25, 34; influence, 60;
    becomes Prime Minister, 24; role
    at Fontainebleau Conference,
    24-6, 34; criticises Bao Dai
    'solution', 59-61; Generals' Affair,
    71; supports Navarre Plan, 114;
    opposes direct negotiations with
    Viet Minh, 37, 52, 116, 118;
    rejects *Expressen* 'peace offer',
    117; role at Berlin Conference,
    119; role at Geneva Conference,
    119-28
Blum, Léon, 30, 37-8, 40, 65
Bollaert, Emile, High Commissioner
    in Indochina (1947-48): appoin-
    ted High Commissioner, 41;
    character and career, 42; visits
    Indochina, 45; abortive peace
    contacts with Ho Chi Minh, 46-52
Bourdet, Claude, 14, 26, 74, 75

165

167

Mondon Report, 108-10
Morand, Colonel, 68, 72
Morlière, General, 29
Moscow, *see* Soviet Union
Mouette, Operation, 118
Moutet, Marius, Socialist Minister of
    Overseas France (1946-47): at
    first favours negotiations with Ho
    Chi Minh, 17; indecisive policy,
    20, 40-1; role at Fontainebleau
    Conference, 25, 34; visits Indo-
    china, 30, 40; turns against
    negotiating with Ho Chi Minh,
    37-8, 41, 43; Socialists criticise
    his policy, 64
MRP (Christian Democrats), *see*
    French policy in Indochina:
    parties
Muret, 92
Mus, Paul, 26, 31, 46-7, 66

Na San, 120
Nationalism, 10, 17, 19, 28, 31-2,
    144-6, 151, *see also*, Indochina;
    Viet Minh; Vietnam; VNQDD
Navarre, General Henri, 110, 116,
    117, 120
Navarre Plan, 106, 107, 108, 114,
    117-8
New York Herald Tribune, 105, 106
Nguyen, Ai Quoc, *see* Ho Chi Minh
Nguyen Hai Than, 10
Nixon, Richard, 124

Observateur, L', 82, 105
OSS (Office of Strategic Services),
    10, 16, 68, 98, 111n, 112n

Paillat, Claude, 14
Palewski, J-P., 83
Papacy, *see* Catholic Church; *Missions
    Etrangères*; Pius XII
Paris-Saigon, 24
Pau (Conference and Agreements),
    56, 87, 88, 108, 109
Peyré, Roger, 67, 68, 71
Pflimlin, Pierre, 1, 2, 155
Phuoc, Do Dei, 70, 72
Piastres: trafficking in, 108, 113;
    devaluation of, 108; Mondon
    Report on, 109-10; effect of
    devaluation on French Indochina
    policy, 107, 110-1
Pignon, Léon; High Commissioner in

Indochina (1948-50): appointed
    High Commissioner, 54; opinion
    of Argenlieu, 13; supports Bao
    Dai policy, 54-5; opinion of Bao
    Dai, 54; and Generals' Affair,
    68-77; sees Tonkin as key to
    Indochina, 82
Pinay, Antoine, 78n, 90, 142
Pius XII, Pope, 60, 138
Pleven, Rene, 64, 67, 73, 81, 82, 84,
    102, 103, 110, 115, 117, 119-20,
    141
Potsdam Conference, 11, 13
Progressive federalism, 2, 7, 34, 65

Queuille, Henri, 67, 70, 71, 72, 73
Quyen, Ngo, 8
Quyet, Chien, 18

Radford, Admiral, 106, 120, 124
Radicals, *see* French policy in
    Indochina: parties
Ramadier, Paul, 37, 39, 40, 43, 44,
    46, 48, 65, 67, 70, 72, 74
Revers, General, 67, 68, 69, 74, 76
Revers Report (1949), 68-70, 74, 81
Reynaud, Paul, 110, 115, 117, 119,
    122
Rivet, Paul, 27, 65-6
RPF (Gaullists), *see* French policy in
    Indochina: parties

Saigon, 14, 15, 23, 30, 46, 94, 108
Sainteny, Jean, 11, 13, 16, 17, 18,
    21, 30, 64
Salan, General, 4, 86, 92, 94, 155
Sarraut, Albert, 30, 87
Savary, Alain, 62, 76, 85, 115, 117,
    120
Schuman, Robert, 2, 4, 52, 56, 57,
    62, 107, 135, 139
Schumann, Maurice, 25, 37, 38, 44,
    50, 122, 124, 133, 134, 144, 145
SDECE (Section de documentation
    exterieure et de contre-espionnage),
    67, 68, 72, 73
SEATO (South East Asia Treaty
    Organisation), 129
Second World War, 3, 9-10
Servan-Schreiber, Jean-Jacques, 106
Sino-Soviet Pact, 121
Socialists (SFIO), *see* French policy
    in Indochina: parties
Soviet Union (Russia), 34, 79, 84,

89, 114, 117, 118, 119, 121-2,
  134, 136, 150, 153
Stalin, Joseph, 120, 133, 135, 152

Tam, Nguyen Tuong, 22
Tam, Nguyen Van, 7, 89-90, 93, 108
Tay Son, 8
Teitgen, Pierre-Henri, 48, 49, 106,
  131n, 140, 145
Témoignage Chrétien, 60, 121
Thorez, Maurice, 24, 134, 136, 144
Tito, 31, 33, 149
Tonkin, 4, 7, 11, 15, 18, 66, 68, 69,
  79, 82, 83, 88, 94, 103, 128, 137,
  139, 143
Tournoux, J-R., 120
Tripartism, 5, 34, 41, 135
Troisième force, 5-6
Truman, President Harry, 101, 102,
  103
Twining, General, 124

United Nations, 3, 19, 27, 87, 89, 98,
  125, 151
United States, *see* American policy in
  Indochina

Valluy, General, 4, 17, 29, 46-7, 48,
  51, 151
Varenne, Alexandre, 18
Vautour, Operation, 120, 121
Viet Minh: founded by Ho Chi Minh,
  10; in Vietnamese provisional
  government, 13; essentially Communist, 6, 11, 31, 48, 134-6; role
  in December 1946 *coup*, 30; aided
  by Chinese Communists, 56, 58,
  67, 68, 80, 84, 151; broadcasts
  Revers Report, 70; benefits from
  piastres traffic, 111; victory at
  Cao Bang, 81; growing strength
  by 1953-54, 114; victory at Dien
  Bien Phu, 120-1; at Geneva Conference, 123, 126, 127, 128; *see
  also* Ho Chi Minh; China; Soviet
  Union
Vietnam: history, 8-9; divisions, 7;
  benefits brought by French, 9;
  revolts against French, 9;
  nationalism, 11, 13, 15, 24, 33,
  47, 55, 60; *see also* Associated
  States; Bao Dai; French policy in
  Indochina; Ho Chi Minh; Indochina; Viet Minh

VNQDD (Viet Nam Quoc Dan Dang),
  10, 17, 22
Warner, Geoffrey, 99, 100, 112n,
  131n, 132n
Werth, Alexander, 74
Williams, Philip, 4, 137
Wilson, Charles, 104, 124

Xuan, General: favours contacts with
  Ho Chi Minh, 57; signs Along Bay
  protocol, 57; supported by part of
  French Left, 61; the Xuan
  'solution', 61-3; involvement in
  Generals' Affair, 68-70, 73, 76;
  failure, 76